Cardiovascular and Coronary Artery Imaging

Cardiovascular and Coronary Artery Imaging

Volume 2

Edited by

AYMAN S. EL-BAZ

University of Louisville, Louisville, KY, United States; University of Louisville at Alamein International University (UofL-AIU), New Alamein City, Egypt

JASJIT S. SURI

AtheroPoint, Roseville, CA, United States

ACADEMIC PRESS

An imprint of Elsevier

Academic Press is an imprint of Elsevier
125 London Wall, London EC2Y 5AS, United Kingdom
525 B Street, Suite 1650, San Diego, CA 92101, United States
50 Hampshire Street, 5th Floor, Cambridge, MA 02139, United States
The Boulevard, Langford Lane, Kidlington, Oxford OX5 1GB, United Kingdom

Notices
Knowledge and best practice in this field are constantly changing. As new research and experience broaden our understanding, changes in research methods, professional practices, or medical treatment may become necessary.

Practitioners and researchers must always rely on their own experience and knowledge in evaluating and using any information, methods, compounds, or experiments described herein. In using such information or methods they should be mindful of their own safety and the safety of others, including parties for whom they have a professional responsibility.

To the fullest extent of the law, neither the Publisher nor the authors, contributors, or editors, assume any liability for any injury and/or damage to persons or property as a matter of products liability, negligence or otherwise, or from any use or operation of any methods, products, instructions, or ideas contained in the material herein.

ISBN: 978-0-12-821983-6

For Information on all Academic Press publications
visit our website at https://www.elsevier.com/books-and-journals

Publisher: Mara Conner
Acquisitions Editor: Tim Pitts
Editorial Project Manager: Tom Mearns
Production Project Manager: Prem Kumar Kaliamoorthi
Cover Designer: Mark Rogers

Typeset by MPS Limited, Chennai, India

Working together
to grow libraries in
developing countries

www.elsevier.com • www.bookaid.org

Dedication

With love and affection to my mother and father, whose loving spirit sustains me still

—Ayman S. El-Baz

To my late loving parents, immediate family, and children

—Jasjit S. Suri

Contents

Mandana Saki, Fatemeh Jafari Pour, Saba Najmi, Mohammad Gholami and Farzad Ebrahimzadeh

9. Cardiac magnetic resonance imaging of cardiomyopathy   149

Ahmed Abdel Khalek Abdel Razek, Germeen Albair Ashmalla and Dalia Fahmy

10. Magnetic resonance imaging of pericardial diseases   159

Ahmed Abdel Khalek Abdel Razek, Germeen Albair Ashmalla and Dalia Fahmy

11. Imaging modalities for congenital heart disease and genetic polymorphism associated with coronary artery and cardiovascular diseases   **169**

Gowtham Kumar Subbaraj, Santhosh Kumar Yasam, Langeswaran Kulanthaivel, Balamurugan Rangasamy, Priyanka Ganapathy, C. Kirubhanand, Selvaraj Jayaraman, Ponnulakshmi Rajagopal, Ramya Sekar, Vidhya Rekha Umapathy and Shazia Fathima Jaffer Hussain

List of Contributors

Ahmed Abdel Khalek Abdel Razek
Department of Diagnostic Radiology, Faculty of Medicine, Mansoura University, Mansoura, Egypt

Hisham Abdeltawab
Bioengineering Department, University of Louisville, Louisville, KY, United States

Ahmad Abdulsaboor
Department of Clinical Pathology, Zagazig University, Zagazig, Egypt

Germeen Albair Ashmalla
Department of Diagnostic Radiology, Faculty of Medicine, Mansoura University, Mansoura, Egypt

Shan Wei Chen
Faculty of Art, Computing and Creative Industry, Universiti Pendidikan Sultan Idris, Tanjong Malim, Perak, Malaysia; Department of Education, Baoji University of Arts and Sciences, Baoji, Shaanxi, P.R. China

Farzad Ebrahimzadeh
Department of Biostatistics, Nutritional Health Research Center, Lorestan University of Medical Sciences, Khorramabad, Iran

Ayman S. El-Baz
University of Louisville, Louisville, KY, United States; University of Louisville at Alamein International University (UofL-AIU), New Alamein City, Egypt

Dalia Fahmy
Department of Diagnostic Radiology, Faculty of Medicine, Mansoura University, Mansoura, Egypt

Kenji Fukushima
Department of Nuclear Medicine (and Cardiology), Saitama Medical University International Medical Center, Hidaka, Saitama, Japan

Priyanka Ganapathy
Department of Physiology, Sree Balaji Medical College and Hospital, Chromepet, Chennai, Tamil Nadu, India

Ahmad Gebreil
Department of Cardiology, University of Louisville, Louisville, KY, United States

Mohammed Ghazal
Electrical, Computer and Biomedical Engineering, Abu Dhabi University, Abu Dhabi, United Arab Emirates

Mohammad Gholami
Social Determinants of Health Research Center, Lorestan University of Medical Sciences, Khorramabad, Iran

Shazia Fathima Jaffer Hussain
Department of Oral and Maxillofacial Pathology, Ragas Dental College and Hospital, Chennai, Tamil Nadu, India

Haidi Ibrahim
School of Electrical and Electronic Engineering, Universiti Sains Malaysia, Nibong Tebal, Penang, Malaysia

Selvaraj Jayaraman
Department of Biochemistry, Saveetha Dental College and Hospitals, Chennai, Tamil Nadu, India

Heba Kandil
Bioimaging Lab, Bioengineering Department, University of Louisville, Louisville, KY, United States; Faculty of Computer and Information Sciences, Mansoura University, Mansoura, ElDakahlia, Egypt

Fahmi Khalifa
Bioengineering Department, University of Louisville, Louisville, KY, United States

C. Kirubhanand
Department of Anatomy, All India Institute of Medical Sciences, Nagpur, Maharashtra, India

Langeswaran Kulanthaivel
Department of Biotechnology, Science Campus, Alagappa University, Karaikudi, Tamil Nadu, India

Ali Mahmoud
Bioimaging Lab, Bioengineering Department, University of Louisville, Louisville, KY, United States

Michinobu Nagao
Department of Diagnostic Imaging and Nuclear Medicine, Tokyo Women's Medical University, Tokyo, Japan

Saba Najmi
Student Research Committee, Lorestan University of Medical Sciences, Khorramabad, Iran

Theam Foo Ng
Centre for Global Sustainability Studies, Universiti Sains Malaysia, Gelugor, Penang, Malaysia

Fatemeh Jafari Pour
Department of Nursing, Behbahan Faculty of Medical Sciences, Behbahan, Iran

Ponnulakshmi Rajagopal
Department of Central Research Laboratory, Meenakshi Ammal Dental College and Hospitals, Chennai, Tamil Nadu, India

Balamurugan Rangasamy
Viral Research and Diagnostic Laboratory (VRDL), Government Villupuram Medical College and Hospital, Mundiyampakkam, Villupuram, Tamil Nadu, India

Mandana Saki
Social Determinants of Health Research Center, Lorestan University of Medical Sciences, Khorramabad, Iran

Abou Bakr M. Salama
Department of Cardiology, University of Louisville, Louisville, KY, United States; Department of Cardiac Surgery, University of Verona, Verona, Italy; Department of Cardiology, Zagazig University, Zagazig, Egypt

Ramya Sekar
Department of Oral Pathology, Meenakshi Ammal Dental College and Hospitals, Chennai, Tamil Nadu, India

Ahmed Mohammed Shaker
Department of Physiology, National Research Institute, Cairo, Egypt

Ahmed Soliman
Bioimaging Lab, Bioengineering Department, University of Louisville, Louisville, KY, United States

Gowtham Kumar Subbaraj
Faculty of Allied Health Sciences, Chettinad Hospital and Research Institute, Chettinad Academy of Research and Education (Deemed to be University), Kelambakkam, Tamil Nadu, India

Fatma Taher
College of Technological Innovation, Zayed University, Dubai, United Arab Emirates

Vidhya Rekha Umapathy
Department of Public Health Dentistry, Sree Balaji Dental College and Hospital, Chennai, Tamil Nadu, India

Shir Li Wang
Faculty of Art, Computing and Creative Industry, Universiti Pendidikan Sultan Idris, Tanjong Malim, Perak, Malaysia; Data Intelligent and Knowledge Management (DILIGENT), Universiti Pendidikan Sultan Idris, Tanjong Malim, Perak, Malaysia

Santhosh Kumar Yasam
Faculty of Allied Health Sciences, Chettinad Hospital and Research Institute, Chettinad Academy of Research and Education (Deemed to be University), Kelambakkam, Tamil Nadu, India

About the editors

Ayman S. El-Baz is a distinguished professor at the University of Louisville, Kentucky, United States and the University of Louisville at AlAlamein International University (UofL–AIU), New Alamein City, Egypt. Dr. El-Baz earned his BSc and MSc degrees in electrical engineering in 1997 and 2001, respectively. He earned his PhD in electrical engineering from the University of Louisville in 2006. Dr. El-Baz was named as a Fellow for Coulter, AIMBE, and NAI for his contributions to the field of biomedical translational research. Dr. El-Baz has almost two decades of hands-on experience in the fields of bioimaging modeling and noninvasive computer-assisted diagnosis systems. He has authored or coauthored more than 700 technical articles (209 journals, 53 books, 104 book chapters, 262 refereed-conference papers, 216 abstracts, and 38 US patents and disclosures).

Jasjit S. Suri is an innovator, scientist, visionary, industrialist, and an internationally known world leader in biomedical engineering. Dr. Suri has spent over 25 years in the field of biomedical engineering/devices and its management. He received his PhD from the University of Washington, Seattle and his Business Management Sciences degree from Weatherhead, Case Western Reserve University, Cleveland, Ohio. Dr. Suri was crowned with the President's Gold medal in 1980 and made Fellow of the American Institute of Medical and Biological Engineering for his outstanding contributions. In 2018 he was awarded the Marquis Life Time Achievement Award for his outstanding contributions and dedication to medical imaging and its management.

Acknowledgments

The completion of this book could not have been possible without the participation and assistance of so many people whose names may not all be enumerated. Their contributions are sincerely appreciated and gratefully acknowledged. However, the editors would like to express their deep appreciation and indebtedness particularly to Dr. Ali H. Mahmoud and Mohamed Elsharkawy for their endless support.

Ayman S. El-Baz
Jasjit S. Suri

CHAPTER 1

Predictors of outcome in ST-segment elevation myocardial infarction

Abou Bakr M. Salama[1,2,3] and Ahmad Abdulsaboor[4]
[1]Department of Cardiology, University of Louisville, Louisville, KY, United States
[2]Department of Cardiac Surgery, University of Verona, Verona, Italy
[3]Department of Cardiology, Zagazig University, Zagazig, Egypt
[4]Department of Clinical Pathology, Zagazig University, Zagazig, Egypt

Because most ST elevation myocardial infarction (STEMI) patients require reperfusion therapy, early risk assessment gives the patient and family an idea of what to expect in the future. Patients who are at an elevated risk of late arrhythmic or nonarrhythmic mortality are identified using late risk stratification. This process has two components: Early in-hospital identification of individuals at elevated risk of recurrent ischemia episodes, and identification of patients with an elevated risk of arrhythmic or nonarrhythmic death following a myocardial infarction (MI) [1].

First of all, the individual risk factors that influence prognosis in patients presented by STEMI that must be controlled properly to prevent recurrence of cardiac events.

The number of coronary heart disease (CHD) risk factors is very high. A family history of early CHD, as well as the four modifiable CHD risk factors (hypertension, smoking, dyslipidemia, and diabetes), predict the development of atherosclerosis and its clinical repercussions [2].

1.1 Clinical predictors

1.1.1 Heart failure

After cardiogenic shock, survival is still dismal. Despite vigorous reperfusion, cardiogenic shock and CHF are still the leading causes of death in STEMI patients having primary PCI. Future research should focus on interventions aimed at lowering mortality in these high-risk individuals [3].

The Killip classification divides individuals with an acute MI into two groups based on whether or not simple physical examination results imply LV dysfunction [4].

Class I: No evidence of heart failure (mortality 6%).

Class II: Findings of mild to moderate heart failure (S3 gallop, rales < halfway up lung fields or elevated jugular venous pressure) (mortality 17%).

Class III: Pulmonary edema (mortality 38%).

Cardiovascular and Coronary Artery Imaging
DOI: https://doi.org/10.1016/B978-0-12-821983-6.00001-1

Class IV: Cardiogenic shock defined as systolic blood pressure <90 and signs of hypoperfusion such as oliguria, cyanosis, and sweating (mortality 67%).

The initial data from 1967 showed that each class had a higher mortality rate. This was before thrombolytic and/or PCI reperfusion treatment. The mortality rates in each class have decreased by 30%—50% due to breakthroughs in therapy.

1.1.2 Tachycardia

Patients with sustained heart rates more than 90 beats per minute had larger and more frequent anterior infarcts, severe LV dysfunction, and a dismal prognosis [5].

1.1.2.1 Electrocardiogram

The following ECG abnormalities, which usually suggest a bigger infarction, are associated with worse outcomes after STEMI. These include:

- Anterior compared to inferior infarcts.
- Higher number of leads showing ST elevation.
- Absence of ST elevation resolution for 90—180 minutes after fibrinolysis.
- Persistant ST elevation is rare except in the presence of ventricular aneurysm.
- Regardless of age, hypertension, diabetes, or renal function, the presence of a Q wave was a substantial predictor of death or hospitalization for ischemic heart disease (IHD) [6].

1.1.2.1.1 Ventricular arrhythmias

The development of ventricular tachycardia (VT) in the peri-MI period (i.e., within the first 48 hours after the MI) is thought to be attributable to temporary ischemia; nevertheless, the incidence of VT/VF and patient mortality rose as the patient's baseline risk increased. Regardless of the underlying baseline risk, VT/VF remained an important predictive marker for the increased risk of clinical adverse events and 90-day mortality in STEMI patients following initial PCI [7].

1.1.2.2 Atrial fibrillation

A common consequence of acute myocardial infarction (AMI) is atrial fibrillation (AF), which is linked to increased morbidity and death in AMI patients [8].

1.1.2.3 Chronic kidney disease

The clinical characteristics of nondialysis-dependent advanced CKD patients with AMI are comparable to those of dialysis patients, and they are likely to have poor outcomes. Intensive efforts are needed to detect AMI in advanced CKD patients in a timely and accurate manner [9].

1.1.2.4 Peripheral artery disease

Intermittent claudication appears to be associated with poorer outcomes in STEMI patients. Men with intermittent claudication are at a higher risk of coronary artery disease than men who have had a heart attack [10].

Other factors might impact the outcome in patients who undergo PPCI including the time between the development of symptoms and PCI (also known as treatment delay), the time from arrival at the hospital to PCI (door-to-balloon time, or door-to-balloon delay), the length of time from initially contacting the healthcare system, presentation time (early vs late), the patient's risk category, hospital and physician factors, and the significance of TIMI 3 flow (patent artery) [11].

1.1.3 Biomarkers

In patients with STEMI, a variety of biomarkers have been linked to risk. Troponin and CK–MB are the two most regularly used.

1.1.4 CK-MB

After myocardial damage, serum CK levels rise between 3–8 hours, peak within 12–24 hours, and recover to baseline within 3–4 days [12]. If the biomarker increases >20% above the level observed at the time of the recurring symptoms, both CK–MB and troponin can be utilized to diagnose episodes of reinfarction [13].

1.1.5 Troponin

Troponin I (cTnI) and T (cTnT) are regulatory proteins found in cardiac muscles that are sensitive and specific markers of myocardial necrosis. Elevated levels have prognostic significance; a value greater than the 99th percentile of the normal population should be considered an indication of MI [14].

1.1.6 High-sensitivity troponin assays

These high-sensitivity assays measure pg/mL levels of circulating troponin rather than ng/mL levels, allowing for not only increased sensitivity but also early diagnosis of myocardial necrosis. cTnI levels rose with time and were a reliable predictor of outcome [15].

1.1.7 Myoglobin

Myoglobin is a protein with a low molecular weight that is found in both cardiac and skeletal muscle. It can be found in the serum as soon as 2 hours after the onset of cardiac necrosis. Because myoglobin has a poor cardiac specificity but a high sensitivity, it can be used to rule out MI if the level is normal within the first 4–8 hours of symptoms [16].

1.2 Brain natriuretic peptide

High baseline BNP was linked to a number of negative clinical outcomes in STEMI patients undergoing primary PCI, including major bleeding, ischemic stroke, and cardiac death. After 3 years, higher BNP concentrations were no longer linked to MACE or all-cause mortality, but remained weakly linked to cardiac death [17].

It has been hypothesized that NT pro-BNP obtained within 24 hours of the onset of chest discomfort is more accurate in predicting mortality at 9 months than the TIMI risk score [18].

1.2.1 Ischemia-modified albumin

Ischemia-modified albumin is a sensitive ischemia marker that prevents albumin from binding to cobalt. Because IMA is a marker of ischemia rather than myocardial cell damage, little is known about its ability to predict long-term cardiac outcomes in patients with established acute myocardial infarction (AMI). However, IMA measured within 24 hours has recently been found to be a strong and independent predictor of cardiac outcome at one year in patients with AMI, which may help identify those who require more aggressive medical management [19].

1.2.2 Unbound free fatty acids

The association of serum unbound free fatty acid (FFAu) levels with mortality in patients presenting with STEMI in the Thrombolysis in Myocardial Infarction (TIMI) II trial found that FFAu was an independent risk factor for death as early as one day of hospitalization and continued to be an independent risk factor for death as late as one year after hospitalization [20].

1.2.3 Circulating microRNAs are new and sensitive biomarkers of myocardial infarction

The human transcriptome is divided into two types of RNA: coding and noncoding. Messenger RNAs (mRNAs) are coding RNAs that represent genes that will be translated into different proteins. Noncoding RNAs (ncRNAs) are a diverse category of molecules that cannot be translated into proteins. They include transfer RNAs (tRNAs), ribosomal RNAs (rRNAs), microRNAs (miRNAs), small nuclear RNAs (snRNAs), small nucleolar RNAs (snoRNAs), long noncoding RNAs (lncRNAs), and Piwi-interacting RNAs (piRNAs) [21,22].

MiRNAs are small regulatory noncoding RNAs with a length of roughly 22 nucleotides that affect the transcriptome [23]. The 21-nucleotide long "lin-4" was the first miRNA to be described in the literature. It was first published in December 1993, when two distinct teams of researchers discovered it in the nematode *C. elegans* [24,25].

In patients with STEMI, higher levels of circulating miR-133a are linked to lower myocardial salvage, larger infarcts, and more severe reperfusion injury. In the setting of STEMI, miR-201a provides high diagnostic and prognostic value, as well as good predictive value for the occurrence of no-reflow [26,27].

1.2.4 Lipoprotein-associated phospholipase A2

In advanced atherosclerotic lesions, lipoprotein-associated phospholipase A2 (Lp-PLA2), also known as platelet-activating factor (PAF) acetyl hydrolase, is prevalent. The bulk and activity of plasma Lp-PLA2 acquired shortly after admission to the hospital for unstable angina or MI failed to predict death or recurrent major cardiovascular events. Another study found that measuring plasma Lp-PLA2 30 days after an acute coronary syndrome but not within 10 days predicts recurrent cardiovascular events [28].

1.2.5 Plasma fibrinogen level

According to one study, elevated plasma fibrinogen levels in STEMI patients following primary PCI are linked to ISR. Larger studies are needed to determine the predictive significance of fibrinogen in comparison to more difficult end-points [29].

1.2.6 Interleukin-6 + , interleukin-10 + , and interleukin-6-interleukin-10 + cytokine

Patients with STEMI can have very high circulating interleukin-6 (IL-6(+)) levels or very low circulating interleukin-6 (IL-6(−)) levels. IL10 was increased both in IL-6(+) STEMI and IL-6(−) STEMI patients, and IL-6(+) IL-10(+) STEMI patients had an increased risk of systolic dysfunction at discharge and death at 6 months. Researchers combined IL-10 and IL-6 in a formula that produced a risk score that exceeded any single cytokine in the prediction of systolic dysfunction and mortality [30].

1.2.7 Routinely feasible multiple biomarker score to predict prognosis after revascularized ST elevation myocardial infarction

After a revascularized acute MI, the long-term prognostic value of an easy-to-do multiple cardiac biomarker score was evaluated in order to evaluate a multimarker strategy to risk classification based on routine biomarkers.

It is possible to use BNP, hsCRP, creatininemia, and troponin I as part of a routine multimarker approach. The most powerful marker is BNP, and this multimarker method provides additional predictive information that aids in the identification of patients at high risk of clinical events [31].

1.2.8 Serum potassium

There is a link between serum potassium levels and in-hospital mortality in patients with acute MI. As a baseline, a blood potassium level of 3.5—4.0 mEq/L was used as a reference. It is worth noting that individuals with serum potassium levels between 4.5 and 5.0 mEq/L, previously thought to be "within normal limits," had a roughly twofold higher risk of death than those with values between 3.5 and 4.0 mEq/L [32].

1.2.9 Glycemic control

In critically ill hyperglycemic patients admitted to an intensive care unit (ICU) with acute coronary syndrome, intensive blood glucose control with intravenous insulin infusion could minimize short-term and 30-day mortality, reinfarction stroke, and rehospitalization for congestive heart failure [33,34].

1.2.10 White blood cell count

In individuals with STEMI, an elevated white blood cell count on presentation has been linked to an increased risk of cardiac mortality. WBCs are a reliable predictor of infarct size as evaluated by cardiac magnetic resonance imaging 30 days following the initial percutaneous coronary intervention (PCI) [35].

1.3 Differential white blood cell count

Numerous research has looked into the relationship between thrombotic and inflammatory pathways in acute coronary syndromes. In acute STEMI, leukocytosis is a typical sign that indicates WBC infiltration into necrotic tissue in response to ischemia and reperfusion. The first leukocytes to be discovered in the injured cardiac region are neutrophils [36].

Neutrophils are the first leukocytes to be detected in the injured cardiac area and are eliminated from myocardial tissue after phagocytosing debris. Monocytes, on the other hand, migrate from capillaries to the extravascular space, where they become macrophages and exceed neutrophils 2—3 days after the acute episode. Macrophage-secreted cytokines increase monocytosis and boost fibroblast proliferation and collagen synthesis. Several studies have found that the number of leukocytes on a patient's initial examination predicts their outcome in both short- and long-term follow-up [37—39].

Increased neutrophil count on admission to the hospital in individuals with AMI is linked to the onset of congestive heart failure [40]. After an AMI, peripheral monocytosis is linked to left ventricular dysfunction and the development of a left ventricular aneurysm. At various stages of the atherosclerotic process, lymphocytes play an important role in controlling the inflammatory response [41].

Lympopenia is a common observation following a stress reaction, second only to elevated corticosteroids, and has high discriminative ability for the diagnosis of acute myocardial infarction in this context [42,43]. A faulty clearance of apoptotic cells due to inadequate phagocytosis of apoptotic cells occurs in subsequent necrosis-inducing production of proinflammatory cytokines (tumor necrosis factor- and interlukin-6) under these pathologic settings. In addition, enhanced lymphocyte apoptosis has been linked to lymphopenia in critical inflammatory conditions [44].

In addition to being an independent measure of mortality, the neutrophil/lymphocyte ratio (N/L) exceeds the predictive information supplied by WBCs. In STEMI patients treated with early revascularization, N/L is a strong independent predictor of long-term mortality whether the link between N/L and long-term mortality is due to a fundamental pathophysiological process or is a marker of the severity of the ischemia episode [45].

Increased N/L is a basic nonspecific inflammatory sign. It may serve as a low-cost novel technique for risk categorization in STEMI because of its widespread availability [45]. Recent research suggests that particular leukocyte subtypes have a stronger predictive value in determining cardiovascular risk. When the N/L ratio (the total number of neutrophils and lymphocytes) is used, the figure is even greater [46]. The N/L ratio is an independent predictor of long-term death in patients undergoing angioplasty [47].

1.3.1 Anemia

Anemia is a risk factor for poor prognosis in individuals with acute coronary syndromes. Anemia is an independent predictor of poor outcome in patients with acute MI [48].

1.3.2 Findings at the time of angiography and percutaneous coronary intervention

Angiographic measures of efficacy of coronary reperfusion at the epicardial artery and microcirculation levels, such as the TIMI grading system and myocardial perfusion grade (MPG), predict unfavorable clinical outcomes, including short- and long-term death [49].

The TIMI flow grade classification was originally used to assess fibrinolytic efficacy. This categorization describes the coronary blood flow in the infarct-related artery, which is typically tested 60—90 minutes after fibrinolytic therapy is administered [50].

Patients with poor procedural success (post-PCI TIMI flow grades of less than two in the IRA) after primary PCI for STEMI have a substantially higher risk of mortality than those with typical post-PCI TIMI flow grades 3 in the IRA [51].

1.3.3 Thrombolysis in myocardial infarction frame count

TIMI frame count (TFC) is the number of frames taken for contrast to reach standardized distal coronary markers in cine. The corrected TIMI frame count (cTFC) is proportional to the time it takes for the contrast to pass through the vessel (in seconds), corrected for vessel length. The cTFC is objective, quantitative, and has been found to be reasonably repeatable. TIMI flow score and cTFC, on the other hand, are both indirect markers of microvascular flow and patency [51].

1.3.4 Left ventricular ejection fraction

The 2013 American College of Cardiology Foundation/American Heart Association (ACCF/AHA) STEMI guideline and the 2012 European Society of Cardiology STEMI guideline both propose assessing resting left ventricular function for risk stratification in patients with acute MI [52].

Left ventricular (LV) dysfunction is a major predictor of death. Despite the fact that current guidelines recommend prophylactic implantable cardioverter-defibrillator (ICD) implantation after STEMI and a depressed LV ejection fraction for 1 month, the prognoses of these patients may be better than those seen in randomized trials of ICDs (1-year mortality 6.8%−19%), particularly because reperfusion treatment has improved and the use of life-saving drugs has increased [53].

Echocardiography should be utilized for routine LVEF assessment after an acute MI in general. However, measures taken during hospitalization may be misleading, as LVEF improvement begins within 3 days and is nearly complete by 14 days. Patients who are reperfused frequently experience this. In two different investigations, roughly 58% of patients with acute STEMI had a significant improvement in LVEF after reperfusion. This could be due to myocardial stunning recovery, at least in part. Patients with better LVEF may have a lower mortality rate than those with no change (1.2% vs 5.6% at 3 years in one study) [54].

Moreover, echocardiography can detect other factors that may, sometimes, complicate the course after myocardial infarction. Conditions such as restrictive diastolic dysfunction, concurrent right ventricular dysfunction, left atrial enlargement, and ischemic mitral regurgitation can be easily detected by echocardiography and usually lead to a worse prognosis [55−60].

References

[1] Becker RC, et al. Early assessment and in-hospital management of patients with acute myocardial infarction at increased risk for adverse outcomes: a nationwide perspective of current clinical practice. The National Registry of Myocardial Infarction (NRMI-2) Participants. Am Heart J 1998;135(5 Pt 1):786−96. Available from: https://doi.org/10.1016/s0002-8703(98)70036-5.

[2] Canto JG, et al. Number of coronary heart disease risk factors and mortality in patients with first myocardial infarction. JAMA 2011;306(19):2120−7. Available from: https://doi.org/10.1001/jama.2011.1654.

[3] French JK, et al. Cardiogenic shock and heart failure post−percutaneous coronary intervention in ST-elevation myocardial infarction: observations from assessment of pexelizumab in acute myocardial infarction. Am Heart J 2011;162(1):89−97. Available from: https://doi.org/10.1016/j.ahj.2011.04.009.

[4] Killip 3rd T, Kimball JT. Treatment of myocardial infarction in a coronary care unit. A two year experience with 250 patients. Am J Cardiol 1967;20(4):457−64. Available from: https://doi.org/10.1016/0002-9149(67)90023-9.

[5] Crimm A, Severance HW, Coffey K, McKinnis R, Wagner GS, Califf RM. Prognostic significance of isolated sinus tachycardia during first three days of acute myocardial infarction. Am J Med 1984;76(6):983−8. Available from: https://doi.org/10.1016/0002-9343(84)90846-5.

[6] Godsk P, Jensen JS, Abildstrøm SZ, Appleyard M, Pedersen S, Mogelvang R. Prognostic significance of electrocardiographic Q-waves in a low-risk population. Europace 2012;14(7):1012−17. Available from: https://doi.org/10.1093/europace/eur409.

[7] Mehta RH, et al. Relationship of sustained ventricular tachyarrhythmias to outcomes in patients undergoing primary percutaneous coronary intervention with varying underlying baseline risk. Am Heart J 2011;161(4):782−9. Available from: https://doi.org/10.1016/j.ahj.2011.01.005.

[8] Saczynski JS, et al. Trends in atrial fibrillation complicating acute myocardial infarction. Am J Cardiol 2009;104(2):169−74. Available from: https://doi.org/10.1016/j.amjcard.2009.03.011.

[9] Shroff GR, Frederick PD, Herzog CA. Renal failure and acute myocardial infarction: clinical characteristics in patients with advanced chronic kidney disease, on dialysis, and without chronic kidney disease. A collaborative project of the United States Renal Data System/National Institutes of Health and the National Registry of Myocardial Infarction. Am Heart J 2012;163(3):399−406. Available from: https://doi.org/10.1016/j.ahj.2011.12.002.

[10] St-Pierre A, Cantin B, Lamarche B, Auger D, Després J, Dagenais GR. Intermittent claudication: from its risk factors to its long-term prognosis in men. The Quebec Cardiovascular Study. Can J Cardiol 2010;26(1):17−21. Available from: https://doi.org/10.1016/s0828-282x(10)70328-7.

[11] Lambert L, Brown K, Segal E, Brophy J, Rodes-Cabau J, Bogaty P. Association between timeliness of reperfusion therapy and clinical outcomes in ST-elevation myocardial infarction. JAMA 2010;303(21):2148−55. Available from: https://doi.org/10.1001/jama.2010.712.

[12] Karras DJ, Kane DL. Serum markers in the emergency department diagnosis of acute myocardial infarction. Emerg Med Clin North Am 2001;19(2):321−37. Available from: https://doi.org/10.1016/s0733-8627(05)70186-3.

[13] Thygesen K, et al. Universal definition of myocardial infarction. Circulation 2007;116(22):2634−53. Available from: https://doi.org/10.1161/circulationaha.107.187397.

[14] Thygesen K, Alpert JS, Jaffe AS, Simoons ML, Chaitman BR, White HD. Third universal definition of myocardial infarction. Circulation 2012;126(16):2020−35. Available from: https://doi.org/10.1161/CIR.0b013e31826e1058.

[15] Eggers Kai M, Venge P, Lindahl B, Lind L. Cardiac troponin I levels measured with a high-sensitive assay increase over time and are strong predictors of mortality in an elderly population. J Am Coll Cardiol 2013;61(18):1906−13. Available from: https://doi.org/10.1016/j.jacc.2012.12.048.

[16] Osman B, Uzun L, Beşirli N, Denizli A. Microcontact imprinted surface plasmon resonance sensor for myoglobin detection. Mater Sci Eng C Mater Biol Appl 2013;33(7):3609−14. Available from: https://doi.org/10.1016/j.msec.2013.04.041.

[17] Jarai R, et al. B-type natriuretic peptide and risk of contrast-induced acute kidney injury in acute ST-segment-elevation myocardial infarction: a substudy from the HORIZONS-AMI trial. Circ Cardiovasc Interv 2012;5(6):813−20. Available from: https://doi.org/10.1161/circinterventions.112.972356.

[18] Khan SQ, Quinn P, Davies JE, Ng LL. N-terminal pro-B-type natriuretic peptide is better than TIMI risk score at predicting death after acute myocardial infarction. Heart 2008;94(1):40−3. Available from: https://doi.org/10.1136/hrt.2006.108985.

[19] Van Belle E, Dallongeville J, Vicaut E, Degrandsart A, Baulac C, Montalescot G. Ischemia-modified albumin levels predict long-term outcome in patients with acute myocardial infarction. The French Nationwide OPERA study. Am Heart J 2010;159(4):570−6. Available from: https://doi.org/10.1016/j.ahj.2009.12.026.

[20] Huber H, Kampf JP, Kwan T, Zhu B, Adams 3rd J, Kleinfeld AM. Usefulness of serum unbound free fatty acid levels to predict death early in patients with ST-segment elevation myocardial infarction (from the Thrombolysis In Myocardial Infarction [TIMI] II trial). Am J Cardiol 2014;113 (2):279−84. Available from: https://doi.org/10.1016/j.amjcard.2013.08.057.

[21] Jacquier A. The complex eukaryotic transcriptome: unexpected pervasive transcription and novel small RNAs. Nat Rev Genet 2009;10(12):833−44. Available from: https://doi.org/10.1038/nrg2683.

[22] Esteller M. Non-coding RNAs in human disease. Nat Rev Genet 2011;12(1):861−74. Available from: https://doi.org/10.1038/nrg3074.

[23] Yates LA, Norbury CJ, Gilbert RJ. The long and short of microRNA. Cell 2013;153(3):516−19. Available from: https://doi.org/10.1016/j.cell.2013.04.003.

[24] Lee RC, Feinbaum RL, Ambros V. The *C. elegans* heterochronic gene lin-4 encodes small RNAs with antisense complementarity to lin-14. Cell 1993;75(5):843−54. Available from: https://doi.org/10.1016/0092-8674(93)90529-y.

[25] Wightman B, Ha I, Ruvkun G. Posttranscriptional regulation of the heterochronic gene lin-14 by lin-4 mediates temporal pattern formation in *C. elegans*. Cell 1993;75(5):855−62. Available from: https://doi.org/10.1016/0092-8674(93)90530-4.

[26] Izarra A, et al. miR-133a enhances the protective capacity of cardiac progenitors cells after myocardial infarction. Stem Cell Rep 2014;3(6):1029−42. Available from: https://doi.org/10.1016/j.stemcr.2014.10.010.

[27] Salama M, et al. MicroRNA-208a: a good diagnostic marker and a predictor of no-reflow in STEMI patients undergoing primary percutaneuos coronary intervention. J Cardiovasc Transl Res 2020;13(6):988−95. Available from: https://doi.org/10.1007/s12265-020-10020-9.

[28] Dullaart RPF, Van Pelt LJ, Kwakernaak AJ, Dikkeschei BD, van der Horst ICC, Tio RA. Plasma lipoprotein-associated phospholipase A2 mass is elevated in STEMI compared to non-STEMI patients but does not discriminate between myocardial infarction and non-cardiac chest pain. Clin Chim Acta Int J Clin Chem 2013;424:136−40.

[29] Lupi A, et al. Plasma fibrinogen levels and restenosis after primary percutaneous coronary intervention. J Thromb Thrombolysis 2012;33(4):308−17. Available from: https://doi.org/10.1007/s11239-011-0628-z.

[30] Anderson JL, Karagounis LA, Becker LC, Sorensen SG, Menlove RL. TIMI perfusion grade 3 but not grade 2 results in improved outcome after thrombolysis for myocardial infarction. Ventriculographic, enzymatic, and electrocardiographic evidence from the TEAM-3 Study. Circulation 1993;87(6):1829−39. Available from: https://doi.org/10.1161/01.cir.87.6.1829.

[31] Roubille F, et al. Routinely-feasible multiple biomarkers score to predict prognosis after revascularized STEMI. Eur J Intern Med 2010;21(2):131−6. Available from: https://doi.org/10.1016/j.ejim.2009.11.011.

[32] Goyal A, et al. Serum potassium levels and mortality in acute myocardial infarction. JAMA 2012;307(2):157−64. Available from: https://doi.org/10.1001/jama.2011.1967.

[33] El-Shenawy R, Moharram A, El-Noamany M, El-Gohary T. Tight Glycemic control in acute coronary syndromes: prognostic implications. Egypt J Crit Care Med 2013;1:5−12. Available from: https://doi.org/10.1016/j.ejccm.2012.12.001.

[34] De Caterina R, Madonna R, Sourij H, Wascher T. Glycaemic control in acute coronary syndromes: prognostic value and therapeutic options. Eur Heart J 2010;31(13):1557−64. Available from: https://doi.org/10.1093/eurheartj/ehq162.

[35] Palmerini T, et al. Relation between white blood cell count and final infarct size in patients with ST-segment elevation acute myocardial infarction undergoing primary percutaneous coronary intervention (from the INFUSE AMI trial). Am J Cardiol 2013;112(12):1860−6. Available from: https://doi.org/10.1016/j.amjcard.2013.08.010.

[36] Bekwelem W, et al. White blood cell count, C-reactive protein, and incident heart failure in the Atherosclerosis Risk in Communities (ARIC) Study. Ann Epidemiol 2011;21(10):739−48. Available from: https://doi.org/10.1016/j.annepidem.2011.06.005.

[37] Cannon P, et al. Comparison of early invasive and conservative strategies in patients with unstable coronary syndromes treated with the glycoprotein IIb/IIIa inhibitor tirofiban. N Engl J Med 2001;344(25):1879−87. Available from: https://doi.org/10.1056/NEJM200106213442501.

[38] Liu R, Nair D, Ix J, Moore DH, Bent S. N-acetylcysteine for the prevention of contrast-induced nephropathy. A systematic review and meta-analysis. J Gen Intern Med 2005;20(2):193−200. Available from: https://doi.org/10.1111/j.1525-1497.2005.30323.x.

[39] Núñez J, et al. Usefulness of the neutrophil to lymphocyte ratio in predicting long-term mortality in ST segment elevation myocardial infarction. Am J Cardiol 2008;101(6):747−52. Available from: https://doi.org/10.1016/j.amjcard.2007.11.004.

[40] Ait-Oufella H, Taleb S, Mallat Z, Tedgui A. Recent advances on the role of cytokines in athero-sclerosis. Arterioscler Thromb Vasc Biol 2011;31(5):969−79. Available from: https://doi.org/10.1161/atvbaha.110.207415.

[41] Ducloux D, Challier B, Saas P, Tiberghien P, Chalopin J-M. CD4 Cell lymphopenia and athero-sclerosis in renal transplant recipients. J Am Soc Nephrol 2003;14(3):767. Available from: https://doi.org/10.1097/01.ASN.0000048718.43419.44.

[42] Onsrud M. Reduced generation of suppressor cells in human mixed lymphocyte culture after radio-therapy. Acta Path Microbiol Scand C Immunol 1982;(1-6):39−45. Available from: https://doi.org/10.1111/j.1699-0463.1982.tb01415.x.

[43] Davis K, Maney DL, Maerz JC. The use of leukocyte profiles to measure stress in vertebrates: a review for ecologists. Funct Ecol 2008;22(5):760−72. Available from: https://doi.org/10.1111/j.1365-2435.2008.01467.x.

[44] Hotchkiss JW, Davies CA, Gray L, Bromley C, Capewell S, Leyland A. Trends in cardiovascular disease biomarkers and their socioeconomic patterning among adults in the Scottish population 1995 to 2009: cross-sectional surveys. BMJ Open 2012;2(3). Available from: https://doi.org/10.1136/bmjopen-2011-000771.

[45] Shen XH, Chen Q, Shi Y, Li HW. Association of neutrophil/lymphocyte ratio with long-term mortality after ST elevation myocardial infarction treated with primary percutaneous coronary inter-vention. Chin Med J 2010;123(23):3438−43.

[46] Horne S, et al. The impact of pre-hospital thrombolytic treatment on re-infarction rates: analysis of the Myocardial Infarction National Audit Project (MINAP), Heart 2009;95(7):559−63. Available from: https://doi.org/10.1136/hrt.2007.126821.

[47] Duffy K, Gurm HS, Rajagopal V, Gupta R, Ellis SG, Bhatt DL. Usefulness of an elevated neutrophil to lymphocyte ratio in predicting long-term mortality after percutaneous coronary intervention. Am J Cardiol 2006;97(7):993−6. Available from: https://doi.org/10.1016/j.amjcard.2005.10.034.

[48] Vrsalovic M, et al. Impact of admission anemia, C-reactive protein and mean platelet volume on short term mortality in patients with acute ST-elevation myocardial infarction treated with primary angioplasty. Clin Biochem 2012;45(16-17):1506−9. Available from: https://doi.org/10.1016/j.clinbiochem.2012.05.026.

[49] Ndrepepa G, et al. Myocardial perfusion grade, myocardial salvage indices and long-term mortality in patients with acute myocardial infarction and full restoration of epicardial blood flow after pri-mary percutaneous coronary intervention, (in engspa). Rev Esp Cardiol 2010;63(7):770−8. Available from: https://doi.org/10.1016/s1885-5857(10)70161-4.

[50] Chesebro JH, et al. Thrombolysis in Myocardial Infarction (TIMI) Trial, Phase I: a comparison between intravenous tissue plasminogen activator and intravenous streptokinase. Clinical findings through hospital discharge. Circulation 1987;76(1):142−54. Available from: https://doi.org/10.1161/01.cir.76.1.142.

[51] Porto I, Hamilton-Craig C, Brancati M, Burzotta F, Galiuto L, Crea F. Angiographic assessment of microvascular perfusion−myocardial blush in clinical practice. Am Heart J 2010;160(6):1015. Available from: https://doi.org/10.1016/j.ahj.2010.08.009.

[52] O'Gara PT, et al. ACCF/AHA guideline for the management of ST-elevation myocardial infarction: executive summary. Circulation 2013;127(4):529–55. Available from: https://doi.org/10.1161/CIR.0b013e3182742c84.

[53] Ottervanger P, et al. Mortality in patients with left ventricular ejection fraction. Am J Cardiol 2007;100(5):793–7. Available from: https://doi.org/10.1016/j.amjcard.2007.03.101.

[54] Ndrepepa G, Mehilli J, Martinoff S, Schwaiger M, Schömig A, Kastrati A. Evolution of left ventricular ejection fraction and its relationship to infarct size after acute myocardial infarction. J Am Coll Cardiol 2007;50(2):149–56. Available from: https://doi.org/10.1016/j.jacc.2007.03.034.

[55] Somaratne B, Whalley GA, Gamble GD, Doughty RN. Restrictive filling pattern is a powerful predictor of heart failure events postacute myocardial infarction and in established heart failure: a literature-based *meta*-analysis. J Card Fail 2007;13(5):346–52. Available from: https://doi.org/10.1016/j.cardfail.2007.01.010.

[56] Kukulski T, et al. Implication of right ventricular dysfunction on long-term outcome in patients with ischemic cardiomyopathy undergoing coronary artery bypass grafting with or without surgical ventricular reconstruction. J Thorac Cardiovasc Surg 2015;149(5):1312–21. Available from: https://doi.org/10.1016/j.jtcvs.2014.09.117.

[57] Mohiedden E, Al-shaer MHE, Elmaghawry LM, Al Zaki MM, Abdelaziz M, Salama AM. Right ventricular functions can predict left ventricular reverse remodeling in patients with ischemic cardiomyopathy after revascularization. Zagazig Univ Med J 2021. Available from: https://doi.org/10.21608/zumj.2021.51617.2032.

[58] Moller JE, et al. Left atrial volume: a powerful predictor of survival after acute myocardial infarction. Circulation 2003;107(17):2207–12. Available from: https://doi.org/10.1161/01.Cir.0000066318.21784.43.

[59] Grigioni F, Enriquez-Sarano M, Zehr KJ, Bailey KR, Tajik AJ. Ischemic mitral regurgitation: long-term outcome and prognostic implications with quantitative Doppler assessment. Circulation 2001;103(13):1759–64. Available from: https://doi.org/10.1161/01.cir.103.13.1759.

[60] Møller JE, Hillis GS, Oh JK, Reeder GS, Gersh BJ, Pellikka PA. Wall motion score index and ejection fraction for risk stratification after acute myocardial infarction. Am Heart J 2006;151(2):419–25. Available from: https://doi.org/10.1016/j.ahj.2005.03.042.

CHAPTER 2

ST-segment elevation myocardial infarction

Abou Bakr M. Salama[1,2,3], Ahmad Gebreil[1] and Ahmed Mohammed Shaker[4]

[1]Department of Cardiology, University of Louisville, Louisville, KY, United States
[2]Department of Cardiac Surgery, University of Verona, Verona, Italy
[3]Department of Cardiology, Zagazig University, Zagazig, Egypt
[4]Department of Physiology, National Research Institute, Cairo, Egypt

2.1 Definition

The first reports that link coronary occlusion to death were in the 19th century through autopsy studies. Over the years, the clear relation of coronary occlusion to death was difficult to prove as almost 30% of autopsies did not have occluding thrombi of coronaries. The clear pathological relation of coronary occlusion to the clinical presentation of heart attack was established in the 20th century and referred to as myocardial infarction (MI) [1−4].

Myocardial infarction, often known as heart attack, is the permanent necrosis of cardiomyocytes caused by a prolonged lack of oxygen delivery. Thrombus formation on top of plaque rupture inside the coronary vasculature causes an abrupt drop in blood supply to a region of the myocardial, resulting in an oxygen supply and demand imbalance [5].

The World Health Organization (WHO) adopted the electrophysiological changes with the clinical presentation for defining MI for epidemiological use [6]. Acute coronary syndromes (ACS) encompass a wide range of clinical manifestations caused by persistent myocardial ischemia, including chest discomfort and alterations in ECG and cardiac damage biomarkers. Myocardial infarction is the most severe type of heart attack, with increased cardiac biomarkers and a distinct temporal profile. This rise is called ST-segment elevation myocardial infarction (STEMI) when it is linked with an elevation of the ST segment in the ECG; otherwise, it is called non−ST-segment elevation myocardial infarction (NSTEMI). It is essential to mention that patients with ischemia pain may or may not have ECG abnormalities. ST elevations in the ECG indicate active and persistent transmural myocardial ischemia and damage (Fig. 2.1). Q waves may form if appropriate oxygen and blood flow are not restored immediately, indicating irreparable damage and a dead zone in the heart. Those without ST elevations and change of cardiac injury biomarkers are diagnosed with unstable angina [7].

Cardiovascular and Coronary Artery Imaging
DOI: https://doi.org/10.1016/B978-0-12-821983-6.00002-3

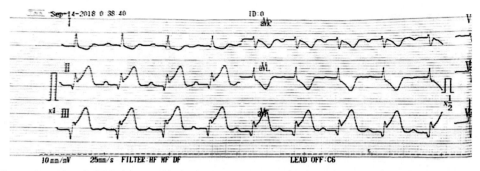

Figure 2.1 6-Leads ECG showing ST elevation in leads II, III and aVf consistent with inferior STEMI.

The ability to establish a clear temporal profile of biomarkers in relation to ongoing pathology, with good correlation to clinical presentation, outcome, and high sensitivity and specificity, prompted the European Society of Cardiology (ESC) and the American College of Cardiology (ACC) task force to report the first definition of MI based on biomarkers [8]. The establishment of a uniform definition of MI was based on a consensus concerning biomarker-based criteria with refinement and adoption of five subtypes. (Fig. 2.2). In mid-2018, the fourth universal definition of myocardial infarction (UDMI) went into effect [9].

Accordingly, MI has the following subtypes:

- Type 1—myocardial injury related to ischemia due to plaque erosion and/or rupture with development of a thrombus on top as a consequence, which is referred to as a primary coronary event. Coronary dissection is included.
- Type 2—Myocardial injury secondary to ischemia due to an increase in the oxygen demand or a decreased supply. Common causes include anemia, hypertension or hypotension, coronary artery spasm, coronary embolism, and arrhythmias.
- Type 3—Sudden unexpected cardiac death, including cardiac arrest.
- Type 4—Coronary angioplasty associated myocardial injury:
  - Type 4a—Myocardial injury associated with percutaneuos coronary intervention (PCI).
  - Type 4b—Myocardial injury due to stent thrombosis.
- Type 5 — Coronary artery bypass grafting (CABG)-associated myocardial injury.

2.2 Epidemiology of ST elevation myocardial infarction

The rate of MI varies greatly among countries, yet it is still very high. The incidence rate of STEMI in Sweden, where the Swedish registry is regarded as the most complete in Europe, was 58 per 100,000 per year in 2015 [10]. In other European countries, the rate could reach 144 per 100,000 [11]. Over the last few years, there has been a global trend of decreasing STEMI and increasing NSTEMI [12,13].

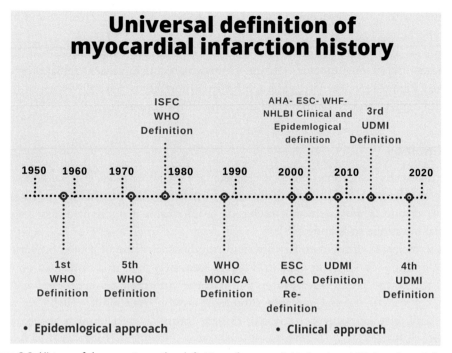

Figure 2.2 History of documents on the definition of myocardial infarction. *ACC*, American College of Cardiology; *AHA*, American Heart Association; *ESC*, European Society of Cardiology; *ISFC*, International Society and Federation of Cardiology; *MONICA*, MONItoring of trends and determinants in CArdiovascular disease; *NHLBI*, National Heart, Lung, and Blood Institute; *UDMI*, Universal Definition of Myocardial Infarction; *WHF*, World Heart Federation; *WHO*, World Health Organization [9].

Ischemic heart disease is the greatest cause of death on the planet. Males have a higher incidence rate than females, developing countries have a higher incidence rate than developed countries, and low-income populations have a higher incidence rate than high-income populations. Few industrialized nations, such as Sweden, have seen an overall drop in STEMI-related deaths, while the incidence is increasing elsewhere and globally [14]. Ischemic heart disease is the major cause of mortality in Egypt, with cardiovascular illnesses accounting for 46% of all deaths and noncommunicable diseases accounting for 25% of premature deaths in 2010 [15].

Men develop ischemic heart disease on average 7–10 years earlier than women; however, the female privilege is eliminated with aging with equal incidence in both sexes after the age of 75 and tendency of females to represent the majority of new patients. There is a considerable difference in presentation between males and females with atypical presentation to be more common with the latter. The incidence and types of complications are also different. Women tend to have fewer interventions than men with poorer outcome in females due to later age of presentation and multiple comorbidities.

Patients' age, color, and gender, as well as the treatment facility itself, may have a significant impact on outcomes. In the United States, being black, female, or older confers a higher mortality rate, although STEMI mortality is generally lower in hospitals with higher patient volumes and busier procedural centers [16,17].

2.3 Etiology

Acute Coronary Syndrome (ACS) is characterized by an imbalance in cardiomyocyte supply and demand, which is generally caused by the rupture of what is known as susceptible plaque, a nonsevere atherosclerotic lesion that is hemodynamically inconsequential but prone to rupture [18].

Atherosclerosis of the coronary arteries is the primary cause of acute coronary syndrome in more than 90% of patients. Plaques form over time as a result of a complex inflammatory and proliferative process and become vulnerable to mechanical and biological factors, culminating in plaque rupture or erosion. As a result, platelet activation and coagulation pathways are activated, causing thrombus development and coronary blockage [19].

Stenoses of less than 70% in the proximal sections of the coronary vasculature are usually the most susceptible lesions. At these sites, the flow dynamics and shear stress influencing the endothelium hasten the development of susceptible plaque [20]. Blood flow turbulence at coronary branching points hastens the development of atherosclerosis at bifurcations [7]. Atheromas with high inflammatory content and a big lipid-rich core surrounded by a thin fibrous cap are more likely to rupture [19].

The following are modifiable and nonmodifiable risk factors for the development of coronary atherosclerosis [19]:

- Age.
- Sex.
- Family history of premature coronary heart disease.
- Smoking or other tobacco use.
- Diabetes mellitus.
- Hypertension.
- Dyslipidemia including hypercholesterolemia and hypertriglyceridemia especially inherited lipoprotein disorders.
- Obesity.
- Sedentary lifestyle and/or lack of exercise.
- Psychosocial stress.
- Poor oral hygiene.
- Type A personality.

- Elevated homocysteine levels.
- The presence of peripheral vascular disease.

Although atherosclerosis is the most common cause of acute coronary syndromes, other causes are equally important because treatment options vary. They include [21]:

- Coronary vasculitis.
- Ventricular hypertrophy including generalized left ventricular hypertrophy due to pressure or volume overload and localized septal of apical hypertrophy.
- Coronary embolization.
- Coronary congenital anomalies.
- Coronary trauma.
- Coronary vasospasm including primary spasm; variant angina, and secondary spasm (e.g., cocaine induced).
- Conditions with increased oxygen requirement; heavy exertion, fever, or hyperthyroidism.
- Conditions with decrease oxygen delivery; severe anemia, hypoxic hypoxia, or cytotoxic hypoxia [22].
- Aortic dissection.

2.4 Pathophysiology

The majority of ACS occurrences are thought to be caused by an episode of acute athero-thrombosis. Angina or myocardial infarction can develop in conditions other than coronary atherosclerosis, however treatment and prognosis are different in these circumstances than when ACS is coupled with underlying atherosclerotic alterations [23].

The atherosclerotic plaque, a localized deposit of extracellular matrix (collagen, elastic fibers, and proteoglycans), cells (inflammatory and noninflammatory), and lipids within the intima of the artery wall, is the disease's clinical hallmark [24]. Certain plaques are classified as "vulnerable" due to their composition and structural fragility; they are mostly made of a massive, necrotic lipid core containing infiltrating macrophages, and other inflammatory cells, and are covered by a thin fibrous cap [25].

The plaque's vulnerability lies in the tendency of the fibrous cap to erode or rupture, releasing proaggregatory factors into the immediate area. Interestingly, some studies have identified more than one vulnerable plaque in patients suffering from an acute coronary event, but, generally, only one is recognized as the culprit lesion [26]. Factors that are involved in rupture of a fibrous cap and subsequent thrombotic events, associated with a particular plaque at a particular moment, are under continuous investigation and consideration, and have included localized elevation of shear, intraplaque hemorrhage, matrix degradation by metalloproteinases, and apoptosis induced by inflammatory cytokines. Acute or chronic psychological stressors have also been implicated [27].

When the fibrous top of a plaque ruptures, the lipid-rich, thrombogenic core is exposed to the circulation, triggering a large and complex cascade of inflammatory and prothrombotic responses [28]. Ruptured plaques have been found concentrated within the proximal segments of epicardial arteries, consistent with other observations suggesting that coronary artery occlusions leading to STEMI tend to cluster within these specific high-risk coronary segments [7,29].

Platelet activation and aggregation then forms a clot on top of the plaque, which can cause a sudden occlusion of the artery lumen, resulting in distal ischemia, which is the cause of the majority of ACS episodes. Ischemia is induced by an abrupt reduction in blood flow produced by a plaque-associated thrombus in a proximal segment of an epicardial artery, especially in STEMI [7]. The resulting myocardial necrosis causes histological and structural changes in both infarct- and noninfarct-related coronary arterial segments, and the extent and severity of the ischemia is influenced by a number of factors, including the presence of collateral blood supply to the infarct area, the location and extent of the infarct, whether or not the ischemia extends from epicardial to endocardial surfaces, and the preexisting ventricular functional status [28].

Ischemia causes hypokinesis in the affected myocardium, which is an immediate loss of contractility. Necrosis starts within 15–30 min after deprivation of blood and in the more prone area, which is the subendocardium. Then, over the next 3–6 h, the necrosis spreads outward to the epicardium, to finally span the entire ventricular wall. At the edges of infarct the myocardium is less affected and reversibly damaged (stunned) and may recover if the blood flow is restored. A compensatory hyperkinesis (increased contractility) occurs in the rest of the viable myocardium [30].

Within 20 min following the suspension of blood flow, ultrastructural evidence of cellular damage and death is visible. The major morphological traits, however, do not appear until 6 h after the infarction. Over the next 12 h, the cell damage worsens and becomes increasingly irreversible, providing a window of opportunity for some myocardium to be saved with thrombolysis and reperfusion [30].

A process of coagulation necrosis of the infarcted myocardium develops between 4 and 12 h after cell death starts during which the necrotic cascade is characterized by progressive swelling of cells, denaturation of cytoplasmic proteins, and breakdown of organelles. Afterwards, the inflammatory component is activated with more neutrophils infiltrating the infarct with their numbers peaking at the 5th day then declining. Macrophages engulf the dead necrotic tissue giving space for deposition of new tissue. The phagocytosed tissue is replaced with granulation tissue, which starts to appear after 3–4 days at the edges of the infarction and spreads inward to the center of infarct consisted of macrophages, fibroblasts, new scar tissue, and new capillaries. Between the 4th and the 7th days postinfarction, the dead tissue is still very soft and may rupture, which is a lethal event accounting for 10% of MI deaths. With time, the maturation of the new deposited connective (scar) tissue and loss of capillaries leaves a stronger thin, firm and noncontracting wall [30].

The hemodynamic stressing of both the healthy myocardium and the scar tissue causes progressive stretching and thinning of the ventricular wall, which can begin the day after the infarction and progress over months, with large transmural infarctions, especially those of the anterior wall, being more visible. Complications such as congestive heart failure, arrhythmias, and free wall rupture are more likely as a result of the remodeling [30].

2.5 Management

2.5.1 Diagnosis

A quick diagnosis of MI is essential for the early implementation of a management plan. The presenting symptoms, ECG signs, and laboratory findings are used to make the diagnosis. Persistent chest pain with radiation to the left arm, neck, jaw, or epigastria is the most common symptom. Symptoms aren't always predictable. Shortness of breath, vomiting, palpitations, or syncope are some of the most common complaints. The relief of chest pain caused by nitrate injection has long been utilized as a diagnostic hint, although it has received less attention recently because it may be misleading [31−33].

It is recommended that ECG be done and interpreted in 10 min of the first medical contact (FMC) whether at the emergency department (ED) or by ambulance service. ST elevation is a clue for coronary occlusion and acute MI in the absence of left bundle branch block (LBBB) and/or left ventricular hypertrophy with the following specifications:

- At least two leads with 2.5 mm ST elevation in men <40 years in V2-V3.
- At least two leads with 2 mm ST elevation in men ≥40 years in V2-V3.
- At least two leads with 1.5 mm ST elevation in women ≥40 years in V2-V3.
- ST elevation ≥1 mm in other leads.
- ST elevation ≥0.5 mm in leads V7-V9.
- ST depression ≥0.5 mm in leads V1-V3 with positive terminal T wave (ST elevation equivalent), posterior leads should be sought [9,34].

Some conditions are associated with nonconclusive ECG findings. In LBBB, a concordant ST elevation is a strong indicator. New LBBB does not specifically predict MI. Right bundle branch block (RBBB) is associated with delayed diagnosis and poor outcome in the context of MI. Paced rhythm hinders diagnosis; if the patient is not pace maker-dependent, reprogramming to allow detection of intrinsic heart activity is essential. ST depression ≥1 mm in at least eight leads with elevation in a VR or V1 is suggestive of left main occlusion. If ECG is inconclusive, ECG monitoring and serial ECGs with comparison will be of great value. In all of the above cases clinical suspicion should be the guide to management other than the ECG findings and primary PCI should never be delayed [35−43].

Biomarkers constitute the cornerstone for diagnosis in the fourth universal definition of MI. At least one value of cardiac troponins rises above the 99th percentile upper reference limit, indicating acute myocardial injury (URL). This will be consistent with MI type 1 if any of the following are present: symptoms of myocardial ischemia, new ischemic ECG changes, development of pathological Q waves, imaging evidence of new ischemic wall motion abnormality or loss of viable myocardium, or identification of coronary thrombus by angiography or autopsy [9]. Primary PCI in the setting of clinical suspension and ECG abnormalities should never be postponed while waiting for laboratory results [33].

2.5.2 Differential diagnosis

Several cardiac and noncardiac conditions may mimic ACS including myocarditis, pericarditis, cardiomyopathies, valvular heart diseases, taku-tsubo cardiomyopathy, cardiac trauma, pulmonary embolism, pulmonary infarction, pneumonia, pleuritic, aortic dissection, cerebrovascular disease, osophageal spasm, peptic ulcer disease, pancreatitis, cholecystitis, musculoskeletal diseases, sickle cell anemia, and herpes zoster diseases. Thorough clinical examination and work-up is required for proper diagnosis [44].

2.5.3 Logistics of management

"Early and complete restoration of blood flow in the infarct-related artery and improvement of myocardial perfusion in the infarct zone" is the major goal of STEMI therapy. To unblock the clogged culprit vessel, two different yet effective reperfusion techniques are commonly used: pharmacological (fibrinolytic medications) and mechanical (primary PCI). Under typical settings, primary PCI is the technique of choice during the first 12 h of symptom onset; 120 min maximum delay and a competent team [45]. Otherwise, patient characteristics, the ready availability of an interventional laboratory, and the availability of rapid transportation for a patient to an interventional site all influence the choice and implementation of each strategy [46]. Regardless of the approach used to promote reperfusion, the most critical aspect is to start treatment as soon as possible. The time between FMC and STEMI diagnosis must be kept to a minimum of 10 min [33].

PCI-based strategy is the recommended initial approach for patients presenting to a hospital with interventional capability, keeping a door-to-wire crossing (or medical contact-to wire crossing) time within 90 min. For patients presenting to a hospital without PCI capability with possibility to transfer to PCI capable facility the door-in to door-out time must be ≤ 30 min and the total system delay ≤ 120 min. For patients who cannot be transferred to another center and undergo PCI within 120 min of first medical contact, a pharmacological strategy should be followed to achieve a door-to-bolus (or medical contact-to-bolus) time of no more than 30 min (Fig. 2.3) [33].

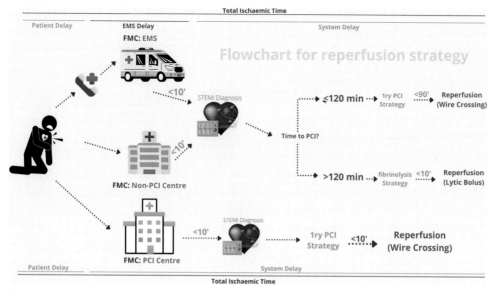

Figure 2.3 Components of ischemia time and flowchart for reperfusion strategy selection.

Depending on whether the first medical contact is made by emergency medical system (EMS) providers or at the hospital emergency department, the management of a patient with STEMI can begin in either prehospital or hospital settings [23].

2.5.4 Prehospital management

Once the EMS personnel arrive on scene and have the first contact with a patient suspected of having STEMI, 162−325 mg of acetyl salicylic acid (chewed) should be administered unless taken by the patient or there is a contraindication. If paramedics are on scene, a 12-lead ECG should be recorded to permit rapid identification of those patients in whom a reperfusion strategy is indicated [23]. The patient should be transferred directly to the primary PCI capable facility if available and on arrival should bypass the emergency department to the cath-lab directly to minimize delays [47].

The life-saving effect of fibrinolytic drugs is maximal in the first hour after symptoms onset (golden hour) and then decreases dramatically with time delays. The approach to administration of fibrinolytic drugs in the prehospital setting has been advocated with the aim of reducing the time-to-needle and increasing the number of lives saved. In the case of remote areas with long transfer time to the nearest facility, prehospital fibrinolysis will be strongly advised [23,48].

Currently, prehospital fibrinolysis is recommended in the following settings: in ambulance with qualified physicians or EMS unit with paramedics who can obtain 12-lead ECGs in the field and transmit the tracings to a qualified interpretation site; paramedics are trained on ECG interpretation and initiation of STEMI management, and medically supervised by online command structures; there is a medical supervisor who can guide STEMI management; and, in addition, there is a program for continuous quality improvement [23,48].

2.5.5 Hospital management

2.5.5.1 Medical management

Supplemental oxygen by nasal cannula should be supplied to all cases with suspected STEMI syndromes and hypoxemia (SaO2 <90% or PaO2 <60 mmHg) to improve the myocardial oxygen supply-demand relationship [23]. Otherwise, routine oxygen supplementation is contraindicated [49]. Patients with more profound arterial desaturation, those with impending respiratory collapse, and patients with flash pulmonary edema may warrant additional efforts at oxygenation using noninvasive ventilation up to endotracheal intubation and mechanical ventilator support [50].

Vasodilators, namely nitroglycerin, alleviate ischemic pain by increasing blood flow to coronary arteries and also help with spasmodic pain [51]. In the prereperfusion era nitroglycerin was considered a standard as it was found to limit infarct size and results in better ventricular sizes. Although not currently strongly recommended, it is still being prescribed for relief of active chest pain with STEMI. However, caution should be paid for its hypotensive effect and associated reflex tachycardia [52].

Dual antiplatelet therapy together with anticoagulation is mandatory for all cases of STEMI. Acetyl salicylic acid is recommended to be administered chewed 162—325 mg, or 75—150 mg IV considering 50% bioavailability unless allergy to it is evident. The chewing approach provides more rapid absorption and can result promptly in almost total blockade of the production of thromboxane A2 [33,53].

Thienopyridines (e.g., clopidogrel or ticlopidine) may be given to patients allergic to aspirin (with hives, nasal polyps, bronchospasm, or anaphylaxis) [46]. They are mandated in patients undergoing PCI. Potent rapidly acting agents, Ticagrelor or Prasugrel, are the agents of choice in patients undergoing primary PCI. In this setting, Clopidogrel is preserved for cases with allergy or contraindication to the aforementioned drugs [54]. Cangrelor may be administered for rapid $P2Y_{12}$ inhibition if no other agent was administered prior to the intervention. Glycoprotein IIb/IIIa have recently been considered as bailout measures for cases with thrombotic complications or no-reflow [55].

Anticoagulation is also recommended to all patients with STEMI; low molecular weight heparin (LMWH) or unfractionated heparin (UFH) is recommended to be routinely used. Bivalirudin is an alternative in cases of heparin-induced thrombocytopenia (HIT) and can also be administered routinely, while the use of fundaparinox is totally contraindicated in patients with planned primary PCI [55,56].

Morphine sulfate is recommended as the analgesic of choice for patients with STEMI-associated pain not readily relieved by nitroglycerine. Treatment must be directed at relieving not only the symptoms of ongoing infarction, but also anxiety and apprehension. Both of the latter issues can contribute to the already heightened adrenergic tone in the infarct patient. Elevated catecholamine levels play known roles in plaque rupture, vasospasm, thrombus propagation and malignant arrhythmias [56]. Morphine has vein dilator properties, in addition to its analgesic effects, and may reduce preload by reducing ventricular cavity volume. Thus, adequate analgesia has broad implications beyond simple pain relief. Morphine may be utilized in the recommended doses of 2–4 mg IV with 2–8 mg increments at 5–15 min intervals. Tranquilizers and benzodiazepines may be considered for relief of anxiety [23].

Beta-adrenergic receptor blocking agents have a variety of favorable pharmacologic effects in STEMI resulting from blockade of beta-1 and beta-2 receptors. The result of lowered heart rate and reduced ventricular contractility is a reduction in myocardial oxygen demand. The use of oral beta-blockers in STEMI patients is recommended to all patients without contraindication regardless of whether they will undergo fibrinolysis or PCI [33,57].

Intravenous beta-blockers should be avoided in patients with evidence of acute decompensated heart failure, those with significant resting bradycardia or systolic hypotension, patients with significant AV conduction abnormalities, and in patients with asthma or reactive airways disease. Because of the possibility of coronary spasm exacerbation, beta-blockers should not be given to patients with cocaine-induced STEMI [58].

The utility of Renin-Angiotensin-Aldosterone System Inhibition in the post-STEMI setting is well established. A *meta*-analysis of large trials with angiotensin converting-enzyme inhibitors (ACEI) indicated benefit resulting from early administration of these drugs in STEMI patients. All patients, unless contraindicated, should administer an ACEI within the first 24 h of STEMI especially in cases with heart failure, left ventricular (LV) dysfunction, diabetes mellitus (DM), and anterior infarctions. Angiotensin receptor blockers (ARBs) are alternatives to ACEI in cases of ACEI intolerance while mineralocoticoid receptor antagonists (MRA) are for patients with LVEF ≤ 40% and heart failure or DM in absence of hyperkalemia or renal failure [23,59–61].

Statins, HMG-CoA inhibitors, are used for chronic management of dyslipidemia and in the secondary prevention of CV disease. However, there are compelling data supporting their early use in the post-infarct patient. There are also compliance benefits from early initiation: patients who begin statin therapy prior to hospital discharge are three times more likely to remain on therapy at 6 months than those who began treatment only after hospital discharge. Data now support early, intensive, and sustained treatment with these agents unless contraindicated to reach low density lipoprotein cholesterol (LDL-C) goal of <1.8 mmol/L, with a second lipid-lowering agent to be added if the goal is not achieved by statins only [62–64].

2.5.5.2 Fibrinolysis in a hospital without percutaneuos coronary intervention capability

Fibrinolysis is indicated in hospitals with no primary PCI facility, when FMC to wire cross in the same facility is >90 min and/or when transfer time to primary PCI capable facility takes > 30 min. A meta-analysis has considered the results of the nine largest clinical trials that randomized patients between fibrinolytic therapy and control [65]. Among these trials, four included STEMI patients presenting within 6 h from the onset of symptoms and the rest included patients first seen up to 24 h after presentation. A significant reduction in the number of deaths during days 0–35 was detected in patients treated with fibrinolysis (9.6%) vs controls (11.5%) regardless of age, sex, heart rate, blood pressure, presence of diabetes, or history of MI (18 lives saved per 1000 patients treated) [23].

The greatest mortality reduction was seen among patients having ST-segment elevation (relative reduction of 21%) and among patients presenting within 3 h of symptom onset (relative reduction of 26%) as well as within the 4–6 h postonset time window (relative reduction of 18%). The beneficial effect on mortality, even though time-dependent, was shown to be significant in patients up to 12 h after symptom onset. Since favorable but nonsignificant outcomes were detected beyond this period of time, it is reasonable to administer fibrinolytic agents if a patient has continuing ischemic symptoms and ST segment elevation. It is striking that the early benefit of fibrinolytics upon survival was sustained at 10 years of follow-up [66,67].

Tissue plasminogen activator (t-PA) is superior to streptokinase (SK) administration with greater percentage of thrombolysis in myocardial infarction (TIMI) grade 3 flows and higher patency rates at 90 min after dosing. Every sword has two edges, and t-PA was also associated with 40% higher risk of hemorrhagic stroke when GISSI-2, ISIS-3 and GUSTO-1 data were analyzed together (3.3 patients per 1000 treated), with no similar net clinical outcome (occurrence of stroke or death) [68].

When SK or t-PA were compared to the newer t-PA variants (reteplase and tenecteplase), no significant difference was found in terms of mortality. Reteplase is bioequivalent to SK and t-PA. Tenecteplase is similar to other t-PA variants, with the advantage of fewer extra-cerebral hemorrhagic episodes and less need for blood transfusion [68].

Fibrin-specific agents (reteplase, tenecteplase, or alteplase) are the drugs of choice for fibrinolysis now. Transfer to PCI capable facility is mandatory in candidate patients after fibrinolysis. Angiography and PCI is indicated after fibrinolysis in patients with shock, reinfarction, and failed fibrinolysis or within 2–24 h of successful fibrinolysis [69–72].

2.5.5.3 Primary percutaneuos coronary intervention

Primary percutaneuos coronary intervention (Primary PCI) is a mechanical reperfusion technique that involves the use of balloons, stents, and/or thrombectomy to produce the maximum optimal opening of the thrombosed artery and adequate coronary flow. This will be the treatment modality of choice for patients with STEMI as long as they have access to a well-equipped institution with trained personnel within the specified time window for primary PCI [33,73].

Years of trials and hundreds of centers experience in primary PCI have led to great development in the techniques and accumulation of evidence to support certain techniques over others. In the presence of experienced operators, radial is the default access to minimize access site bleeding, need for transfusion, and other vascular complications [74−76]. Stenting is preferred to balloon angioplasty [77], while drug eluting stents (DES) especially the new generation are proved to be superior to bare metal stents (BMS) as they reduce the rate of restenosis [78−80].

However, in few cases, balloon angioplasty may be the strategy of choice. For example, in patients who are planned to undergo bypass surgery for left main or multivessel coronary disease, as well as in patients with thrombocytopenia in whom clopidogrel is contraindicated. When the infarct related artery is too small to place a stent balloon angioplasty will be sufficient [81,82].

Many of the past modalities have no routine role in primary PCI now: deferred stenting, thrombus aspiration, and glycoprotein IIb/IIIa administration. Deferring stenting was proposed to reduce microvascular obstruction after primary PCI. Recent studies using cardiac magnetic resonance shows no benefit of using this strategy as well as higher need for target vessel revascularization after deferred stenting [83,84]. Thrombus aspiration is associated with increased risk of stroke and should be reserved only for cases with high thrombus burden with maximum protective precautions against stroke [85,86].

Primary PCI is not without risks. Local vascular problems, including bleeding, hematomas, pseudo aneurysms, and arteriovenous fistulae, occur in 2%−3% of patients. About two-thirds of patients have significant bleeding, which may necessitate transfusion [87−89]. When all types of bleeding are considered, the rate of bleeding rises to nearly 7%, with cerebral hemorrhage being the most serious but having a lower incidence than fibrinolysis (0.05% vs 1%, P .001) [90]. Lower heparin doses, finer catheters, more operator expertise, and the use of radial access have all contributed to a decrease in hemorrhage.

After PCI, up to 2% of patients develop severe contrast-induced nephropathy (CIN) [91]. CIN is more common in patients with cardiogenic shock, underlying renal insufficiency, and the elderly [92−94]. In very rare circumstances, radiographic contrast material can cause anaphylaxis [95]. Arrhythmia can develop as a side effect of primary PCI, with a 4.3% chance of ventricular tachycardia or fibrillation. It is linked to longer hospital admissions but a similar long-term prognosis to people who do not have arrhythmias [96].

The incidence rate of complications is inversely related to the procedural volume at the PCI center. Centers with elective PCI annual rate of 200 cases or more report lower incidences of urgent bypass surgery and death after primary PCI [90].

2.6 Prevention

Primary prevention depends entirely on lowering the rate of progress of atherosclerosis by prompt control of the aforementioned risk factors. Healthy diet, regular exercise, smoking cessation, and tight control of hypertension, diabetes, and dyslipidemia to the best evidenced targets are the cornerstone for protection [97].

2.7 Complications

Mechanical and electrical complications of myocardial infarction exist. Heart failure, mitral regurgitation, ventricular wall aneurysm, rupture free wall, and cardiogenic shock are mechanical problems. Thromboembolism is prevalent, with the risk of rein-farction, pulmonary embolism, and stroke being significant. Both tachy and Brady arrhythmias are electrophysiological problems. Dressler's syndrome, pericarditis, and sudden cardiac death are all potential complications [98].

2.8 Prognosis

Around 30% of STEMI patients die within the first 24 h of the index event, with half dying before reaching the hospital; however, these rates have been steadily declining in recent years. Almost 10% of survivors die within the first year, and half of those who survive are rehospitalized. The extent of the infarct, the success of reperfusion, and remaining functions are all factors that influence the prognosis. Successful reperfusion within the prescribed timeframes, intact ventricular functions, and long-term treatment with ACE inhibitors, beta blockers, and statins are all connected to a better prognosis. Patients with diabetes, a prior vascular event, failed or delayed reperfusion, and/or impaired ventricular functions, on the other hand, are predicted to have a bad prognosis [99].

Clinical, laboratory, and imaging methods are among the many tools available for prognostication. Clinical models such as the TIMI risk score for STEMI, the GRACE score, and the Killip class of heart failure are widely used. The predictive power of laboratory markers such as cTns, N-terminal pro B-type natriuretic peptide (NT pro-BNP), and high sensitive C-reactive protein (hs-CRP) has been extensively studied, but it is still insufficient to guide clinical decisions. Although many studies have linked inflammatory indicators to the occurrence of no-reflow phenomena during primary PCI, no one sign has been proven to predict the likelihood of this debilitating event [21,23,57,100—102].

Echocardiographic models have been used in trial to predict outcome of STEMI [103]. Currently many approaches for cardiac regeneration are under investigation including the use of stem cells or induction of cardiomyocytes proliferation. Although the trials are still very primitive some approaches showed extremely promising results with high potential to reach clinical trials [104−106].

2.9 Conclusion

Thrombolytic drugs and primary PCI are the two reperfusion strategies currently available to open the infarct-related artery. Achieving an early diagnosis and complete restoration of blood flow, with resultant improvement in myocardial perfusion, is the target of STEMI management. According to current data, there is still an important percentage of eligible patients not receiving reperfusion therapy within recommended time frames with delayed diagnosis in many cases. Major efforts are being undertaken to increase awareness of the symptoms associated with myocardial infarction and the importance of rapid treatment to decrease both complications and mortality.

References

[1] Hammer A. Wiener Zeitung (in German) Ein Fall von thrombotischem Verschlusse einer der Kranzarterien des Herzens: am Krankenbette konstatirt. Wien: Druckderk; 1878.
[2] Obrastzow WP, Straschesko ND. in German Zur Kenntnis der Thrombose der Koronararterien des Herzens. Berlin: Hirschwald; 1910.
[3] Herrick JB. Clinical features of sudden obstruction of the coronary arteries. J Am Med Assoc 1912; LIX(23):2015−22. Available from: https://doi.org/10.1001/jama.1912.04270120001001.
[4] Friedberg CK, Horn H. Acute myocardial infarction not due to coronary artery occlusion. J Am Med Assoc 1939;112(17):1675−9. Available from: https://doi.org/10.1001/jama.1939.02800170021007.
[5] Costa MA, et al. Impact of stent deployment procedural factors on long-term effectiveness and safety of sirolimus-eluting stents (Final results of the multicenter prospective STLLR trial). Am J Cardiol 2008;101(12):1704−11. Available from: https://doi.org/10.1016/j.amjcard.2008.02.053.
[6] WHO. The work of WHO, 1971: annual report of the Director-General to the World Health Assembly and to the United Nations; 1972. Available from: https://apps.who.int/iris/handle/10665/85845.
[7] Wang N, Lan D, Chen W, Matsuura F, Tall AR. ATP-binding cassette transporters G1 and G4 mediate cellular cholesterol efflux to high-density lipoproteins. Proc Natl Acad Sci U S A 2004;101 (26):9774−9. Available from: https://doi.org/10.1073/pnas.0403506101.
[8] No Authors. Myocardial infarction redefined—A consensus document of The Joint European Society of Cardiology/American College of Cardiology Committee for the Redefinition of Myocardial Infarction. Eur. Heart J 2000;21(18):1502−13. Available from: https://doi.org/10.1053/euhj.2000.2305.
[9] Thygesen K, et al. Fourth universal definition of myocardial infarction (2018. Eur Heart J 2019;40 (3):237−69. Available from: https://doi.org/10.1093/eurheartj/ehy462.
[10] Jernberg T, et al. The Swedish web-system for enhancement and development of evidence-based care in heart disease evaluated according to recommended therapies (SWEDEHEART). Heart 2010;96(20):1617. Available from: https://doi.org/10.1136/hrt.2010.198804.
[11] Widimsky P, et al. Reperfusion therapy for ST elevation acute myocardial infarction in Europe: description of the current situation in 30 countries. Eur Heart J 2010;31(8):943−57. Available from: https://doi.org/10.1093/eurheartj/ehp492.

[12] McManus DD, Gore J, Yarzebski J, Spencer F, Lessard D, Goldberg RJ. Recent trends in the incidence, treatment, and outcomes of patients with STEMI and NSTEMI. Am J Med 2011;124 (1):40−7. Available from: https://doi.org/10.1016/j.amjmed.2010.07.023.

[13] Sugiyama T, Hasegawa K, Kobayashi Y, Takahashi O, Fukui T, Tsugawa Y. Differential time trends of outcomes and costs of care for acute myocardial infarction hospitalizations by ST elevation and type of intervention in the United States, 2001−2011. J Am Heart Assoc 2015;4(3):e001445. Available from: https://doi.org/10.1161/JAHA.114.001445.

[14] WHO, Monitoring health for the SDGs; 2019. Available from: https://www.who.int/news/item/04-04-2019-uneven-access-to-health-services-drives-life-expectancy-gaps-who.

[15] Rahim HFA, et al. Non-communicable diseases in the Arab world. Lancet 2014;383(9914): 356−67. Available from: https://doi.org/10.1016/S0140-6736(13)62383-1.

[16] Kang S-H, et al. Sex differences in management and mortality of patients with ST-elevation myocardial infarction (from the Korean Acute Myocardial Infarction National Registry. Am J Cardiol 2012;109(6):787−93. Available from: https://doi.org/10.1016/j.amjcard.2011.11.006.

[17] Kytö V, Sipilä J, Rautava P. Gender and in-hospital mortality of ST-segment elevation myocardial infarction (from a Multihospital Nationwide Registry Study of 31,689 Patients). Am J Cardiol 2015;115(3):303−6. Available from: https://doi.org/10.1016/j.amjcard.2014.11.001.

[18] Bangalore S, Qin J, Sloan S, Murphy SA, Cannon CP. What is the optimal blood pressure in patients after acute coronary syndromes? Circulation 2010;122(21):2142−51. Available from: https://doi.org/10.1161/circulationaha.109.905687.

[19] Bonaca MP, et al. American College of Cardiology/American Heart Association/European Society of Cardiology/World Heart Federation Universal Definition of Myocardial Infarction Classification System and the Risk of Cardiovascular Death. Circulation 2012;125(4):577−83. Available from: https://doi.org/10.1161/circulationaha.111.041160.

[20] Chatzizisis YS, Coskun AU, Jonas M, Edelman ER, Feldman CL, Stone PH. Role of endothelial shear stress in the natural history of coronary atherosclerosis and vascular remodeling: molecular, cellular, and vascular behavior. J Am Coll Cardiol 2007;49(25):2379−93. Available from: https://doi.org/10.1016/j.jacc.2007.02.059.

[21] Haaf P, et al. B-type natriuretic peptide in the early diagnosis and risk stratification of acute chest pain. Am J Med 2011;124(5):444−52. Available from: https://doi.org/10.1016/j.amjmed.2010.11.012.

[22] Juliard J-M, et al. Can we provide reperfusion therapy to all unselected patients admitted with acute myocardial infarction. J Am Coll Cardiol 1997;30(1):157−64. Available from: https://doi.org/10.1016/S0735-1097(97)00119-8.

[23] Antman EM, et al. Focused update of the ACC/AHA 2004 guidelines for the management of patients with ST-elevation myocardial infarction. Circulation 2007;117(2):296−329. Available from: https://doi.org/10.1161/CIRCULATIONAHA.107.188209.

[24] Falk E. Pathogenesis of atherosclerosis. J Am Coll Cardiol 2006;47(8, Supplement):C7−12. Available from: https://doi.org/10.1016/j.jacc.2005.09.068.

[25] Naghavi M, et al. From vulnerable plaque to vulnerable patient. Circulation 2003;108(15):1772−8. Available from: https://doi.org/10.1161/01.CIR.0000087481.55887.C9.

[26] Asakura M, et al. Extensive development of vulnerable plaques as a pan-coronary process in patients with myocardial infarction: an angioscopic study. J Am Coll Cardiol 2001;37(5):1284−8. Available from: https://doi.org/10.1016/S0735-1097(01)01135-4.

[27] Shen B-J, et al. Anxiety characteristics independently and prospectively predict myocardial infarction in men: the unique contribution of anxiety among psychologic factors. J Am Coll Cardiol 2008;51 (2):113−19. Available from: https://doi.org/10.1016/j.jacc.2007.09.033.

[28] Davì G, Patrono C. Platelet Activation and Atherothrombosis. N Engl J Med 2007;357 (24):2482−94. Available from: https://doi.org/10.1056/NEJMra071014.

[29] Libby P. Molecular bases of the acute coronary syndromes. Circulation 1995;91(11):2844−50. Available from: https://doi.org/10.1161/01.CIR.91.11.2844.

[30] DeFilippi CR, et al. Association of serial measures of cardiac troponin T using a sensitive assay with incident heart failure and cardiovascular mortality in older adults. JAMA 2010;304(22):2494−502. Available from: https://doi.org/10.1001/jama.2010.1708.

[31] Henrikson CA, et al. Chest pain relief by nitroglycerin does not predict active coronary artery disease. Ann Intern Med 2003;139(12):979—86. Available from: https://doi.org/10.7326/0003-4819-139-12-200312160-00007.

[32] De Torbal A, et al. Incidence of recognized and unrecognized myocardial infarction in men and women aged 55 and older: the Rotterdam Study. Eur Heart J 2006;27(6):729—36. Available from: https://doi.org/10.1093/eurheartj/ehi707.

[33] Ibanez B, et al. 2017 ESC Guidelines for the management of acute myocardial infarction in patients presenting with ST-segment elevation. Eur Heart J 2018;39(2):119—77. Available from: https://doi.org/10.1093/eurheartj/ehx393.

[34] Lopez-Sendon J, Coma-Canella I, Alcasena S, Seoane J, Gamallo C. Electrocardiographic findings in acute right ventricular infarction: sensitivity and specificity of electrocardiographic alterations in right precordial leads V4R, V3R, V1, V2and V3. J Am Coll Cardiol 1985;6(6):1273—9. Available from: https://doi.org/10.1016/S0735-1097(85)80213-8.

[35] Sgarbossa EB, et al. Electrocardiographic diagnosis of evolving acute myocardial infarction in the presence of left bundle-branch block. N Engl J Med 1996;334(8):481—7. Available from: https://doi.org/10.1056/NEJM199602223340801.

[36] Sgarbossa EB, Pinski SL, Gates KB, Wagner GS, The G-I. Early electrocardiographic diagnosis of acute myocardial infarction in the presence of ventricular paced rhythm. Am J Cardiol 1996;77 (5):423—4. Available from: https://doi.org/10.1016/S0002-9149(97)89377-0.

[37] Shlipak MG, Lyons WL, Go AS, Chou TM, Evans GT, Browner WS. Should the electrocardiogram be used to guide therapy for patients with left bundle-branch block and suspected myocardial infarction? JAMA 1999;281(8):714—19. Available from: https://doi.org/10.1001/jama.281.8.714.

[38] Madias JE. The nonspecificity of ST-segment elevation ≥5.0 mm in V1—V3 in the diagnosis of acute myocardial infarction in the presence of ventricular paced rhythm. J Electrocardiol 2004;37 (2):135—9. Available from: https://doi.org/10.1016/j.jelectrocard.2004.01.008.

[39] Wong C-K, et al. Patients with prolonged ischemic chest pain and presumed-new left bundle branch block have heterogeneous outcomes depending on the presence of ST-segment changes. J Am Coll Cardiol 2005;46(1):29—38. Available from: https://doi.org/10.1016/j.jacc.2005.02.084.

[40] Chang AM, Shofer FS, Tabas JA, Magid DJ, McCusker CM, Hollander JE. Lack of association between left bundle-branch block and acute myocardial infarction in symptomatic ED patients. Am J Emerg Med 2009;27(8):916—21. Available from: https://doi.org/10.1016/j.ajem.2008.07.007.

[41] Krishnaswamy A, Lincoff AM, Menon V. Magnitude and consequences of missing the acute infarct-related circumflex artery. Am Heart J 2009;158(5):706—12. Available from: https://doi.org/10.1016/j.ahj.2009.08.024.

[42] Lopes RD, et al. Diagnosing acute myocardial infarction in patients with left bundle branch block. Am J Cardiol 2011;108(6):782—8. Available from: https://doi.org/10.1016/j.amjcard.2011.05.006.

[43] Widimsky P, et al. Primary angioplasty in acute myocardial infarction with right bundle branch block: should new onset right bundle branch block be added to future guidelines as an indication for reperfusion therapy? Eur Heart J 2012;33(1):86—95. Available from: https://doi.org/10.1093/eurheartj/ehr291.

[44] Katritsis DG, et al. Optimal timing of coronary angiography and potential intervention in non-ST-elevation acute coronary syndromes. Eur Heart J 2011;32(1):32—40. Available from: https://doi.org/10.1093/eurheartj/ehq276.

[45] West RM, et al. Impact of hospital proportion and volume on primary percutaneous coronary intervention performance in England and Wales. Eur Heart J 2011;32(6):706—11. Available from: https://doi.org/10.1093/eurheartj/ehq476.

[46] Antman EM, et al. ACC/AHA guidelines for the management of patients with ST-elevation myocardial infarction—Executive summary. Circulation 2004;110(5):588—636. Available from: https://doi.org/10.1161/01.cir.0000134791.68010.fa.

[47] Bagai A, et al. Emergency department bypass for ST-segment—elevation myocardial infarction patients identified with a prehospital electrocardiogram. Circulation 2013;128(4):352—9. Available from: https://doi.org/10.1161/CIRCULATIONAHA.113.002339.

[48] Welsh RC, et al. Time to treatment and the impact of a physician on prehospital management of acute ST elevation myocardial infarction: insights from the ASSENT-3 PLUS trial. Heart 2005;91 (11):1400. Available from: https://doi.org/10.1136/hrt.2004.054510.

[49] Stub D, et al. Air vs oxygen in ST-segment—elevation myocardial infarction. Circulation 2015;131 (24):2143—50. Available from: https://doi.org/10.1161/CIRCULATIONAHA.114.014494.

[50] Moholdt T, et al. Aerobic interval training increases peak oxygen uptake more than usual care exercise training in myocardial infarction patients: a randomized controlled study. Clin Rehabil 2012;26 (1):33—44. Available from: https://doi.org/10.1177/0269215511405229.

[51] Chunawala Z, Chang PP, DeFilippis AP, Hall ME, Matsushita K, Caughey MC. Recurrent admissions for acute decompensated heart failure among patients with and without peripheral artery disease: The ARIC Study. J Am Heart Assoc 2020;9(21):e017174. Available from: https://doi.org/10.1161/JAHA.120.017174.

[52] Shufelt K, Yusuf S, Cairns JA, Camm AJ. Evidence-based cardiology. 2nd edition London: BMJ Books; 2003.

[53] Hohlfeld T, et al. Prospective, randomised trial of the time dependent antiplatelet effects of 500 mg and 250 mg acetylsalicylic acid i.v. and 300 mg p. o. in ACS (ACUTE). Thromb Haemost 2017;117(03):625—35. Available from: https://doi.org/10.1160/th16-08-0650.

[54] Wiviott SD, et al. Prasugrel vs clopidogrel in patients with acute coronary syndromes. N Engl J Med 2007;357(20):2001—15. Available from: https://doi.org/10.1056/NEJMoa0706482.

[55] Steg PG, et al. Effect of cangrelor on periprocedural outcomes in percutaneous coronary interventions: a pooled analysis of patient-level data. Lancet 2013;382(9909):1981—92. Available from: https://doi.org/10.1016/S0140-6736(13)61615-3.

[56] Montalescot G, et al. Intravenous enoxaparin or unfractionated heparin in primary percutaneous coronary intervention for ST-elevation myocardial infarction: the international randomised open-label ATOLL trial. Lancet 2011;378(9792):693—703. Available from: https://doi.org/10.1016/S0140-6736(11)60876-3.

[57] Salama AM, et al. MicroRNA-208a: a good diagnostic marker and a predictor of no-reflow in STEMI patients undergoing primary percutaneuos coronary intervention. J Cardiovasc Transl Res 2020;13(6):988—95. Available from: https://doi.org/10.1007/s12265-020-10020-9.

[58] Salama ABM, et al. Abstract 294: microrna-208a: a marker of no-reflow in STEMI patients undergoing primary percutaneuos coronary intervention. Circ Res 2020;127(Suppl_1):A294. Available from: https://doi.org/10.1161/res.127.suppl_1.294.

[59] Fox KM. Efficacy of perindopril in reduction of cardiovascular events among patients with stable coronary artery disease: randomised, double-blind, placebo-controlled, multicentre trial (the EUROPA study). The Lancet 2003;362(9386):782—8. Available from: https://doi.org/10.1016/S0140-6736(03)14286-9.

[60] Pfeffer MA, et al. Valsartan, captopril, or both in myocardial infarction complicated by heart failure, left ventricular dysfunction, or both. N Engl J Med 2003;349(20):1893—906. Available from: https://doi.org/10.1056/NEJMoa032292.

[61] Zannad F, et al. Eplerenone in patients with systolic heart failure and mild symptoms. N Engl J Med 2011;364(1):11—21. Available from: https://doi.org/10.1056/NEJMoa1009492.

[62] Boekholdt SM, et al. Very low levels of atherogenic lipoproteins and the risk for cardiovascular events: a meta-analysis of statin trials. J Am Coll Cardiol 2014;64(5):485—94. Available from: https://doi.org/10.1016/j.jacc.2014.02.615 /08/05/ 2014.

[63] Sabatine MS, et al. Evolocumab and clinical outcomes in patients with cardiovascular disease. N Engl J Med 2017;376(18):1713—22. Available from: https://doi.org/10.1056/NEJMoa1615664.

[64] Fathia Abd Elwahid Mannaa KGA-W, Baha-Eldin Abdallah Elsayed A, Abdel-hamid fatehy M, Mohammed Shaker A. Exercise as a physiotherapy potentiates thermogenesis and obesity management through elevation of myokine irisin. J Innov Pharm Biol Sci (JIPBS) 2018;05(04):74—80.

[65] Fibrinolytic G. Therapy Trialists' Collaborative, Indications for fibrinolytic therapy in suspected acute myocardial infarction: collaborative overview of early mortality and major morbidity results from all randomised trials of more than 1000 patients. Lancet 1994;343(8893):311—22. Available from: https://doi.org/10.1016/S0140-6736(94)91161-4.

[66] Björklund E, et al. Pre-hospital thrombolysis delivered by paramedics is associated with reduced time delay and mortality in ambulance-transported real-life patients with ST-elevation myocardial infarction. Eur Heart J 2006;27(10):1146–52. Available from: https://doi.org/10.1093/eurheartj/ehi886.

[67] Bonnefoy E, et al. Comparison of primary angioplasty and pre-hospital fibrinolysis in acute myocardial infarction (CAPTIM) trial: a 5-year follow-up. Eur Heart J 2009;30(13):1598–606. Available from: https://doi.org/10.1093/eurheartj/ehp156.

[68] Gabriel R. Evidencias en cardiología II. De los ensayos clínicos a las conductas terapéuticas. Revista Española de Cardiología (English Edition) 2003;56(10):1036 [Online]. Available: /18855857/0000005600000010/v0_201403070112/13052425/v0_201403070113/en/main.assetsER.

[69] Gershlick AH, et al. Rescue angioplasty after failed thrombolytic therapy for acute myocardial infarction. N Engl J Med 2005;353(26):2758–68. Available from: https://doi.org/10.1056/NEJMoa050849.

[70] Authors/Task Force M, et al. ESC Guidelines for the management of acute myocardial infarction in patients presenting with ST-segment elevation: the task force on the management of ST-segment elevation acute myocardial infarction of the European Society of Cardiology (ESC). Eur Heart J 2012;33(20):2569–619. Available from: https://doi.org/10.1093/eurheartj/ehs215.

[71] Armstrong PW, et al. Fibrinolysis or primary PCI in ST-segment elevation myocardial infarction. N Engl J Med 2013;368(15):1379–87. Available from: https://doi.org/10.1056/NEJMoa1301092.

[72] Madan M, et al. Relationship between time to invasive assessment and clinical outcomes of patients undergoing an early invasive strategy after fibrinolysis for ST-segment elevation myocardial infarction. JACC Cardiovasc Interv 2015;8(1):166.

[73] Boersma E, The Primary Coronary Angioplasty vs. Thrombolysis -2 Trialists' Collaborative G. Does time matter? A pooled analysis of randomized clinical trials comparing primary percutaneous coronary intervention and in-hospital fibrinolysis in acute myocardial infarction patients. Eur Heart J 2006;27(7):779–88. Available from: https://doi.org/10.1093/eurheartj/ehi810.

[74] Jolly SS, et al. Radial vs femoral access for coronary angiography and intervention in patients with acute coronary syndromes (RIVAL): a randomised, parallel group, multicentre trial. Lancet 2011;377(9775):1409–20. Available from: https://doi.org/10.1016/S0140-6736(11)60404-2.

[75] Romagnoli E, et al. Radial vs femoral randomized investigation in ST-segment elevation acute coronary syndrome: The RIFLE-STEACS (Radial vs femoral randomized investigation in ST-elevation acute coronary syndrome) Study. J Am Coll Cardiol 2012;60(24):2481–9. Available from: https://doi.org/10.1016/j.jacc.2012.06.017.

[76] Valgimigli M, et al. Radial vs femoral access in patients with acute coronary syndromes undergoing invasive management: a randomised multicentre trial. Lancet 2015;385(9986):2465–76. Available from: https://doi.org/10.1016/S0140-6736(15)60292-6.

[77] Nordmann AJ, Hengstler P, Harr T, Young J, Bucher HC. Clinical outcomes of primary stenting vs balloon angioplasty in patients with myocardial infarction: a meta-analysis of randomized controlled trials. Am J Med 2004;116(4):253–62. Available from: https://doi.org/10.1016/j.amjmed.2003.08.035.

[78] Kastrati A, et al. Meta-analysis of randomized trials on drug-eluting stents vs. bare-metal stents in patients with acute myocardial infarction. Eur Heart J 2007;28(22):2706–13. Available from: https://doi.org/10.1093/eurheartj/ehm402.

[79] Räber L, et al. Effect of biolimus-eluting stents with biodegradable polymer vs bare-metal stents on cardiovascular events among patients with acute myocardial infarction: The COMFORTABLE AMI randomized trial. JAMA 2012;308(8):777–87. Available from: https://doi.org/10.1001/jama.2012.10065.

[80] Sabaté M, et al. Clinical outcomes in patients with ST-segment elevation myocardial infarction treated with everolimus-eluting stents vs bare-metal stents (EXAMINATION): 5-year results of a randomised trial. Lancet 2016;387(10016):357–66. Available from: https://doi.org/10.1016/S0140-6736(15)00548-6.

[81] Valgimigli M, et al. Tirofiban and sirolimus-eluting stent vs abciximab and bare-metal stent for acute myocardial infarctiona randomized trial. JAMA 2005;293(17):2109–17. Available from: https://doi.org/10.1001/jama.293.17.2109.

[82] Laarman GJ, et al. Paclitaxel-eluting vs uncoated stents in primary percutaneous coronary intervention. N Engl J Med 2006;355(11):1105–13. Available from: https://doi.org/10.1056/NEJMoa062598.

[83] Carrick D, et al. A randomized trial of deferred stenting vs immediate stenting to prevent no- or slow-reflow in acute ST-segment elevation myocardial infarction (DEFER-STEMI). J Am Coll Cardiol 2014;63(20):2088–98. Available from: https://doi.org/10.1016/j.jacc.2014.02.530.

[84] Kelbæk H, et al. Deferred vs conventional stent implantation in patients with ST-segment elevation myocardial infarction (DANAMI 3-DEFER): an open-label, randomised controlled trial. Lancet 2016;387(10034):2199–206. Available from: https://doi.org/10.1016/S0140-6736(16)30072-1.

[85] Jolly SS, et al. Stroke in the TOTAL trial: a randomized trial of routine thrombectomy vs. percutaneous coronary intervention alone in ST elevation myocardial infarction. Eur Heart J 2015;36 (35):2364–72. Available from: https://doi.org/10.1093/eurheartj/ehv296.

[86] Li J-F, et al. Clinical impact of thrombus aspiration and interaction with D-dimer levels in patients with ST-segment elevation myocardial infarction undergoing primary percutaneous coronary intervention. Front Cardiovasc Med 2021;8:706979. Available from: https://doi.org/10.3389/fcvm.2021.706979.

[87] Grines CL, et al. A comparison of immediate angioplasty with thrombolytic therapy for acute myocardial infarction. N Engl J Med 1993;328(10):673–9. Available from: https://doi.org/10.1056/NEJM199303113281001.

[88] Aversano T, et al. Thrombolytic therapy vs primary percutaneous coronary intervention for myocardial infarction in patients presenting to hospitals without on-site cardiac surgerya randomized controlled trial. JAMA 2002;287(15):1943–51. Available from: https://doi.org/10.1001/jama.287.15.1943.

[89] Piper WD, et al. Predicting vascular complications in percutaneous coronary interventions. Am Heart J 2003;145(6):1022–9. Available from: https://doi.org/10.1016/S0002-8703(03)00079-6.

[90] Keeley EC, Boura JA, Grines CL. Primary angioplasty vs intravenous thrombolytic therapy for acute myocardial infarction: a quantitative review of 23 randomised trials. Lancet 2003;361(9351):13–20. Available from: https://doi.org/10.1016/S0140-6736(03)12113-7.

[91] Bartholomew BA, et al. Impact of nephropathy after percutaneous coronary intervention and a method for risk stratification. Am J Cardiol 2004;93(12):1515–19. Available from: https://doi.org/10.1016/j.amjcard.2004.03.008.

[92] Hochman JS, et al. Early revascularization in acute myocardial infarction complicated by cardiogenic shock. N Engl J Med 1999;341(9):625–34. Available from: https://doi.org/10.1056/NEJM199908263410901.

[93] DeGeare VS, et al. Angiographic and clinical characteristics associated with increased in-hospital mortality in elderly patients with acute myocardial infarction undergoing percutaneous intervention (a pooled analysis of the primary angioplasty in myocardial infarction trials). Am J Cardiol 2000;86 (1):30–4. Available from: https://doi.org/10.1016/S0002-9149(00)00824-9.

[94] Sadeghi HM, et al. Impact of renal insufficiency in patients undergoing primary angioplasty for acute myocardial infarction. Circulation 2003;108(22):2769–75. Available from: https://doi.org/10.1161/01.CIR.0000103623.63687.21.

[95] Goss JE, Chambers CE, Heupler JFA. Systemic anaphylactoid reactions to Iodinated contrast media during cardiac catheterization procedures: Guidelines for prevention, diagnosis, and treatment. Cathet Cardiovasc Diagn 1995;34(2):99–104. Available from: https://doi.org/10.1002/ccd.1810340403.

[96] Mehta RH, et al. Sustained ventricular tachycardia or fibrillation in the cardiac catheterization laboratory among patients receiving primary percutaneous coronary intervention: incidence, predictors, and outcomes. J Am Coll Cardiol 2004;43(10):1765–72. Available from: https://doi.org/10.1016/j.jacc.2003.09.072.

[97] Pell JP, et al. Smoke-free legislation and hospitalizations for acute coronary syndrome. N Engl J Med 2008;359(5):482–91. Available from: https://doi.org/10.1056/NEJMsa0706740.

[98] Chang AM, Walsh KM, Shofer FS, McCusker CM, Litt HI, Hollander JE. Relationship between cocaine use and coronary artery disease in patients with symptoms consistent with an acute coronary syndrome. Academic Emerg Med 2011;18(1):1–9. Available from: https://doi.org/10.1111/j.1553-2712.2010.00955.x.

[99] Terkelsen CJ, et al. System delay and mortality among patients with STEMI treated with primary percutaneous coronary intervention. JAMA 2010;304(7):763–71. Available from: https://doi.org/10.1001/jama.2010.1139.

[100] Boersma E, et al. Predictors of outcome in patients with acute coronary syndromes without persistent ST-segment elevation. Circulation 2000;101(22):2557–67. Available from: https://doi.org/10.1161/01.CIR.101.22.2557.

[101] Reffelmann T. The "no-reflow" phenomenon: basic science and clinical correlates. Heart 2002;87(2):162–8. Available from: https://doi.org/10.1136/heart.87.2.162.

[102] James SK, et al. N-terminal pro–brain natriuretic peptide and other risk markers for the separate prediction of mortality and subsequent myocardial infarction in patients with unstable coronary artery disease. Circulation 2003;108(3):275–81. Available from: https://doi.org/10.1161/01.CIR.0000079170.10579.DC.

[103] Mohiedden E, Al-shaer MHE, Elmaghawry LM, Al Zaki MM, Abdelaziz M, Salama AM. Right ventricular functions can predict left ventricular reverse remodeling in patients with ischemic cardiomyopathy after revascularization. Zagazig Univ Med J 2021. Available from: https://doi.org/10.21608/zumj.2021.51617.2032.

[104] Abouleisa RRE, et al. Transient cell cycle induction in cardiomyocytes to treat subacute ischemic heart failure. Circulation 2022;145(17):1339–55. Available from: https://doi.org/10.1161/circulationaha.121.057641.

[105] Abouleisa RRE, et al. Cell cycle induction in human cardiomyocytes is dependent on biosynthetic pathway activation. Redox Biol 2021;46:102094. Available from: https://doi.org/10.1016/j.redox.2021.102094.

[106] Abouleisa R, et al. Abstract 10492: preclinical evaluation of transient and cardiomyocyte specific gene therapy for the treatment of subacute ischemic heart failure. Circulation 2021;144(Suppl_1):A10492. Available from: https://doi.org/10.1161/circ.144.suppl_1.10492.

CHAPTER 3

The effect of patient-centered education in adherence to the treatment regimen in patients with coronary artery disease

Mandana Saki[1], Fatemeh Jafari Pour[2], Saba Najmi[3], Mohammad Gholami[1] and Farzad Ebrahimzadeh[4]

[1]Social Determinants of Health Research Center, Lorestan University of Medical Sciences, Khorramabad, Iran
[2]Department of Nursing, Behbahan Faculty of Medical Sciences, Behbahan, Iran
[3]Student Research Committee, Lorestan University of Medical Sciences, Khorramabad, Iran
[4]Department of Biostatistics, Nutritional Health Research Center, Lorestan University of Medical Sciences, Khorramabad, Iran

3.1 Introduction

Coronary artery disease (CAD) is the most important cardiovascular disorder and a health problem in developing and developed countries and is one of the chronic diseases that limit life in the long run [1]. Coronary artery disease is a pervasive heart disease in which the arteries become narrow and the heart muscle is deprived of enough blood and oxygen. In this case, there may be no problem at rest, but when the heart has to do more work, the coronary arteries can not supply enough oxygen and blood according to the needs of these muscles, resulting in chest pain and angina [2]. Chronic disease management is complex and requires the involvement of patients and healthcare workers [3]. Economic and industrial development and the expansion of communication have mechanized life and subsequently led to changes in lifestyle and increased incidence of cardiovascular diseases [4]. A person's lifestyle is closely related to a person's health, so that a healthy lifestyle promotes a person's health. The most important risk factors for cardiovascular disease are poor nutrition, sedentary lifestyle, smoking, obesity, and high blood pressure. Diabetes and hyperlipidemia are all rooted in an unhealthy lifestyle. Therefore by modifying lifestyle and changing high-risk behaviors, the prevalence of this disease can be reduced [5]. Adherence to the treatment regimen in these patients includes adherence to pharmacological and nonpharmacological methods. In addition to medication, CAD patients should be informed about diet, physical activity, and control of signs and symptoms. Patients should be educated and empowered to choose the appropriate behavior to maintain physiological stability, which can include monitoring the symptoms of the disease, adherence to the treatment regimen, as well as the appropriate response in case of symptoms [6].

Cardiovascular and Coronary Artery Imaging
DOI: https://doi.org/10.1016/B978-0-12-821983-6.00003-5
35

Adherence to a proper diet as well as long adherence to cardiovascular drugs is the cornerstone of management and prevention of cardiovascular diseases [7]. Adherence to treatment programs is an important challenge in patients with chronic diseases and one of the main concerns and clinical problems of healthcare systems [8]. Therefore adherence to treatment is more important in chronic diseases, including heart disease, in which patients must follow the prescribed treatment for a long time [9]. If the treatment plans of patients suffering from severe consequences of the disease such as recurrence of the disease and disability progression are not followed, the need for immediate treatment and hospitalization becomes necessary [10].

Evidence shows that a quarter of patients generally do not adhere to their treatment regimen [11]. Lack of follow-up treatment and care in patients is one of the factors that can increase the risk of complications along with increased mortality, disability, and cost of healthcare. For this reason, people with CAD need to strengthen their skills and acquire the necessary competencies in the field of self-care. Involving the patient in monitoring his health status is very important in maintaining health [12]. One of the most effective measures in this field is educating and following up on patients after discharge from the hospital, which plays an important role in patient rehabilitation [13]. In chronic diseases, education is a key part of the care program that encourages patients to actively participate in self-care. If the training is provided properly and in a timely manner, the need for medication and hospitalization for vascular risks such as stroke in the future will be significantly reduced [14].

Considering that diet-training education and exercise programs have very important effects on a patient's recovery process, one of the key goals in patient care is to increase the adherence to the treatment regimen and the recommendations provided by the treatment group [15].

Patient-centered care is a goal and a tool to improve health outcomes and is recognized as an important priority for improving healthcare [16]. Patient-centered care is defined as care that builds partnerships between physicians, patients, and their families to ensure that the clinical decisions are based on patients' wishes, needs, and preferences [17].

In the patient-centered approach, cardiovascular patients need long-term care in various situations of daily life, requiring self-care requires and the acquisition of health-related information. Evidence suggests that obtaining this information in cardiovascular patients can play an important role in improving health outcomes such as reducing stress, increasing satisfaction, increasing perception of control, adhering to a diet, and improving patient communication with healthcare providers [18].

Health services around the world are moving toward patient-centered approaches. The basis of this work is to involve the patient in improving his own health [19]. Giving patients the opportunity to participate in their own care will enhance care, increase patient responsibility and commitment to health behaviors, and facilitate care and treatment [20]. However, nonadherence to the treatment regimen in heart patients is not only a major obstacle to the effective provision of healthcare [21] but also one of the factors that can lead to readmission of these patients [22] and one of the reasons for treatment failure, increased morbidity, prolongation of treatment, and increased costs of healthcare [23]. Thus it is necessary to provide solutions to increase adherence to the treatment regimen in heart patients. Therefore due to the importance of this subject, the current study was performed to assess the effect of patient-centered education on adherence to treatment regimen in patients with CAD. In this study, a major question arises as to what effect patient-centered education has on adherence to the treatment regimen. And only by providing favorable outcomes, we can emphasize the effectiveness of patient-centered education in adherence to the treatment regimen in order to control the disease and improve the patients' health .

3.2 Methods

3.2.1 Type of research

Parallel randomized controlled study.

3.2.2 Research environment

Cardiac Care Units (CCUs) of Teaching Hospitals in Khorramabad city.

3.2.3 Research community

The population in this study was all patients with coronary artery disease (acute myocardial infarction) referred to teaching hospitals affiliated to Lorestan University of Medical Sciences in 2019.

3.2.4 Sample

All patients with acute myocardial infarction who met the inclusion criteria and were admitted to the cardiac intensive care unit.

3.2.5 Sample size

The sample size was obtained by the formula: $n = \dfrac{\left(z_{1-\frac{\alpha}{2}} + z_{1-\beta}\right)^2 (s_1^2 + s_2^2)}{(\mu_1 - \mu_2)^2}$

$$\alpha = 0/05 \; \beta = 0/20 \; S_1 = 2/27$$

$$S_2 = 0/92 \; \mu_1 = 23/3 \; \mu_2 = 24/3$$

Assuming 10% attrition, 52 patients were divided into intervention and control groups.

3.2.6 Sampling method

In the present study, the sampling was done through nonprobability consecutive method and patients were then allocated into intervention and control groups using stratified randomization. We did not consider blinding for our participants because our intervention was educational in nature.

3.2.7 Inclusion criteria

(1) Willingness to enter the study; (2) No mental illness; (3) Age between 30—65 years; (4) Ability to speak; (5) diagnosed coronary heart disease (myocardial infarction) by a doctor; (6) Ability to perform their daily activities; (7) Familiarity with Persian language; (8) No memory impairment (such as Alzheimer's); (9) Not participating in rehabilitation-educational programs; and (10) Hospitalization in the intensive care units.

3.2.8 Exclusion criteria

(1) Reluctance to continue attending the study; (2) Fail to attend more than one session in training sessions; (3) Drug and alcohol abuse; (4) Being on the list for heart surgery; and (5) Unstable hemodynamic conditions.

3.2.9 Data collection tool

In this study, a two-part questionnaire was used: The first part was questions related to demographic information including gender, age, marital status, level of education, family history of cardiovascular disease, medical history, number of hospitalizations, etc. The second part was related to the scale of adherence to the treatment regimen [24]. This scale contained items in three dimensions [medication (six items and score of 24)—diet (13 items and score of 46) —activity pattern (seven items and score of 18)]. The validity and reliability of the scale were tested by content validity and test-retest and interrater reliability. Test-retest reliability was accounted for 90% and the Pearson correlation coefficient in this questionnaire was diet ($r = 0.86$), medication ($r = 0.91$), and activity pattern ($r = 0.95$). The total score of the adherence to treatment scale based on a scale of 0 to 100 was classified as poor (0—33.3), average (33.3—66.6), and good (66.6—100).

3.2.10 Procedure

In order to carry out this research, after obtaining the permission of the Ethics Committee, the researcher referred to the teaching hospitals for sampling. The sampling was done through nonprobability consecutive method and patients were then allocated into intervention and control groups using the stratified randomization and with the help of a table of random numbers. In order to prevent contamination of the samples, sampling was first performed for the control group and then for the intervention group. Written informed consent was obtained from the participants. Thus the researcher provided necessary explanations on how to complete the questionnaire. At the beginning of the study, the participants from both intervention and control groups filled out the questionnaire. The patients in the control group were not trained by the researcher and only received the usual training of the center, such as educational pamphlets which their contents were briefly designed and provided to the patients at their request. The intervention group, in addition to usual care, received the necessary training for patients to participate in their treatment (patient-centered education). The educational content was developed in three care dimensions including diet, medication, and activity pattern. Patient-centered educational intervention consisted of two sessions in person with 2-day intervals for 45−60 minutes (according to the patient's needs) after discharge from the hospital and after the sampling of the control group in the hospital clinic. Three 30-minute telephone follow-ups were performed at the end of the fourth week, the end of the eighth week, and the end of the twelfth week after the last training session for the intervention group. After the intervention, the questionnaire was completed by both intervention and control groups. At the end of the study, an educational booklet was given to the control group in terms of observing the ethical issues. Educational materials were presented in the form of lectures, questions, and answers and educational booklets (in simple and understandable language). The educational content was prepared based on scientific sources and according to the cardiologists' and nursing professors' suggestions, which talks about issues such as heart disease, complications, risk factors, and self-care in three dimensions: diet, medication, physical activity, stress control, and smoking cessation. It should be noted that the sampling lasted from May 2019 for 7 months.

3.2.11 Session 1: interview

In this session, a comprehensive interview with the patients was conducted. The patients were first asked to state their educational needs regarding self-care, illness, information about daily life, as well as information about cardiovascular risk. In this meeting, while determining the educational needs of patients, prioritization of these requirements was considered.

3.2.12 Session 2: patients' participation in the design and implementation of educational goals

During this session, the patient learned how to follow the medication regimen and the correct use of medications and about how to follow a healthy diet in accordance with cardiovascular disease and physical activity and its positive effects on the cardiovascular system with the patient's participation (based on preprepared educational content).

Educational intervention was presented in three areas of medication, diet, and physical activity using a patient-centered and face-to-face method. At the end of this session, all patients with the help of the researcher wrote an action plan for themselves and then an educational booklet was given to the patients in the intervention group.

3.2.13 How to analyze data

Data were analyzed using SPSS statistical analysis software version 22. Chi-square, Wilcoxon, and analysis of covariance tests in the significant level of 0.05 were used based on the type of variable.

3.3 Findings

3.3.1 Comparison of demographic and contextual variables in two groups of intervention and control

In this study, the mean age of patients in the intervention group was 53.6 ± 8.3 years and in the control group was 49.2 ± 11.9 years. There was a significant difference between the two groups in terms of age group ($P = .033$). There was a significant difference between the two groups in terms of gender ($P < .001$). There was no significant difference between the two groups in terms of marriage ($P = .760$). There was no statistically significant difference between the two groups in terms of education ($P = .519$). There was a significant difference between the two groups in terms of occupation ($P = .001$). There was no significant difference between the two groups in terms of heart disease history ($P = .433$). Other details of these comparisons are given in Table 3.1.

3.3.2 Comparison of treatment adherence and its dimensions in two groups of intervention and control

Table 3.2 compares the mean scores of adherence to treatment in the diet dimension between the intervention and control groups. Wilcoxon test showed that the mean scores in the diet dimension of the subjects in the intervention group at the beginning and end of the study were 57.02 ± 10.85 and 80.11 ± 50.50, respectively, and the mean change in the scores of the intervention group at the beginning and end of the study was 23.09 ± 10.57. The mean scores of the diet in the control group at the beginning and end of the study were 58.41 ± 12.89 and 58.54 ± 12.83 and the mean change in the scores of the control group at the beginning and end of the study was 0.13 ± 0.64. Therefore a nonsignificant change was observed between the scores of the diet in the control group ($P = .109$), but in the intervention group there was a significant change ($P < .001$). Based on the analysis of covariance model (by adjusting the baseline values of diet dimension, age group, gender, and occupation), a statistically

Table 3.1 Frequency distribution of demographic and underlying characteristics of patients in intervention and control groups.

Variable		Group		P
		Intervention N (%)	Control N (%)	
Age category	40 <	5 (9.60)	11 (21.20)	.033
	40–59	27 (51.90)	32 (61.50)	
	60 ≥	20 (38.50)	9 (17.3)	
Gender	Male	38 (73.10)	17 (32.70)	.001 >
	Female	14 (26.90)	35 (67.30)	
Marital status	Single	5 (9.60)	7 (13.50)	.760
	Married	47 (90.40)	47 (86.50)	
education	Illiterate	21 (40.40)	19 (36.50)	.519
	Uunder diploma	17 (32.70)	14 (26.90)	
	Diploma	7 (13.50)	13 (25.00)	
	University	7 (13.50)	6 (11.50)	
Occupation	Employee	7 (13.50)	4 (7.70)	.001
	Housewife	11 (21.20)	31 (59.60)	
	Retired/disabled	6 (11.50)	3 (5.80)	
	Other	28 (53.80)	14 (26.90)	
History of heart disease	Yes	29 (88.80)	24 (46.20)	.433
	No	23 (44.20)	28 (53.80)	

significant difference was observed between the mean change of diet dimension scores in the intervention and control groups.

Table 3.3 compares the mean scores of adherence to treatment in the physical activity dimension between the intervention and control groups. Wilcoxon test showed that the mean scores in the physical activity dimension of the intervention group at the beginning and end of the study were 32.17 ± 19.91 and 45.12 ± 15.84, respectively. The mean change of intervention group scores at the beginning and end of the study was 12.96 ± 9.28. The mean scores of physical activity in the control group at the beginning and end of the study were 26.42 ± 15.40 and 88.26 ± 15.46 and the mean change in control scores at the beginning and end of the study was 0.46 ± 2.54. Therefore a nonsignificant change ($P = .197$) was observed between the scores of physical activity area in control, and a significant change ($P < .001$) was observed in the intervention group. Also, analysis of covariance (by adjusting the baseline values of physical activity, age group, gender, and occupation) showed that there was a statistically significant difference between the mean change in scores of the physical activity dimension in the intervention and control groups.

Table 3.4 compares the mean scores of adherence to treatment in terms of drug regimen between the two groups of intervention and control. Wilcoxon test showed

Table 3.2 Comparison of mean scores of adherence to treatment in the diet dimension at the beginning and end of the study and between the intervention and control groups.

Group								Comparison between two groups
Intervention				Control				
Beginning of the study	End of the study	Change		Beginning of the study	End of the study	Change		
M (SD)	M (SD)	M (SD)	P^a	M (SD)	M (SD)	M (SD)	P^a	P^b
57.02 (10.85)	80.11 (5.50)	23.09 (10.57)	> .001	58.41 (12.89)	58.54 (12.83)	0.13 (0.64)	.109	> .001

[a]Only the effect of the base values of the dependent variable is adjusted.
[b]In addition to adjusting the effect of the base values of the dependent variable, the effect of age group, gender and occupation has also been adjusted.

Table 3.3 Comparison of mean scores of adherence to treatment in the physical activity dimension at the beginning and end of the study and between the intervention and control groups.

	Group								Comparison between two groups
	Intervention				Control				
	Beginning of the study	End of the study	Change		Beginning of the study	End of the study	Change		
	M (SD)	M (SD)	M (SD)	P^a	M (SD)	M (SD)	M (SD)	P^a	P^b
	32.17 (19.91)	45.12 (15.84)	12.96 (9.28)	.001 >	26.42 (15.40)	26.88 (15.46)	0.46 (2.54)	.197	.001 >

[a]Only the effect of the base values of the dependent variable is adjusted.
[b]In addition to adjusting the effect of the base values of the dependent variable, the effect of age group, gender and occupation has also been adjusted.

Table 3.4 Comparison of mean scores of adherence to treatment in the medication dimension at the beginning and end of the study and between the intervention and control groups.

	Group									Comparison between two groups
	Intervention				Control					
	Beginning of the study	End of the study	Change		Beginning of the study	End of the study	Change			
	M (SD)	M (SD)	M (SD)	P^a	M (SD)	M (SD)	M (SD)	P^a	P^b
	50.04 (32.65)	83.97 (6.30)	34.93 (31.94)	$> .001$	64.58 (29.60)	79.49 (16.48)	2.78 (5.71)	.107	$> .001$

[a]Only the effect of the base values of the dependent variable is adjusted.
[b]In addition to adjusting the effect of the base values of the dependent variable, the effect of age group, gender and occupation has also been adjusted.

that the mean scores of the drug regimen in the intervention group at the beginning and end of the study were 50.04 ± 32.65 and 83.97 ± 6.30, respectively, and the mean change in the scores of the intervention group at the beginning and end of the study was 34.93 ± 31.94. The mean scores of the medication regimen in the control group at the beginning and end of the study were 64.58 ± 29.60 and 79.49 ± 16.48 and the mean change in the scores of the control group at the beginning and end of the study was 2.78 ± 5.71. A nonsignificant change ($P = .107$) was observed between the scores of the medication dimension in the control group, and a significant change was observed in the intervention group ($P < .001$). Analysis of covariance model (by adjusting the baseline values of drug dimension, age group, gender, and occupation) showed a significant difference between the mean change of scores after intervention and control in the two groups of intervention and control.

3.4 Discussion

The findings revealed that patients in the intervention group after the intervention had a significant change in adherence to treatment, which means that this change was greater in the intervention group than in the control group. The results of this study showed that patient-centered education in patients suffering from CAD during two training sessions after discharge from the hospital is effective in getting patients to adhere to the treatment regimen. This study is in accordance with other studies [25–28] that indicated the effect of implementing a follow-up care approach on adherence to the treatment regimen in patients suffering from myocardial infarction. In our research, the mean score of self-management and adherence to treatment after education and after follow-up showed a significant difference between the intervention and control groups. There was a significant difference between the two groups in case of self-management and adherence to the treatment regimen [25]. This research is in accordance with our study because it shows the need for education and follow-up after discharge and its positive impact on adherence to the treatment regimen.

Nazer Mozaffari et al. [26] investigated the impact of telephone follow-up on the self-efficacy of nutritional behaviors and physical activity in patients with coronary artery bypass graft. In their study, the mean scores of nutritional behaviors and physical activity in the control and experimental groups before the intervention were not statistically significant. However, it was statistically significant after the intervention. According to the findings of this study, telephone follow-up by a nurse can improve self-efficacy in adherence to diet and physical activity.

The study by Polsook et al. [27] showed that at the end of a 4-week program to increase self-efficacy in patients after myocardial infarction, the mean score of adherence to the medication regimen was higher in the intervention group than in the control group. Based on a study by Unverzagt et al. [29], patients' commitment to their health, education, and regular follow-up calls can increase adherence to treatment in patients suffering from heart failure. Lee et al. [30] showed that early identification of patients with poor adherence, lifestyle modification, educational and motivational programs to improve health results and adherence are very essential. A study by Silva et al. [31] carried out to follow up on treatment in patients suffering from heart failure showed that patients that lived with their relatives and had three or more previous sessions had higher adherence scores. Zakerimoghadam et al. [32] in a study assessed the self-management program after discharge to follow the treatment regimen of patients suffering from ischemic heart disease. There was no significant difference between the two groups regarding demographic characteristics and adherence to the treatment regimen before the intervention, while after the intervention, adherence to the treatment regimen of patients in the intervention group improved. In our study, a self-management program is one of the indices of patient-centered training and positive and significant results with regard to patient-centered education and adherence to the treatment regimen were obtained, with a significant difference between the control group and the test group after the intervention. A study by Moeini et al. [33] was conducted to assess the effect of a web-based family-centered support training program on adherence to the treatment regimen of patients suffering from heart failure after discharge and showed that the mean score of adherence to the treatment regimen in the intervention and control groups immediately and one month after the intervention were significantly different and the intervention group had a better treatment regimen compared with the control group. The findings also showed that the mean score of adherence to the treatment regimen in the control group before, immediately, and one month after the intervention was not significantly different, while this difference in the intervention group showed a significant increase. The mean score of adherence to the treatment regimen in the intervention group had a significant difference in both times after the intervention, immediately and one month after the intervention.

The results of this study are in line with the findings of Hung et al. [34], which assessed patients with telephone counseling on nutrition and physical activity after bone marrow transplantation. In their research, patients in the telephone follow-up group followed the treatment regimen and there was a significant difference between the intervention and control groups. The findings of this research are in accordance with this study regarding improved diet and physical activity in the intervention group after follow-up.

Deif et al. [35] carried out a study about the benefits of an educational program on adherence to the treatment regimen in patients suffering from chronic kidney disease in Egypt. The results of this study indicated that frequent contacts with nurses help patients learn how to solve their problems and gain self-management skills that are effective in increasing adherence to the treatment regimen. These two studies are different with regard to the study population and the scale for assessing adherence to the treatment regimen, but they are the same in the case of the educational program and increasing adherence to the treatment regimen.

A study by Deka et al. [36], which examined the effect of Internet-based intervention on adherence to the activity program of patients suffering from heart failure, is not in line with the recent research. In a study by Deka, patients were educated once a week for 8 weeks through group and online discussions, but adherence to the activity program in these patients was not significantly different from the control group. The reason for the difference between the study of Deka and our research may be the small sample size. In addition, the education method in the study of Deka was online, but in our study it was in person and face to face.

A study by Shively et al. [37] was carried out on the effect of patient self-management activation in patients suffering from heart failure. This study showed that the self-management program was beneficial in improving patients' adherence to the diet. One of the differences between this study and our research was in the follow-up period of patients. In their study, the follow-up period was two periods of 3 and 6 months; while in our study, follow-up was done for 12 weeks. Plus, in our study, several educational methods like workshops, booklets, and telephone follow-up were applied, which strengthens the teachings provided to patients.

3.5 Limitations

It was possible to receive training through various media in the interval between the intervention and the completion of the questionnaires after the end of intervention. Other limitations include lack of the cooperation of the participants in completing the self-report questionnaire.

3.6 Conclusion

The results of this study showed that a patient-centered education program increases adherence to the treatment regimen in three areas of diet, physical activity, and medication in patients with CAD. The results also emphasize the importance of having a program and continuing a training program both during and after hospitalization. Continuing education in an appropriate way can increase the patient's skill, participation, and consistency in following the treatment regimen. These findings can be a turning point in improving adherence to the treatment regimen in coronary artery patients and thus reduce costs and readmission and also increase patient satisfaction.

Because this intervention is a simple and low-cost nursing intervention, critical care nurses can use it in patient care programs.

References

[1] American Diabetes Association. 9. Cardiovascular disease and risk management: standards of medical care in diabetes—2018. Diabetes Care 2018;41(Suppl. 1):S86−104 Jan 1.

[2] Nayeleh E. Perceptions of patients with coronary artery disease about their therapeutic regimen. IJN 2010;23(63):26−34.

[3] Vahedparast H, Mohammadi E, Ahmadi F. The challenge of adherence from treatment-care regimens among patients with chronic diseases: a qualitative study. Iran South Med J 2017;19 (6):989−1004.

[4] Kreatsoulas C, Anand SS. The impact of social determinants on cardiovascular disease. Can J Cardiol 2010;26(Suppl C):8C−13C. Available from: https://doi.org/10.1016/s0828-282x(10) 71075-8.

[5] Soleimani Moghadam R, Mohammadi S, Kargar Kakhki N, Mohammadi M, Ghadimifar A, Ahmadnejad A, et al. Evaluation the predictors in patients with cardiovascular disease based on walker health-promoting lifestyle. IJDLD. 2018;17(3):157−64.

[6] Zakeri Bazmandeh, M.A. Effect the application of continuous care model on self-management & adherence to treatment in patients with myocardial infarction (MI) referred to Ali ebne Abi Taleb hospital in Rafsanjan city in 2016. Doctoral dissertation, School of Nursing and Midwifery, Kerman University of Medical Sciences, Kerman, Iran.

[7] Santo K, Kirkendall S, Laba TL, Thakkar J, Webster R, Chalmers J, et al. Interventions to improve medication adherence in coronary disease patients: a systematic review and meta-analysis of randomised controlled trials. Eur J Prev Cardiol 2016;23(10):1065−76. Available from: https://doi.org/ 10.1177/2047487316638501.

[8] Jin J, Sklar GE, Min Sen Oh V, Chuen Li S. Factors affecting therapeutic compliance: a review from the patient's perspective. Ther Clin Risk Manag 2008;4(1):269−86. Available from: https:// doi.org/10.2147/tcrm.s1458.

[9] Poshtchaman Z, Jadid Milani M, Atashzadeh Shoorideh F, Akbarzadeh Bagheban A. The effect of two ways of using the phone and SMS follow-up care on treatment adherence in Coronary Artery Bypass Graft patients. Cardio Nurs J 2014;3(2):6−14.

[10] Masror Roudsari D, Dabiri Golchin M, Haghani H. Relationship between adherence to therapeutic regimen and health related quality of life in hypertensive patients. IJN 2013;26(85):44−54.

[11] Tao D, Xie L, Wang T, Wang T. A meta-analysis of the use of electronic reminders for patient adherence to medication in chronic disease care. J Telemed Telecare 2015;21(1):3−13. Available from: https://doi.org/10.1177/1357633X14541041.

[12] Esmaeilpour H, Kolagari S, Yazdi K, Azimi HR, Mir Ahmadi AA. Effect of training and post discharge follow-up on self- care behavior of patients with ischemic heart disease. Koomesh 2017;19 (2):448−57.

[13] Najafi SS, Shaabani M, Momennassab M, Aghasadeghi K. The nurse-led telephone follow-up on medication and dietary adherence among patients after myocardial infarction: a randomized controlled clinical trial. Int J Community Based Nurs Midwifery 2016;4(3):199−208.

[14] Deyirmenjian M, Karam N, Salameh P. Preoperative patient education for open-heart patients: a source of anxiety. Patient Educ Couns 2006;62(1):111−17. Available from: https://doi.org/ 10.1016/j.pec.2005.06.014.

[15] Piette JD, List J, Rana GK, Townsend W, Striplin D, Heisler M. Mobile health devices as tools for worldwide cardiovascular risk reduction and disease management. Circulation 2015;132 (21):2012−27. Available from: https://doi.org/10.1161/CIRCULATIONAHA.114.008723.

[16] De Boer D, Delnoij D, Rademakers J. The importance of patient-centered care for various patient groups. Patient Educ Couns 2013;90(3):405−10. Available from: https://doi.org/10.1016/j. pec.2011.10.002.

[17] Rathert C, Wyrwich MD, Boren SA. Patient-centered care and outcomes: a systematic review of the literature. Med Care Res Rev 2013;70(4):351−79. Available from: https://doi.org/10.1177/1077558712465774.

[18] Gholami M, Fallahi Khoshknab M, Seyed Bagher Madah S, Ahmadi F, Khankeh H, Naderi N. Information needs of patients with cardiovascular disease in health information seeking process: a qualitative study. 3 JNE 2014;2(4):33−49.

[19] Baljani M.Sc. E, Rahimi M.Sc. ZH, Heidari M.Sc. SH, Azimpour M.Sc. A. The Effect of self management interventions on medication adherence and life style in cardiovascular patients. Avicenna J Nurs Midwifery Care 2012;20(3):58−68.

[20] Manouchehri H, Zagheri-Tafreshi M, Nasiri M, Ashrafi H. Patients participation in health care decision makings in Hospitals affiliated with saveh school of medical sciences, 2016. J Health Care 2018;19(4):251−61.

[21] John J, Haseena T. Compliance with therapeutic regimen in patients with coronary artery disease. IJSR 2015;4(11):385−8.

[22] Rahnama M, Sajjadian I, Raoufi A. The effectiveness of acceptance and commitment therapy on psychological distress and medication adherence of coronary heart patients. J Nurs Edu 2017;5(4):34−43.

[23] Mousavizadeh SN, Ashktorab T, Ahmadi F, Zandi M. Evaluation of barriers to adherence to therapy in patients with diabetes. J Diabetes Nurs 2016;4(3):94−108.

[24] Heydari A, Ziaee ES, Gazrani A. Relationship between awareness of disease and adherence to therapeutic regimen among cardiac patients. Int J Community Based Nurs Midwifery 2015;3(1):23−30.

[25] Zakeri MA, Khoshnood Z, Dehghan M, Abazari F. The effect of the continuous care model on treatment adherence in patients with myocardial infarction: a randomised controlled trial. J Res Nurs 2020;25(1):54−65. Available from: https://doi.org/10.1177/1744987119890666.

[26] Nazer Mozafari M, Jahani Y, Najafi S, Hoseinrezaei H. Effect of telephone follow-up (Tele-nursing) on nutritional self-efficacy & physical activity in patients with coronary artery bypass graft in Shiraz Namazi hospital in 2015. [in Persian]. Iran J Anesthesiology Crit Care 2017;38(4):53−63.

[27] Polsook R, Aungsuroch Y, Thongvichean T. The effect of self-efficacy enhancement program on medication adherence among post-acute myocardial infarction. Appl Nurs Res 2016;32:67−72. Available from: https://doi.org/10.1016/j.apnr.2016.05.002.

[28] Andey A, Krumme AA, Patel T, Choudhry NK. The impact of text messaging on medication adherence and exercise among postmyocardial infarction patients: randomized controlled pilot trial. JMIR Mhealth Uhealth 2017;5(8):e110. Available from: https://doi.org/10.2196/mhealth.7144.

[29] Unverzagt S, Meyer G, Mittmann S, Samos FA, Unverzagt M, Prondzinsky R. Improving treatment adherence in heart failure. Dtsch Arztebl Int 2016;113(25):423−30. Available from: https://doi.org/10.3238/arztebl.2016.0423.

[30] Lee YM, Kim RB, Lee HJ, Kim K, Shin MH, Park HK, et al. Relationships among medication adherence, lifestyle modification, and health-related quality of life in patients with acute myocardial infarction: a cross-sectional study. Health Qual Life Outcomes 2018;16(1):100. Available from: https://doi.org/10.1186/s12955-018-0921-z.

[31] da Silva AF, Cavalcanti AC, Malta M, Arruda CS, Gandin T, da Fé A, et al. Treatment adherence in heart failure patients followed up by nurses in two specialized clinics. Rev Lat Am Enferm 2015;23(5):888−94. Available from: https://doi.org/10.1590/0104-1169.0268.2628.

[32] Zakerimoghadam M, Ebrahimi S, Haghani H. The effect of self-management program after discharging on therapeutic adherence in patient with ischemic heart disease. IJNR 2016;11(1):17−24.

[33] Moeini M, Shafiei D. The impact of a web-based family-oriented supportive education program in adherence to treatment of the heart failure patients after discharge from hospital; a randomized clinical trial. [in Persian]. J Clin Nurs Midwife 2019;7(4):286−95.

[34] Hung YC, Bauer JD, Horsely P, Coll J, Bashford J, Isenring EA. Telephone-delivered nutrition and exercise counselling after auto-SCT: a pilot, randomised controlled trial. Bone Marrow Transpl 2014;49(6):786−92. Available from: https://doi.org/10.1038/bmt.2014.52.

[35] Deif HI, Elsawi K, Selim M, NasrAllah MM. Effect of an educational program on adherence to therapeutic regimen among Chronic Kidney Disease Stage5 (CKD5) patients under maintenance hemodialysis. JEP 2015;6(5):21−33.

[36] Deka P, Pozehl B, Williams MA, Norman JF, Khazanchi D, Pathak D. MOVE-HF: an internet-based pilot study to improve adherence to exercise in patients with heart failure. Eur J Cardiovasc Nurs 2019;18(2):122−31. Available from: https://doi.org/10.1177/1474515118796613.

[37] Shively MJ, Gardetto NJ, Kodiath MF, Kelly A, Smith TL, Stepnowsky C, et al. Effect of patient activation on self-management in patients with heart failure. J Cardiovasc Nurs 2013;28(1):20−34. Available from: https://doi.org/10.1097/JCN.0b013e318239f9f9.

CHAPTER 4

Artificial intelligence in cardiovascular imaging

Shan Wei Chen[1,2], Shir Li Wang[1,3], Theam Foo Ng[4] and Haidi Ibrahim[5]

[1]Faculty of Art, Computing and Creative Industry, Universiti Pendidikan Sultan Idris, Tanjong Malim, Perak, Malaysia
[2]Department of Education, Baoji University of Arts and Sciences, Baoji, Shaanxi, P.R. China
[3]Data Intelligent and Knowledge Management (DILIGENT), Universiti Pendidikan Sultan Idris, Tanjong Malim, Perak, Malaysia
[4]Centre for Global Sustainability Studies, Universiti Sains Malaysia, Gelugor, Penang, Malaysia
[5]School of Electrical and Electronic Engineering, Universiti Sains Malaysia, Nibong Tebal, Penang, Malaysia

4.1 Introduction

Cardiovascular diseases (CVDs) rank as the first leading cause of global mortality and pose a great threat to human health [1]. The deaths caused by CVDs in the world exceed 15 million every year. The high incidence rate of CVD has resulted in a significant increase in patients' demand for medical resources. Due to the limited medical resources, the medical attention and care required by patients cannot be met in time, resulting in missing the best treatment time and high medical costs.

Cardiovascular imaging diagnosis is one of the main methods to detect CVDs. At present, computed tomography (CT), ultrasonic diagnosis (USD), magnetic resonance imaging (MRI), nuclear medicine, and other cardiovascular imaging technologies have been widely used in the diagnosis of CVDs, and their clinical value has been widely recognized. However, the main problem is that the processing of cardiovascular images is time-consuming and is easily affected by the level of imaging and doctors' subjective factors, resulting in inconsistent results of disease detection or disease degree judgment, which is the limitation of existing cardiovascular imaging technology.

Artificial intelligence (AI) is an intelligent technology based on computer science. Through the interdisciplinary and multidisciplinary research on AI, this theory and method of simulating human intelligence are applied to all aspects of social life [2].

The application of AI in the medical field is mainly focused on medical image recognition, such as coronary computed tomography, ultrasonic cardiogram diagnosis, electrocardiogram (ECG), and optical coherence tomography [3]. The application of AI in the medical image field can not only shorten the image processing time but also make the diagnosis result more reliable based on the objective analysis of big data. Its usage improves the accuracy of disease diagnosis, greatly alleviates the contradiction between medical resources and the number of patients, and helps patients get timely

Cardiovascular and Coronary Artery Imaging
DOI: https://doi.org/10.1016/B978-0-12-821983-6.00004-7

51

treatment. CVD diagnosis based on AI technology and medical images not only makes image examination faster and safer but also provides patients with economic and accurate medical solutions and improves patients' treatment experience [4].

This chapter introduces the research of AI in CVD image detection from two aspects, namely machine learning and deep learning, and looks forward to the application of AI in CVD detection, to provide new ideas for the research of computer-aided CVD diagnosis and help to further improve public medical services.

4.2 Artificial intelligence

AI is a branch of computer science. By understanding the essence of intelligence, it attempts to produce a new intelligent machine that can respond in a similar way to human intelligence. After decades of development, the research of AI covers various fields of expert system, natural language processing, robot, biological signal, image recognition, and medical applications.

4.2.1 The concept of artificial intelligence

Generally, any agent or device that can perceive and understand its surrounding environment and take appropriate actions to maximize its goals is AI [5]. AI has the characteristics of machines and intelligent devices. Its main feature is that it can automatically predict an outcome through some operations on the collected data to achieve the purpose of autonomous learning.

From a macro perspective, weak AI and strong AI are the two broad classifications of AI [6]. A weak AI refers to a programmed system or machine that operates within a predetermined or predefined range of functions. Strong AI, often known as general AI, is a type of AI that has the same or more intellectual than humans and can mimic all their intelligent activities. AI can easily surpass human beings in certain aspects, such as calculation, addition, multiplication, and so on. At present, this kind of weak AI is widely used.

4.2.2 The history of artificial intelligence

The history of AI can be traced back to the 1940s at least. For example, W. McCulloch and W. Pitts proposed the first artificial neuron model [7]. In 1949, D. Hebb proposed the Hebbian learning rule [8] to update the connection strength between neurons. However, the formal birth of the concept of AI will wait until the Dartmouth conference in 1956. Since then, the development history of AI for more than 60 years has had its ups and downs. It has experienced three tides, but it also encountered two winters. The first tide was from 1956 to the 1960s. In the summer of 1956, J. McCarthy, M. Minsky, N. Rochester, and C. Shannon launched a two-month Dartmouth Conference on AI, the famous Dartmouth conference [9]. According to the conference, if learning and other aspects of intelligence can be adequately characterized, a machine can be used to simulate intelligence, to teach the machine to utilize language, develop abstract notions, solve problems that humans can solve, and even improve itself.

Many participants in the conference later won the Turing Award (including J. McCarthy, M. Minsky and H. Simon). Because most of the participants had a deep logic research background, the first AI upsurge driven by Dartmouth conference took symbolic logic as the main starting point, that is, the so-called symbolism in later generations. In theory, if we can use some symbolic logic to represent the existing knowledge and problems to be solved, we can solve all kinds of intelligent tasks through the logical problem solver. Following this line of thought, A. Newell and H. Simon demonstrated the reasoning computer program known as Logic Theorist at the Dartmouth conference, which later proved many mathematical theorems. In addition, the first upsurge also emerged some influential achievements, such as several reasoning provers, chess programs, checkers programs, question and answer, and planning systems. During this period, F. Rosenblatt proposed the perceptron model [10], which attracted the attention of many researchers at that time.

At the beginning of the first tide, AI researchers were very optimistic about the future. In 1957, H. Simon put forward: "now there are machines in the world that can think, learn and create. Their ability will be improved rapidly, and the scope of problems to be handled will be extended to the scope of human thinking application in the foreseeable future." He also predicted that computers would become chess champions within 10 years, but IBM's dark blue system wouldn't become chess champion until 40 years later. Because the researchers found that the difficulty of the development of AI was far more than originally thought, the first upsurge of AI soon subsided and entered the first winter of more than 10 years.

The second tide occurred between 1975 and 1991. The landmark event of the second tide of AI was when Japan launched an ambitious five-generation computer plan in 1982. The goal of the plan was to establish an intelligent computing system that could run Prolog efficiently within 10 years. Around that same time, successful cases began to appear in the international expert system. Some expert systems even played a practical role in business. For example, the expert system R1 of Digital Equipment Corporation (DEC) could automatically purchase software and hardware components for Virtual Address eXtension (VAX) computer systems according to the needs of users. In the mid-1980s, the neural network method also ushered in a revolution. The proposal of the backpropagation learning algorithm [11] made neural networks again the focus of research and become a connectionist method keeping pace with symbolism. In the late 1980s, AI began to combine mathematical theory to form a more practical application. For example, the hidden Markov model (HMM) began to be used in speech recognition, providing a mathematical framework for understanding problems and effectively dealing with practical applications. Other examples include information theory for machine translation, Bayesian network for uncertain reasoning, and expert system to provide an effective representation and strict reasoning for uncertain knowledge.

Symbolism is still AI's dominant school of thought in the second tide. Whether Prolog computer language was used by the fifth-generation computers in Japan or List Processor (LISP) was used by the expert system MYCIN, its core was the reasoning of symbolic logic. However, researchers gradually found that there were many insurmountable difficulties in semiotic methods, such as the lack of concise logic with sufficient representation ability, and the time-consuming logic problem solver. On the other hand, connectionist methods (such as neural networks) did not find their place in key applications. With the failure of Japan's five-generation computer program in 1991, the second tide retreated, and AI fell into the second winter of nearly 20 years.

The third tide started in 2006. In 2006, G. Hinton and R. Salakhutdinov wrote that multihidden layer neural networks could describe the essential attributes of data, and the difficulty of deep neural network training could be overcome with the help of the unsupervised layer-by-layer initialization method [12]. It is widely believed in the industry that this paper sounded the horn of deep learning toward prosperity and opened the third upsurge of AI. In 2012, A. Krizhevsky, I. Sutskever, and G. Hinton proposed a novel deep learning neural network called AlexNet, which became the champion of the ImageNet Large Scale Visual Recognition Competition (ILSVRC) in 2012. Since then, deep learning has attracted extensive attention in the industry. With the growth of data sets and model scales, the recognition accuracy of deep learning neural networks was widely received, and today are widely used in the fields of speech recognition, face recognition, machine translation, and in the applications of various domains. In 2016, AlphaGo, a Go program based on deep learning developed by Google DeepMind team, defeated Lee Sedol, the Go world champion of human players, further promoting the development of the third tide and making the AI, machine learning, deep learning, and neural network the focus of public attention.

4.2.3 Briefly division of artificial intelligence

AI can be roughly divided into two categories: The first category is represented by expert systems, such as multiagent systems, fuzzy logic, and rough sets. It inputs the knowledge and wisdom of humans and experts into the computer program system and makes reasoning and decision based on the knowledge base. The other category is represented by machine learning, which no longer relies on the direct input of knowledge into the system by human beings. Instead, the system continuously learns by itself based on experience (data) and judges and solves new problems by improving the parameters of the prediction model or extracting deep abstract cognition. Fig. 4.1 shows the fundamental classification of AI.

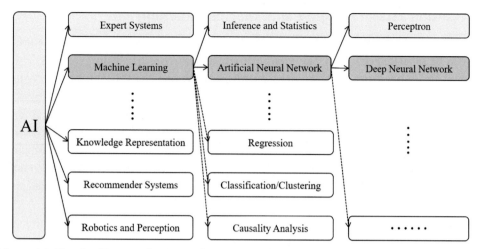

Figure 4.1 The classification of AI. *AI*, artificial intelligence.

AI methods represented by machine learning have self-learning ability and more development potential. Therefore machine learning has become the most representative branch of AI. Machine learning can also be divided into two main categories: The first one uses almost pure mathematical methods, that is, inferential statistical methods, learning problem models, and parameters from known data (samples), plus various techniques to predict new problems. Linear regression, logistic regression, support vector machines, decision trees, K-nearest neighbor, K-average, EM algorithms, and algorithms related to Bayesian inference and Markov processes all belong to this category; the second one uses the Artificial Neural Network (ANN) method. Taking the human cognitive system and nervous system as the starting point, by studying the cognitive rules of the human neuron system and simulating the human nervous system with a computer, the ability to learn and solve problems can be achieved. Perceptron, backpropagation algorithm, Hopfield network, Boltzmann machine, limited Boltzmann machine, deep confidence network, convolutional neural network, and recurrent neural network all belong to this field.

Artificial neural networks (ANN) can also be divided into two categories: The first one is shallow networks. Like the early perceptron, it consisted of only one input layer and one output layer. In addition, the inferential statistical types of machine learning methods mentioned above generally fall into this category; the second one is deep neural network. It has one or more hidden layers in addition to the input layer and output layer. Through the learning algorithm, the abstract expression of data is realized in the hidden layer, just like the human cognitive system. Deep learning can achieve higher intelligence. One can always abstract deeper cognition from the information one obtains from experience, namely perception. That is the goal deep learning pursues.

4.3 Cardiovascular imaging with machine learning

According to the complexity of AI, the methods of applying AI to cardiovascular imaging can be separated into two categories: namely, applications based on general machine learning and applications based on deep learning. At present, the CVD diagnosis method based on machine learning is mainly to train on specific data sets, obtain the diagnosis model, and then apply it to new data sets to complete specific diagnosis tasks.

Machine learning is mainly used in the diagnosis of CVD, such as coronary artery computed tomography, computer-aided diagnosis based on ultrasonic cardiogram, computer-aided diagnosis based on ECG, Single-Photon Emission Computed Tomography, Positron Emission Tomography, and nuclear magnetic resonance imaging matching to different imaging forms [13].

According to the different classifications above, we searched the subject and content of the research papers in Google Scholar from 2016 to 2021 using the keywords CVD, machine learning, coronary computed tomography, ultrasonic cardiogram, ECG, SPECT, and PECT, and the results are shown in Fig. 4.2.

4.3.1 The diagnosis based on coronary artery computed tomography

Coronary artery calcification is one of the most important indicators to measure the severity of coronary heart disease. Coronary computed tomography angiography (CCTA) is a noninvasive coronary imaging technology widely used in coronary heart disease detection and clinical decision-making, which is used to diagnose and rule out obstructive coronary artery diseases, such as coronary artery stenosis detection, and evaluation of the degree of coronary atherosclerosis. However, these technologies still have limitations in terms of cost-effectiveness and clinical accuracy. The introduction of machine learning can effectively overcome these limitations.

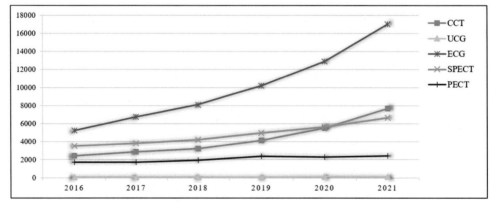

Figure 4.2 Research on the application of machine learning in cardiovascular imaging from 2016 to 2021.

Takx et al. [14] used *K*-nearest neighbor (KNN) algorithm and supper vector machine (SVM) classifier to automatically detect 1793 low-dose chest CT scanning images and score coronary artery calcification. The experimental results show that the score generated by this method has strong consistency and reliability compared with those obtained by doctors. In the work carried out by Isgum et al. [15], the same machine learning algorithm was used to score the automatic calcification on the images of 133 patients with low-dose CT attenuation correction (CTAC) myocardial perfusion (85 men, 48 women, average age 69 years), and the results were similar to those of manual scoring, The method of automatic calcification score can avoid additional radiation dose and scanning time. Motwani et al. [16] followed 10,030 patients with suspected coronary artery disease for 5 years, and all patients received CCTA treatment. The authors evaluated 25 clinical parameters and 44 CCTA parameters, including segmental stenosis score, segmental interpersonal score, modified Duke index, number of noncalcified plaque segments, number of mixed calcified plaque segments, number of calcified plaque segments, age, gender, standard cardiovascular risk factors, and Framingham Risk Score. The information gain ranking method was used for feature selection, and the experimental results show that machine learning achieved a higher area under the curve (AUC) in predicting all-cause mortality.

In addition, machine learning has also made good progress in the classification and prediction of coronary heart disease. Liu et al. [17] use the random forest machine learning model to predict the possibility of CVD events within 90 days through five validation trials, which are all-cause mortality, myocardial infarction, repeat revascularization, contrast-induced acute kidney injury, and renal replacement therapy. Through the follow-up of 185 patients with moderate coronary heart disease for 90 days, it was shown that the accuracy of this model was comparable to current noninvasive cardiac imaging methods. Nakanishi et al. [18] followed 6814 patients with suspected coronary heart disease with the same method. The experimental results showed that the machine learning algorithm had a higher AUC value than the clinical method.

To sum up, the diagnosis method based on CCTA uses machine learning to select the features of the original scanning data, and then classify, detect, or segment the features according to the target task. Generally, this method is an end-to-end training model, which reduces manual participation as much as possible, optimizes the model through big data, and finally obtains an automatic diagnosis system. The system is very effective for doctors' auxiliary diagnosis and greatly reduces the misdiagnosis problem of human operation.

4.3.2 The diagnosis based on ultrasonic cardiogram

Ultrasonic diagnosis (USD) is a noninvasive technique that uses the special physical characteristics of ultrasound to examine the anatomical structure and functional state of the heart and large blood vessels. Radiologists usually make estimations and judg-ments based on their own experience when reading and analyzing 2D ultrasonic car-diogram (UCG), which can cause misdiagnoses and missed diagnoses. To improve efficiency and reduce the rate of misdiagnosis and missed diagnosis, relevant medical enterprises have developed commercial software for 2D echocardiography analysis, such as EchoPAC of General Electric medical group [19], QLAB of Philips [20], etc. Although the aforementioned software can complete the segmentation and anatomy of the samples to be tested and blood tracking, doctors still need to manually select the required images for analysis and diagnosis [21]. Therefore classifying large databases and accurately identifying views is challenging and energy-consuming work.

Khamis et al. [22] proposed a fully automatic apical UCG view classification method, which uses the apical views of 309 clinical UCG segments for training. The algorithm is composed of spatial feature extraction and a supervised dictionary learning method. The recognition and classification of UCG views finally achieved an average accuracy of 95%. Knackstedt et al. [23] evaluated the endocardial boundary ejection fraction by visual esti-mation and manual tracking in 255 patients with sinus heart rate and used the machine learning software (autolv, TomTec arena 1.2, TomTec imaging systems, Germany) to measure the fully automatic ejection fraction and the average longitudinal strain of both wings. The experimental results show that the accuracy of measurement using machine learning software is 98%, and the average analysis time is only (8 ± 1) s/person. In addi-tion, Dong [13] and others applied deep learning in the 3D echocardiography data of the 2014 Cetus challenge to segment the left ventricular endocardium of 3ducg. Compared with experts, the results of this method have higher accuracy and diagnostic efficiency.

To sum up, the training in UCG can be a good auxiliary diagnosis. It can not only help doctors evaluate the accuracy, but also segment the data in 2D and 3D in an end-to-end way. These results are comparable to the division results of doctors.

4.3.3 The diagnosis based on electrocardiogram

Arrhythmia refers to another group of diseases in CVD. It is caused by aberrant sino-atrial node activation or excitement that occurs outside the sinoatrial node. Excitation slowly travels when blood is obstructed or is conveyed through an irregular channel.

Arrhythmia can occur alone or with other CVD (such as coronary heart disease). An electrocardiograph (ECG) is a conventional method for the clinical diagnosis of arrhythmia. ECG is composed of a group of one-dimensional time-series signals. However, due to the need for manual examination and secondary interpretation, and the low signal-to-noise ratio of time-series signals, doctors' diagnosis errors can occur, so it has certain limitations in clinical applications.

It has been found that the use of a machine learning approach can effectively enhance diagnostic accuracy and decrease the analysis cost. Machine learning models such as SVM and wavelet transform can effectively identify different waveforms (QRS complex, P wave, and T wave); calculate clinically important parameters, such as heartbeats per minute, axis deviation, and interval length; and detect ST segments, such as atrial fibrillation and ventricular conduction delay. In 2005, Zhao et al. [24], using 11343 ECG signal data, extracted the transform coefficient as the feature of each ECG by using wavelet transform, and applied autoregressive modeling to obtain the time structure of ECG waveform. Finally, SVM with a Gaussian kernel was used to classify different heart rhythms, and the final accuracy of this method reached 99.68%. In 2018, Alfaras et al. [25] designed an end-to-end detection system for processing and analyzing ECG sensing data in wearable devices, automatically detecting heartbeat, and classifying arrhythmia in 47 patients in combination with an echo state network with ring topology, as a supervised machine learning algorithm. In the classification results of arrhythmia, the system can achieve 96.8% accuracy, 89.1% return rate, 80.5% accuracy, and 84.4% F1 score. To sum up, we should first identify and classify the one-dimensional waveform and then extract and classify the features in the processing of ECG signals based on machine learning. This method is superior to the performance of clinicians and has practical clinical application value.

4.3.4 The diagnosis based on nuclear medicine technology

In nuclear medicine, single-photon emission computed tomography (SPECT) and positron emission tomography (PET) are two CT modalities. SPECT is used to assess myocardial perfusion imaging (MPI), which is linked to coronary artery blockage.

In the process of SPECT scanning, it is necessary to manually define the mitral valve plane.

In 2015, Arsanjani et al. [26], using the LogitBoost algorithm, predicted revascularization through the control test of baseline ECG, ECG, clinical response during stress, and post ECG probability of 713 samples (372 cases of revascularization and 341 cases of non-revascularization). This study is helpful to predict the early revascularization of patients with suspected coronary artery disease. The model is trained and tested by using tenfold cross-validation. The final experimental results show that the specificity of using LogitBoost is 74.7% ± 4.2%, and the judgment results of the two experts are 67.2% ± 4.9% and 66.0% ± 5.0%. The judgment result of ($P < .05$) of the machine learning is better than that of professional doctors. The AUC of operator characteristics calculated by the machine learning was 0.81 ± 0.02, which was similar to that of Reader 1 (0.81 ± 0.02), but better than that of Reader 2 (0.72 ± 0.02, $P < .01$) and the standard measure of perfusion (independent perfusion measurement): (0.77 ± 0.02, $P < .01$).

In 2017, Betancur et al. [27] used the SVM method to automatically locate the mitral valve plane, which plays a very important role in the accurate evaluation of MPI. They trained and verified the SPECT scanning results of 392 patients. The final test results showed that in the image processing results of attenuation correction and nonattenuation correction, the AUC value of the SVM method is very close to that of professional doctors (nonattenuation correction: the value of SVM is 0.79, doctor 1 and doctor 2 are 0.8 and 0.77, respectively; attenuation correction: the value of SVM is 0.82, doctor 1 and doctor 2 are 0.81 and 0.79, respectively).

Dey et al. [28] studied 51 patients using PET to study the relationship between quantitative plaque characteristics of coronary angiography and coronary vascular dysfunction and impaired myocardial blood flow reserve. The results of the machine learning showed that the risk score of AUC was 0.83 and the quantitative stenosis of AUC was 0.66.

4.3.5 Other diagnostic methods

Machine learning algorithms are not only used in the above cardiovascular imaging modes, but also in magnetic resonance imaging (MRI), intravascular ultrasound (IVUS), and optical coherence tomography (OCT). Dawes et al. [29] used a machine learning survival model that uses 3D cardiac motion to predict and analyze pulmonary hypertension in MRI images of 256 patients through the 3D mode of supervised cardiac systolic movement. The results showed that the AUC value of deep learning reached 0.73. Zhang et al. [30] proposed seven independent SVM classifiers based on seven different feature subsets to conduct machine learning training on intravascular ultrasound images of 61 patients to identify high-risk coronary plaques prone to serious adverse cardiac incidents. The results showed that the accuracy of this machine learning method in predicting fibrotic aneurysms and nonfibrotic aneurysms was 85.9% and 81.7%, respectively. This experiment proves that it is feasible to detect the location specificity of high-risk coronary plaque in the future by using the machine learning method of focal vascular characteristics and demographic variables.

4.4 Cardiovascular imaging with deep learning

Deep learning refers to machine learning based on multilayer neural networks. Different from traditional machine learning, deep learning technology can obtain stronger representation learning ability through continuously accumulated data and deeper models [31].

According to different imaging forms, deep learning is mainly used in the diagnosis of CVD, such as CCTA, computer-aided diagnosis of ultrasonic cardiogram, computer-aided diagnosis based on ECG, cardiovascular MRI, etc. [32].

We searched the subject and content of the research papers in Google Scholar from 2016 to 2021 using the keywords CVD, deep learning, coronary computed tomography, arrhythmia, myocardial infarction, serum potassium, ECG, cardiovascular magnetic resonance, SPECT, and OCT, and the results are shown in Fig. 4.3.

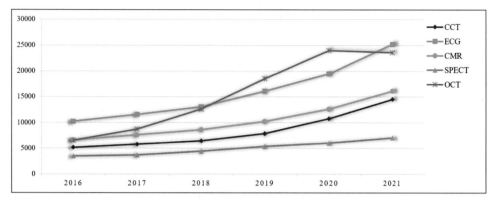

Figure 4.3 Research on the application of deep learning in cardiovascular imaging from 2016 to 2021.

4.4.1 The diagnosis based on coronary artery computed tomography

Deep learning in CT is mainly used in the examination of coronary arteries and the anatomical location and segmentation of different tissues and organs. CT has significant advantages in calcification development. Coronary artery calcification (CAC) scanning and CCTA can qualitatively and quantitatively evaluate the situation of arteriosclerosis.

The research of Wolterink et al. [33] and Wu et al. [34] showed that deep learning based on a convolutional neural network (CNN) can automatically recognize and extract the coronary artery tree in CCTA image, and recognize the functional stenosis of coronary artery based on the texture feature of coronary artery calcification. In the research of Wolterink et al. [35], CNN can automatically calculate the coronary artery centerline and mark the coronary artery tree segment to locate the lesion, to further improve the ability of coronary artery segmentation and location. Lessmann et al. [36] found that CNN has significant specificity for detecting aortic and coronary calcification in chest nonenhanced CT. This shows that virtual anatomy can also accurately detect atherosclerosis through deep learning without using contrast agents. ITU et al. [37] predicted the decrease of coronary artery fractional flow reserve (FFR) in patients with coronary heart disease by extracting the coronary artery tree. Its calculation accuracy is comparable to that of traditional computational fluid dynamics. However, due to the partial volume effect (PVE), the lumen area of the small-diameter coronary artery will be overestimated. The results of Yu, Li et al. show that [38], compared with any measurement using CCTA images alone, deep learning has higher sensitivity and accuracy in measuring AUC, stenosis severity, calcified wind block, and total plaque volume.

In terms of segmentation, location, and classification of the heart and its tissues, Commandeur et al. [39] segmented 250 chest CT images and epicardial adipose tissue

CT images by using CNN. The correlation between the segmentation results of thoracic and epicardial adipose tissue by the automatic segmentation model and the manual segmentation results of cardiologists reached 0.945 and 0.926, respectively. The results showed that the segmentation results based on a deep learning algorithm were very close to those of clinical experts, and the segmentation time was only 3 seconds. Zreik et al. [40] introduced a deep neural network (DNN) into the prediction of CAD. The experimental data were from 166 CCTA scanning data collected from 2012 to 2016. Firstly, CNN was used to segment the left ventricular myocardium of the CCTA image, then it was encoded by an automatic coder algorithm, and the encoded statistical data were extracted as classification features. Ten times cross-validation was used and the best SVM parameters are selected for classification. The results showed that the average AUC reached 0.75.

4.4.2 The diagnosis based on electrocardiogram

In the computer-aided diagnosis of ECG, deep learning is mainly used for the prediction and diagnosis of CVD such as myocardial ischemia and arrhythmia, as shown in Fig. 4.4.

4.4.2.1 The arrhythmia diagnosis

In 2016, Rahhal et al. [41], King's University of Saudi Arabia, used self-encoder for unsupervised feature learning and then used a fully connected neural network for supervised learning to detect abnormal ECG. This study mainly carried out an automatic diagnosis of ventricular arrhythmia and supraventricular arrhythmia. Hannun et al. [42] of Stanford University conducted supervised feature learning through a CNN and performed atrial fibrillation, atrial flutter, atrioventricular block, dyadic

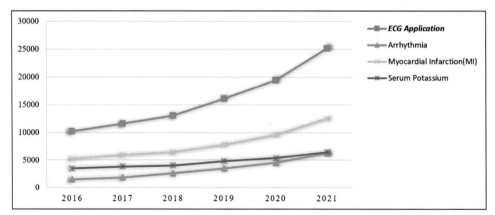

Figure 4.4 Research on deep learning in ECG assisted diagnosis from 2016 to 2021. *ECG*, electrocardiogram.

rhythm, early repolarization, borderline rhythm, sinus rhythm, and noise classification of 12 rhythms of supraventricular tachycardia, triad, ventricular tachycardia, and venturi phenomenon. The research team reported for the first time that the end-to-end deep convolution network can widely distinguish the most common and important rhythm diagnosis in a single-lead ECG. The training sample size of this study was large. A total of 91,232 electrocardiograms were collected from 53,549 patients. The average area under the subject working characteristic curve on the test data set was 0.97. Besides, the harmonic mean of positive predictive value and sensitivity exceeded the average level of cardiologists (0.837 vs 0.780). Yily et al. [43] realized normal sinus rhythm, atrial premature beat, atrial flutter, atrial fibrillation, supraventricular tachycardia, preexcitation, ventricular premature beat, ventricular duplex, ventricular triplet, ventricular tachycardia, ventricular rhythm, atrial flutter, ventricular fusion wave, left bundle branch block, and right bundle branch block automatic diagnosis of 17 arrhythmias including second phase block and pacing rhythm.

With the continuous expansion of the application of deep learning in ECG automatic diagnosis, the research on ECG rhythm diagnosis combined with a variety of neural network algorithms is gradually increasing. Sayantan et al. [44] used the MIT-BIH arrhythmia database to classify the heartbeat of ECG through a deep belief network and active learning. This method achieved higher accuracy than traditional algorithms in the detection of abnormal rhythms such as atrial fibrillation and premature beat. Yao and Chen [45] classified arrhythmias in a single-lead ECG through a multiscale convolutional neural network. The research of Oh et al. [46] and Philip a Warrick et al. [47] realized the automatic detection of arrhythmia by combining a convolutional neural network and long-term and short-term memory networks.

4.4.2.2 The myocardial infarction diagnosis

Myocardial ischemia is a common disease in clinical cardiology. The interpretation of the ST segment of ECG is very important for the early warning, early detection, and timely treatment of myocardial ischemia and myocardial infarction (MI). It has important value for increasing the survival rate and improving the prognosis of patients [48]. In 2006, Rokos et al. [49] proposed the rationality of establishing a regional ST-segment elevated myocardial infarction (STEMI) network model. Later, several studies confirmed the effectiveness of deep learning in the automatic diagnosis of ST-segment related ischemia or MI. Xiao et al. [50], combined with the image-based method, realized the automatic recognition of ischemic ST-segment changes by using the CNN model in the long-term ST database of PhysioNet. Liu et al. [51] used a real-time multilead convolutional neural network to detect the occurrence of MI.

Chang et al. [52] used the hidden Markov model and Gaussian mixture model to classify MI. Recently, Rokos [53] and Zhao et al. [54], using the data of 667 patients with STEMI in the hospital, found that the area under the working characteristic curve of subjects predicted by deep learning can reach 0.974, and the sensitivity and specificity can reach 90% and 98%, respectively. Mehta et al. [55] enriched the differential diagnosis of STEMI by using AI algorithms. These studies suggest that the research results of deep learning in the early diagnosis of myocardial ischemia and MI may help improve the survival and prognosis of patients with myocardial ischemia and MI.

4.4.2.3 Other diagnostic methods based on electrocardiogram

The incidence of asymptomatic left ventricular dysfunction (ALVD) in the general population is 3 to 6%, which can decrease the quality of life and life span. Attia et al. [56], by training a revolutionary neural network and using the paired data of 12 lead ECG and echocardiogram of 44,959 patients from Mayo Clinic, constructed a model for predicting ventricular dysfunction using 12 lead ECG under the condition of ejection fraction $\leq 35\%$. Through the test of the control group of 52,870 independent patients, the sensitivity, specificity, and accuracy of AUC for the model were 0.93%, 86.3%, 85.7%, and 85.7% respectively. The positive screening rate of the model was four times that of the traditional method, which is better than the BNP and NT-proBNP methods commonly used in clinical practice.

Galloway et al. [57] used 1,576,581 ECG data of 449,380 patients from Mayo Clinic, and established a deep convolutional neural network (DCNN) model using ECG data of two leads (leads I and II) or four leads (leads I, II, V3, and V5). After 4 hours of ECG recording, the model was used to count the serum potassium of patients, and the statistical trend of decreasing level was found to predict the hyperkalemia of chronic kidney disease. The experimental outcome of the test set showed that the AUC of the DCNN model was from 0.853 to 0.883, the sensitivity was from 88.9% to 91.3%, and the specificity was from 54.7% to 63.2%. The predictive diagnosis of patients with serum potassium levels ≤ 5.5 m mEq/L was realized.

4.4.3 Cardiovascular magnetic resonance imaging

Cardiac magnetic resonance imaging (CMRI) has significant advantages for the imaging of cardiac tissue. It is mainly used to segment the internal structure of the heart and carry out a series of quantitative evaluations based on it. The segmentation of cardiac structure by CMRI can effectively quantify cardiac function.

The results of deep learning by Bai et al. show that [58] the accuracy of its segmentation algorithm is equivalent to that of human experts, which provides the possibility of an automatic diagnosis of heart disease. The results of some series of studies show that [59,60], CMRI can realize fully automatic and high-quality segmentation of the right ventricle, left ventricle, endocardium, and epicardium, to estimate cardiac quality and functional parameters more reliably. Based on the accurate segmentation of the left ventricle, relevant studies used multiview CNN based on the regression method to directly calculate left ventricular ejection fraction (LVEF), which is of great significance for the evaluation of cardiac function. Xu et al. [61] used CNN to directly depict the myocardial infarction area in the noncontrast cardiac magnetic resonance imaging sequence; this method has high accuracy and consistency, which is conducive to the rapid diagnosis of myocardial infarction. Other in-depth learning studies on CMRI also include segmentation of the aortic valve (for quantitative blood flow fraction) [62], segmentation of blood and myocardium in congenital heart disease [63], and positioning of the long and short diameter of the left ventricle [64].

4.4.4 Other diagnostic methods

In addition to the above imaging modes, deep learning is applied in SPECT and OCT. Betancur et al. [65] established and trained a DCNN using SPECT and MPI data of 1638 multicenter populations (a combination of patients and nonpatients). The total perfusion defect (TPD) was investigated and evaluated using SPECT and myocardial perfusion imaging (MPI) combined with a 10-fold cross-validation process. The final results showed that the sensitivity of each patient increased from 79.8% of traditional quantitative methods to 82.3% of DCNN, and the sensitivity per vessel increased from 64.4% of traditional quantitative methods to 69.8% of DCNN. Experiments show that compared with the existing quantitative methods, deep learning can significantly improve the automatic interpretation of MPI.

OCT is an interference imaging method that can provide high-resolution images of the coronary artery wall to detect the deposition of plaque under the artery wall. Abdolmanafi et al. [66] used the OCT data sets of 33 patients to train three CNNs, Alexnet, VGG-19, and inception-v3, for the judgment and recognition of Kawasaki disease. The outcomes show that the accuracy, sensitivity, and specificity of the three deep learning models can reach (0.99 ± 0.01), which shows that deep learning is effective in the automatic interpretation of OCT.

Gessert et al. [67] trained resnet50-v2 and densenet-121 using the intravascular optical coherence tomography (IVOCT) images data set of St. Jude Medical Ilumien OPTIS, so that these two deep learning models could directly learn the classification of atherosclerotic plaque from the image. Good experimental outcomes were obtained on the test set, and the accuracy, sensitivity, and specificity reached 91.7%, 90.9%, and 92.4%, respectively. The results show that the decision support system based on deep learning can effectively identify and judge atherosclerotic plaque, and its auxiliary diagnosis of atherosclerotic plaque is feasible.

4.5 Discussion

According to the introduction above, we summarize the application of AI in cardiovascular images, as shown in Fig. 4.5, to analyze the challenges it faces, and then provide specific recommendations.

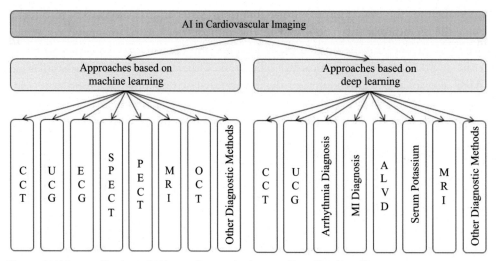

Figure 4.5 The application of AI in cardiovascular image. *AI,* artificial intelligence.

4.5.1 Open challenges

The introduction of AI in the medical field can help to realize a rapid clinical diagnosis. Especially in recent years, deep learning has made significant research advancements in medical applications [68]. However, the accurate diagnosis and early prediction of CVD is still an ongoing unsolved problem that requires the research attention of experts in medical and AI areas. To fully apply AI methods to the daily clinical image analysis and diagnosis of CVDs, at least the following problems need to be solved:

1. Small sample problem. Traditional AI learning algorithms have made good progress in many fields, thanks to many training samples. However, for medical data, especially in the field of CVD, researchers are often unable to collect data on a large scale. This is because there are problems such as social ethics, privacy, and security, and based on the property rights of data, the sample banks of different hospitals are generally unavailable for use, resulting in the inability to obtain enough samples for training [69]. A small sample size will inevitably lead to overfitting. The general data increment method cannot increase the feature diversity of samples and will not essentially improve the overfitting.

2. Data annotation problem. Medical data labeling needs professional doctors to ensure the reliability of training data. However, due to the difference in human subjectivity, a database is usually labeled and detected repeatedly by multiple doctors, resulting in high costs and time [70].

3. Sample balance problem. For medical data, it is usually impossible to predict the number of positive and negative samples in advance, such as the number of patients with benign and malignant tumors. Therefore many data sets are unbalanced

samples, that is, the number of positive and negative samples varies greatly, which eventually leads to a large gap between sensitivity and specificity, that is, the robustness of the model is poor [71].

4. The problem of low signal-to-noise ratio. Due to the limited size of cardiovascular morphology and structure and the small difference between tissues, the current interlaminar resolution of tomography sometimes cannot fully capture the lesions, which increases the difficulty of subsequent segmentation tasks and reduces the diagnostic efficiency and accuracy [72].

5. The universality of the model is low. Current machine algorithms are often trained on specific data sets and lack the test of other data sets, resulting in poor universality of the model and good results on a data set, but they cannot achieve ideal performance after changing a data set [73].

4.5.2 Recommendations

To enhance the safety and effective use of AI technology in cardiovascular angiography, the review of the relevant articles has offered some insightful and targeted suggestions on the challenges faced by AI in cardiovascular angiography.

1. Medical data sharing and expanded sample data set. Management departments should focus on the identification of data property rights and their ownership, under the framework of existing intellectual property rights, combined with ethical factors, through legislation, clearly stipulate the ownership of personal data and integrate data ownership, find potential solutions for the identification and ownership of medical big data property rights, balance personal interests with the social and public welfare, and remove the legal, economic, and ethical barriers to sharing big medical data. Expanded sample data set. Based on medical small sample data, more effective image data can be generated through technical means. For example, using the few class synthesis oversampling methods proposed by Chawla et al. [74], the categories with small sample sizes in the data set are repeatedly sampled. This execution mechanism can meet all the conditions required for small sample data sets.

2. Completion of data annotation database. It is suggested that government or private investment should first establish a labeling network integrating medical labeling experts, attract many labeling experts to participate in it, and use independent labeling, cross quality control, and other methods to label medical data with high quality. On this basis, the medical annotation database is established to provide users with paid or free access to the database. Relying on continuous accumulation and continuous improvement of the medical annotation database, the problem of data annotation will be effectively solved in the end.

3. Sample balance problem. Starting from early data collection, improve the clinical medical database and make the collected data samples tend to be balanced as much

as possible. Starting with the later data processing (the application of generating a countermeasure network in medical small sample data) Zhang Kai used the technical means of adjusting the threshold and under-sampling to solve the problem of sample imbalance based on existing samples [75].

4. The problem of low signal-to-noise ratio. This problem can still be solved from two aspects: one is medical image denoising. Researchers can continue to deeply study image denoising, and use wavelet transform, digital filtering, or other methods to denoise medical images to reduce the segmentation difficulty of cardiovascular angiography. On the other hand, researchers can also study the reconstruction of low signal-to-noise ratio medical images, but the current research is difficult because it involves the further development of basic mathematics and physics. It is believed that over time, the research results in this field will be gradually enriched, and finally solve the problem of the signal-to-noise ratio of cardiovascular angiography.

5. The universality of the model is low. Combined with the solution of medical annotation database and medical data sharing, on the one hand, let the established AI model be tested on as many data sets as possible. On the other hand, researchers need to establish a general medical image data set to increase the universality of the model.

4.6 Summary

AI has made great research progress in cardiovascular imaging detection in recent years and has been widely used in the rapid diagnosis and treatment of cardiovascular diseases. Through the investigation and classification of studies, a brief conclusion can be drawn as follows.

The applications of AI in cardiovascular imaging detection can be divided based on complexity into two methods, namely the machine learning-based method and the deep learning based-method. The former is mainly used in CCTA, computer-aided diagnosis based on ultrasonic cardiogram and computer-aided diagnosis based on ECG, SPECT, PET, nuclear MRI, etc. The latter is mainly used in computer-aided diagnosis of ultrasonic cardiogram and computer-aided diagnosis based on ECG, cardiovascular MRI, and so on. The two categories of methods do not show much difference in the scope of applications.

The main problems in the current research are: (1) Small sample; (2) data annotation; (3) sample balance; (4) low ratio of signal-to-noise; and (5) low universality of model.

In response to these issues above, we put forward the following recommendations: (1) Medical data sharing and expanded sample data set; (2) establish a data annotation database; (3) improve the clinical medical database and use technical means such as threshold adjusting and under-sampling to solve the problem of sample balance; (4) medical image denoising and medical image reconstruction; and (5) establish a general medical image data set to solve the problem of universality.

Although the implementation of the above suggestions is not easy, they offer valuable references for the follow-up research in this field and deserve to receive more research attention to improve the quality of healthcare.

References

[1] Muhammad Z., Kim J., Yoon C. An Automated ECG Beat Classification System Using Convolutional Neural Networks. 2016 6th Int Conf IT Converg Secur, 2016.

[2] Kahn CE. From images to actions: opportunities for artificial intelligence in radiology. Radiology 2017;285(3):719–20. Available from: https://doi.org/10.1148/radiol.2017171734.

[3] Panayides AS, et al. AI in medical imaging informatics: current challenges and future directions. IEEE J Biomed Heal Inform 2020;24(7):1837–57. Available from: https://doi.org/10.1109/JBHI.2020.2991043.

[4] Dilsizian ME, Siegel EL. Machine meets biology: a primer on artificial intelligence in cardiology and cardiac imaging. Curr Cardiol Rep 2018;20(12). Available from: https://doi.org/10.1007/s11886-018-1074-8.

[5] Yu KH, Beam AL, Kohane IS. Artificial intelligence in healthcare. Nat Biomed Eng 2018;2(10):719–31. Available from: https://doi.org/10.1038/s41551-018-0305-z.

[6] Jatin B. Applications of artificial intelligence & associated technologies. Proc Int Conf Emerg Technol Eng Biomed Manag Sci 2016;(March):25–30.

[7] McCulloch WS, Pitts W. A logical calculus of the ideas immanent in nervous activity. Bull Math Biophys 1943;5:115–33. Available from: https://doi.org/10.1007/978-3-030-01370-7_61.

[8] Hebb DO, Leeper R. Review of the organization of behavior: a neuropsychological theory. Wiley; 1950. p. 203–4.

[9] Moor J. Artificial intelligence conference: the next fifty years. AI Mag 2006;27(4):87–91.

[10] Rosenblatt F. The perceptron: a probabilistic model for information storage and organization in the brain. Psychol Rev 1958;65(6):386–408. Available from: https://doi.org/10.1037/h0042519.

[11] Rumelhart DE, Hinton GE, Williams RJ. Learning representations by back-propagating errors. Nature 1986;323(6088):533–6. Available from: https://doi.org/10.1038/323533a0.

[12] Hinton GE, Salakhutdinov RR. Reducing the dimensionality of data with neural networks. Science 2006;313(5786):504–7. Available from: https://doi.org/10.1016/B978-0-08-044894-7.00081-6.

[13] Zhao Mengdie SJ. Review on machine learning approaches for cardiovascular disease diagnosis. Beijing Biomed Eng 2020;39(2):208–14.

[14] Takx RAP, et al. Automated coronary artery calcification scoring in non-gated chest CT: Agreement and reliability. PLoS One 2014;9(3). Available from: https://doi.org/10.1371/journal.pone.0091239.

[15] Išgum I, et al. Automatic determination of cardiovascular risk by CT attenuation correction maps in Rb-82 PET/CT. J Nucl Cardiol 2018;25(6):2133–42. Available from: https://doi.org/10.1007/s12350-017-0866-3.

[16] Motwani M, et al. Machine learning for prediction of all-cause mortality in patients with suspected coronary artery disease: a 5-year multicentre prospective registry analysis. Eur Heart J 2017;38(7):500–7. Available from: https://doi.org/10.1093/eurheartj/ehw188.

[17] Liu Y, Haoxing R, Hanna F. A machine learning model in predicting hemodynamically significant coronary artery disease a prospective cohort study. Cardiovasc Digit Heal J 2018;(7):112. Available from: https://doi.org/10.1016/j.cvdhj.2022.02.002.

[18] Nakanishi R, et al. Machine learning in predicting coronary heart disease and cardiovascular disease events: results from the multi-ethnic study of Atherosclerosis (Mesa). J Am Coll Cardiol 2018;71(11):A1483. Available from: https://doi.org/10.1016/s0735-1097(18)32024-2.

[19] Bayoumy S, Habib M, Abdelmageed R. Impact of maternal diabetes and obesity on fetal cardiac functions. Egypt Hear J 2020;72(1):10–16. Available from: https://doi.org/10.1186/s43044-020-00077-x.

[20] Stenberg B, Chandler C, Wyrley-Birch H, Elliott ST. Post-operative 3-dimensional contrast-enhanced ultrasound (CEUS) vs Tc99m-DTPA in the detection of post-surgical perfusion defects in kidney transplants — preliminary findings. Ultraschall der Med 2014;35(3):273—8. Available from: https://doi.org/10.1055/s-0033-1355964.

[21] Amedro P, et al. Speckle tracking echocardiography in healthy children: comparison between the QLAB by Philips and the EchoPAC by General Electric. Int J Card. Imaging 2019;35(5):799—809. Available from: https://doi.org/10.1007/s10554-018-01516-2.

[22] Khamis H, Zurakhov G, Azar V, Raz A, Friedman Z, Adam D. Automatic apical view classification of echocardiograms using a discriminative learning dictionary. Med Image Anal 2017;36:15—21. Available from: https://doi.org/10.1016/j.media.2016.10.007.

[23] Knackstedt C, et al. Fully automated vs standard tracking of left ventricular ejection fraction and longitudinal strain the FAST-EFs multicenter study. J Am Coll Cardiol 2015;66(13):1456—66. Available from: https://doi.org/10.1016/j.jacc.2015.07.052.

[24] Qibin Z., Liqing Z., ECG feature extraction and classification using wavelet transform and support vector machines. Proc. 2005 Int. Conf. Neural Networks Brain Proceedings, ICNNB'05, vol. 2, pp. 1089—1092, 2005. Available from: https://doi.org/10.1109/icnnb.2005.1614807.

[25] Alfaras M, Soriano MC, Ortín S. A fast machine learning model for ECG-Based heartbeat classification and arrhythmia detection. Front Phys 2019;7. Available from: https://doi.org/10.3389/fphy.2019.00103.

[26] Arsanjani R, et al. Prediction of revascularization after myocardial perfusion SPECT by machine learning in a large population. J Nucl Cardiol 2015;22(5):877—84. Available from: https://doi.org/10.1007/s12350-014-0027-x.

[27] Betancur J, et al. Automatic valve plane localization in myocardial perfusion SPECT/CT by machine learning: anatomic and clinical validation. J Nucl Med 2017;58(6):961—7. Available from: https://doi.org/10.2967/jnumed.116.179911.

[28] Dey D, et al. Relationship between quantitative adverse plaque features from coronary computed tomography angiography and downstream impaired myocardial flow reserve by 13N-ammonia positron emission tomography: a pilot study. Circ Cardiovasc Imaging 2015;8(10):1—9. Available from: https://doi.org/10.1161/CIRCIMAGING.115.003255.

[29] Dawes TJW, et al. Machine learning of three-dimensional right ventricular motion enables outcome prediction in pulmonary hypertension: a cardiac MR imaging study. Radiology 2017;283(2):381—90.

[30] Zhang L, Wahle A, Chen Z, Lopez JJ, Kovarnik T, Sonka M. Predicting locations of high-risk plaques in coronary arteries in patients receiving statin therapy. IEEE Trans Med Imaging 2018;37(1):151—61. Available from: https://doi.org/10.1109/TMI.2017.2725443.

[31] Lecun Y, Bengio Y, Hinton G. Deep learning. Nature 2015;521(7553):436—44. Available from: https://doi.org/10.1038/nature14539.

[32] Lyu T, Ding Z, Yuan Y, Lin J, Wang G, Zhang P. Value of deep learning in automatic diagnosis and prediction of cardiovascular diseases by electrocardiogram. Chin J Cardiovasc Med 2021;26(3).

[33] Wolterink JM, Leiner T, de Vos BD, van Hamersvelt RW, Viergever MA, Išgum I. Automatic coronary artery calcium scoring in cardiac CT angiography using paired convolutional neural networks. Med Image Anal 2016;34:123—36. Available from: https://doi.org/10.1016/j.media.2016.04.004.

[34] Wu D, et al. Automated anatomical labeling of coronary arteries via bidirectional tree LSTMs. Int J Comput Assist Radiol Surg 2019;14(2):271—80. Available from: https://doi.org/10.1007/s11548-018-1884-6.

[35] Wolterink JM, Hamersvelt RWv, Viergever MA, Leiner T, Išgum I. Coronary artery centerline extraction in cardiac CT angiography using a CNN-based orientation classifier. Med Image Anal 2019;51:46—60. Available from: https://doi.org/10.1016/j.media.2018.10.005.

[36] Lessmann N, et al. Automatic calcium scoring in low-dose chest CT using deep neural networks with dilated convolutions. IEEE Trans Med Imaging 2018;37(2):615—25. Available from: https://doi.org/10.1109/TMI.2017.2769839.

[37] Itu L, et al. A machine-learning approach for computation of fractional flow reserve from coronary computed tomography. J Appl Physiol 2016;121(1):42—52. Available from: https://doi.org/10.1152/japplphysiol.00752.2015.

[38] Yu L, Guo Y, Wang Y, Yu J, Chen P. Segmentation of fetal left ventricle in echocardiographic sequences based on dynamic convolutional neural networks. IEEE Trans Biomed Eng 2017;64 (8):1886−95. Available from: https://doi.org/10.1109/TBME.2016.2628401.

[39] Commandeur F, et al. Deep learning for quantification of epicardial and thoracic adipose tissue from non-contrast CT. IEEE Trans Med Imaging 2018;37(8):1835−46. Available from: https://doi.org/10.1109/TMI.2018.2804799.

[40] Zreik M, et al. Deep learning analysis of the myocardium in coronary CT angiography for identification of patients with functionally significant coronary artery stenosis. Med Image Anal 2018;44:72−85. Available from: https://doi.org/10.1016/j.media.2017.11.008.

[41] Rahhal MMA, Bazi Y, Alhichri H, Alajlan N, Melgani F, Yager RR. Deep learning approach for active classification of electrocardiogram signals. Inf Sci (NY) 2016;345:340−54. Available from: https://doi.org/10.1016/j.ins.2016.01.082.

[42] Hannun AY, et al. Cardiologist-level arrhythmia detection and classification in ambulatory electrocardiograms using a deep neural network. Nat Med 2019;25(1):65−9. Available from: https://doi.org/10.1038/s41591-018-0268-3.

[43] Yıldırım Ö, Pławiak P, Tan RS, Acharya UR. Arrhythmia detection using deep convolutional neural network with long duration ECG signals. Comput Biol Med 2018;102:411−20. Available from: https://doi.org/10.1016/j.compbiomed.2018.09.009.

[44] Sayantan G, Kien KP, Kadambari VK. Classification of ECG beats using deep belief network and active learning. Med Biol Eng Comput 2018;56(10):1887−98. Available from: https://doi.org/10.1007/s11517-018-1815-2.

[45] Yao Z., Chen Y., Arrhythmia classification from single lead ECG by multi-scale convolutional neural networks. IEEE Eng Med Biol Soc Annu Conf, vol. 2018, no. June, pp. 344−347, 2018. Available from: https://doi.org/10.1109/EMBC.2018.8512260.

[46] Oh SL, Ng EYK, Tan RS, Acharya UR. Automated diagnosis of arrhythmia using combination of CNN and LSTM techniques with variable length heart beats. Comput Biol Med 2018;102:278−87. Available from: https://doi.org/10.1016/j.compbiomed.2018.06.002.

[47] Warrick PA, Homsi MN. Ensembling convolutional and long short-term memory networks for electrocardiogram arrhythmia detection. Physiol Meas 2018;0−12.

[48] Rokos IC, et al. Appropriate cardiac cath lab activation: optimizing electrocardiogram interpretation and clinical decision-making for acute ST-elevation myocardial infarction. Am Heart J 2010;160(6). Available from: https://doi.org/10.1016/j.ahj.2010.08.011 995−1003.e8.

[49] Rokos IC, et al. Rationale for establishing regional ST-elevation myocardial infarction receiving center (SRC) networks. Am Heart J 2006;152(4):661−7. Available from: https://doi.org/10.1016/j.ahj.2006.06.001.

[50] Xiao R, Xu Y, Pelter MM, Mortara DW, Hu X. A deep learning approach to examine ischemic ST changes in ambulatory ECG recordings AMIA Jt Summits Transl Sci Proc AMIA Jt Summits Transl Sci 2018;2017:256−62[Online]. Available from: http://www.ncbi.nlm.nih.gov/pubmed/29888083%0Ahttp://www.pubmedcentral.nih.gov/articlerender.fcgi?artid = PMC5961830.

[51] Liu W, et al. Real-time multilead convolutional neural network for myocardial infarction detection. IEEE J Biomed Heal Inform 2018;22(5):1434−44. Available from: https://doi.org/10.1109/JBHI.2017.2771768.

[52] Chang PC, Lin JJ, Hsieh JC, Weng J. Myocardial infarction classification with multi-lead ECG using hidden Markov models and Gaussian mixture models. Appl Soft Comput J 2012;12 (10):3165−75. Available from: https://doi.org/10.1016/j.asoc.2012.06.004.

[53] Rokos IC. Artificial intelligence for STEMI detection: the 'Shanghai Algorithm' provides a step forward. Int J Cardiol 2020;317:231−2. Available from: https://doi.org/10.1016/j.ijcard.2020.07.002.

[54] Zhao Y, et al. Early detection of ST-segment elevated myocardial infarction by artificial intelligence with 12-lead electrocardiogram. Int J Cardiol 2020;317:223−30. Available from: https://doi.org/10.1016/j.ijcard.2020.04.089.

[55] Mehta S, et al. Enriching artificial intelligence ST-elevation myocardial infarction (STEMI) detection algorithms with differential diagnoses. Eur Heart J 2020;41(Suppl 2):2020. Available from: https://doi.org/10.1093/ehjci/ehaa946.1776.

[56] Attia ZI, et al. Screening for cardiac contractile dysfunction using an artificial intelligence—enabled electrocardiogram. Nat Med 2019;25(1):70—4. Available from: https://doi.org/10.1038/s41591-018-0240-2.

[57] Galloway CD, et al. Development and validation of a deep-learning model to screen for hyperkalemia from the electrocardiogram. JAMA Cardiol 2019;4(5):428—36. Available from: https://doi.org/10.1001/jamacardio.2019.0640.

[58] Bai W, et al. Automated cardiovascular magnetic resonance image analysis with fully convolutional networks. J Cardiovasc Magn Reson 2018;20(1):1—12. Available from: https://doi.org/10.1186/s12968-018-0471-x.

[59] Avendi MR, Kheradvar A, Jafarkhani H. A combined deep-learning and deformable-model approach to fully automatic segmentation of the left ventricle in cardiac MRI. Med Image Anal 2016;30:108—19. Available from: https://doi.org/10.1016/j.media.2016.01.005.

[60] Zotti C, Luo Z, Lalande A, Jodoin PM. Convolutional neural network with shape prior applied to cardiac MRI segmentation. IEEE J Biomed Heal Inform 2019;23(3):1119—28. Available from: https://doi.org/10.1109/JBHI.2018.2865450.

[61] Xu C, et al. Direct delineation of myocardial infarction without contrast agents using a joint motion feature learning architecture. Med Image Anal 2018;50:82—94. Available from: https://doi.org/10.1016/j.media.2018.09.001.

[62] Bratt A, et al. Machine learning derived segmentation of phase velocity encoded cardiovascular magnetic resonance for fully automated aortic flow quantification. J Cardiovasc Magn Reson 2019;21(1):1—11. Available from: https://doi.org/10.1186/s12968-018-0509-0.

[63] Dou Q, et al. 3D deeply supervised network for automated segmentation of volumetric medical images. Med Image Anal 2017;41:40—54. Available from: https://doi.org/10.1016/j.media.2017.05.001.

[64] Emad O., Yassine I.A., Fahmy A.S., Automatic localization of the left ventricle in cardiac MRI images using deep learning. Proc Annu Int Conf IEEE Eng Med Biol Soc EMBS, vol. 2015-Novem, pp. 683—686, 2015. Available from: https://doi.org/10.1109/EMBC.2015.7318454.

[65] Betancur J, et al. Deep learning for prediction of obstructive disease from fast myocardial perfusion SPECT: a multicenter study. JACC Cardiovasc Imaging 2018;11(11):1654—63. Available from: https://doi.org/10.1016/j.jcmg.2018.01.020.

[66] Abdolmanafi A, Duong L, Dahdah N, Adib IR, Cheriet F. Characterization of coronary artery pathological formations from OCT imaging using deep learning. Biomed Opt Express 2018;9(10):4936. Available from: https://doi.org/10.1364/boe.9.004936.

[67] Gessert N, et al. Automatic plaque detection in IVOCT pullbacks using convolutional neural networks. IEEE Trans Med Imaging 2019;38(2):426—34. Available from: https://doi.org/10.1109/TMI.2018.2865659.

[68] Shen D, Wu G, Suk H-I. Deep learning in medical image analysis. Annu Rev Biomed Eng 2017;19(4):221—48. Available from: https://doi.org/10.3390/jimaging7040074.

[69] Willemink MJ, et al. Preparing medical imaging data for machine learning. Radiology 2020;295(1):4—15. Available from: https://doi.org/10.1148/radiol.2020192224.

[70] Deselaers T, Deserno TM, Müller H. Automatic medical image annotation in ImageCLEF 2007: overview, results, and discussion. Pattern Recognit Lett 2008;29(15):1988—95. Available from: https://doi.org/10.1016/j.patrec.2008.03.001.

[71] Sun K. Research progress on application of random forest in medical image analysis. Beijing Biomed Eng 2018;37(4):413—18.

[72] Baisong Z, Xiangrui Z, Xiangqian C, Gang ZHU, Yu W. Influence of intraoperative fluoroscopy images' quality on the accuracy of bi-planar positioning method. Beijing Biomed Eng 2017;36(4):372—7.

[73] Zhou DX. Universality of deep convolutional neural networks. Appl Comput Harmon Anal 2020;48(2):787—94. Available from: https://doi.org/10.1016/j.acha.2019.06.004.

[74] Chawla NV, Bowyer KW, Hall LO, Kegelmeyer WP. SMOTE: synthetic minority over-sampling technique. J Artif Intell Res 2002;30(16):321—57. Available from: https://doi.org/10.1002/eap.2043.

[75] Yu H, Mu C, Sun C, Yang W, Yang X, Zuo X. Support vector machine-based optimized decision threshold adjustment strategy for classifying imbalanced data. Knowl Syst 2015;76:67—78. Available from: https://doi.org/10.1016/j.knosys.2014.12.007.

CHAPTER 5

Valvular assessment and flow quantification

Ahmed Abdel Khalek Abdel Razek, Germeen Albair Ashmalla and Dalia Fahmy
Department of Diagnostic Radiology, Faculty of Medicine, Mansoura University, Mansoura, Egypt

5.1 Introduction

Regarding valvular disease, the aim of cardiac MRI is to assess the abnormal valve (stenosis/regurge) together with ventricular function and flow disturbance to guide treatment plan. Various techniques are used: SSFP, ECG gating, Cine sequences, and phase contrast with velocity encoded gradients (VENC). Recently 4D flow Mr and wall shear stress sequences were introduced to expand our knowledge of hemodynamics of flow disturbance and degenerative changes in vascular wall responsible for development of aneurysm.

5.2 Techniques

5.2.1 Assessment of valve structure

Cardiovascular magnetic resonance (CMR) provided radiologists with the ability to visualize valvular anatomical structure and mobility in several imaging planes. Balanced steady-state free-precession (SSFP) sequences are frequently used for valvular assessment as they provide high signal-to-noise ratio (S/N). It provides significant contrast between the myocardial muscles and blood pool that enables better delineation of myocardial wall and effective volumetric-based functional measurements (Figs. 5.1 and 5.2) [1,2].

Prospective or retrospective electrocardiographic (ECG) gating is necessary for the acquisition of data from several cardiac cycles in a single breath-hold. The exact positioning of the slices in a plane chosen to create a right angle with that of the selected valve using a slice thickness (ST) of 4–6 mm is mandatory to avoid partial volume effects. Typically, noncine T1WI, T2 WI, fat saturated TSE sequences are utilized for visualization and tissue characterization of valve masses or vegetations [1–4].

Cardiovascular and Coronary Artery Imaging
DOI: https://doi.org/10.1016/B978-0-12-821983-6.00005-9

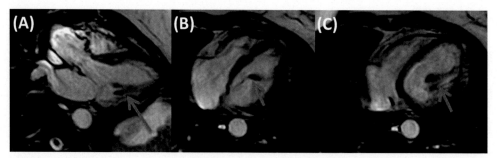

Figure 5.1 Parachute-like asymmetric mitral valve: (A,B,C): cine SSFP image in three chamber and four chamber views show asymmetric elongation of single antrolateral papillary muscle (arrow) attached to leaflets of the mitral valve with subsequent eccentric mitral orifice.

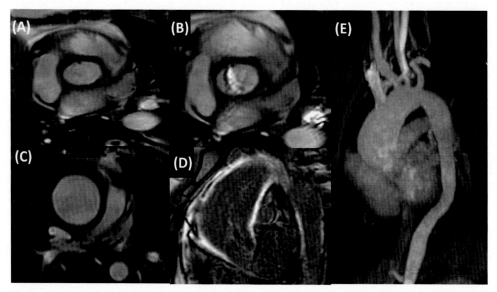

Figure 5.2 Ascending aortic aneurysm with inflammatory aortitis and bicusped aortic valve: (A,B) Short axis SSFP image during systole and diastole at the level of the aortic valve show mildly thickened bicuspid valve. (C) Short axis SSFP image shows dilated mid ascending aorta (6.6 cm) with thickened aortic wall. (D) LGE-shows enhancement of Aaortic wall. (E) 3D CE-MRA demonstrates the AAA and its extent.

5.2.2 Evaluation of ventricular volume and function

The timing of when to perform valvu-plasty or valve replacement is determined by the degree of severity of valvular disease. Grading of valvular stenosis or regurge depends upon several factors: accurate evaluation of ejection fraction (EF) and ventricular dimensions and volumes. Accurate measurement of left ventricle (LV) size and volumes is a crucial component of valvular evaluation. As mentioned earlier, SSFP techniques are perfect for the measurement of myocardial mass, ventricular volume (VV), and function via a postprocessing software that enables drawing of inner and outer margins of the LV as well as the endocardial border of the RV. Then the software uses Simpson method to give the final calculations [2,3].

5.2.3 Flow visualization

CMR cine sequences enable direct visualization of forward and backward blood flow across the diseased valve. Qualitative analysis depends on direct visualization of flow voids across in the flowing blood through the valve. Flow void represent intravoxel spin dephasing caused by turbulent flow. Gradient echo imaging (GRE) demonstrates different phase shifts with subsequent dephasing and signal loss that occur in turbulent blood. The detection of dephasing depends upon the echo time (ET) (i.e., the longer the ET, the larger and more pronounced the jet). In valve stenosis, a vena contracta could be evaluated as a high SI central jet of laminar flow surrounded by low signal voids; however, this method is not widely used or recommended. In malfunctioning valve regurgitant jets are visualized as dark flow voids [1−4].

5.2.3.1 Flow quantification

Phase-contrast utilizes velocity-encoding (VENC) gradients to produce a phase shift that is representative of the velocity of mobile protons. This sequence shows the velocity of spins (positive and negative) in the direction of the applied velocity encoding gradients for each voxel. The velocity encoding value chosen for each valve and each patient is variable, as it must fit with the highest possible velocity not causing aliasing. The axis of encoding should be kept parallel to the direction of blood flow across the valve to assure accurate measurements. Nonmobile spins appear gray while those having maximum velocity in the direction with encoding (in-plane) appear white while those moving in the opposite direction (regurgitation) appear black. Further quantification of blood flow and velocity across the valves is done utilizing dedicated software [2−6].

5.3 Individual valvular assessment

5.3.1 Aortic valve

5.3.1.1 Aortic regurgitation

Cardiac magnetic resonance imaging techniques enable detailed assessment of both the aorta as well as its valve through accurate measurement of LV volume during systole and diastole with subsequent functional calculations. It also provides clear identification of LV myocardial wall remodeling and aortic valve (AV) morphology. The key in diagnosis of aortic regurgitation (AR) is by detecting and calculating the aortic regurgitant volume (RVol), followed by looking for potential aortopathy.

5.3.1.2 Cine imaging for valve morphology and left ventricle volumes

SSFP and GRE cine sequences enable evaluation of the aortic valve and root morphological features. When it comes to calculations, two-dimensional (2D) and three-dimensional (3D) ECHO often under-estimate LV volumes in comparison to CMR. A multicenter observational study found that an LV end-diastolic volume >246 mL (calculated by CMR) can be used as diagnostic indicator to select patients in need of AV replacement [3,4].

5.3.1.3 Cardiovascular magnetic resonance quantification of aortic regurgitation severity

Peak systolic velocity (PSV) and flow in the aortic valve can be calculated with phase-contrast (PC) velocity mapping. The imaging plane should be put perpendicular to the axis of AV and exactly in the middle between the aortic annulus and sino-tubular junction. In the absence of obvious stenosis, a maximum VENC of 150 or 200 cm/s is usually adequate. If aliasing is observed, then the VENC is increased by 50 cm/s until the disappearance of aliasing. Aortic Rvol is measured from the area under the retrograde diastolic flow curve. Another method to calculate aortic RVol in cases without pulmonary artery regurgitation is by subtracting the pulmonic forward flow from the aortic forward flow. Regurgitant fraction (RF) is calculated with the equation RF = (regurgitant volume/forward volume) × 100% [4,7,8].

5.3.2 Mitral valve

5.3.2.1 Mitral regurgitation

CMR is used to evaluate the mitral valve regurgitation as well as myocardial muscle remodeling and viability, which in turn direct surgical decisions. Cine images can be taken in the different planes of the mitral valve (MV) leaflets. Evaluation of LGE of the inferior left ventricular wall and papillary muscles may show ischemic changes. Secondary mitral regurgitation (Mr) can be recognized through assessment of LV functional impairment and LV dilatation [2−4].

Primary Mr caused by mitral valve prolapse (MVP) is a good illustration of the way CMR is a helpful tool in severity evaluation of mitral valve regurgitation. In this particular disease, regurgitation develops in mid-late systole, and CMR show leaflets mal-coaptation and eccentric regurgitant jet. Volumetric measurement of Rvol by ECHO or CMR are more accurate for evaluation of Mr grade than calculation of the estimated regurgitant orifice area (EROA) or evaluation of the vena contracta on color-flow images [7−9].

5.3.2.2 Cardiovascular magnetic resonance quantification of mitral regurgitation severity

RVol and RF are considered the appropriate indicators of Mr severity. Continuous movement of mitral valve annulus along with high velocity of turbulent regurgitant

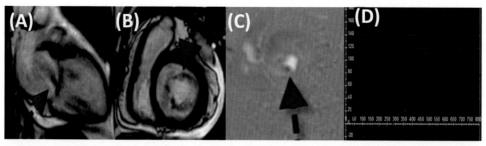

Figure 5.3 Moderate mitral regurgitation with preserved left ventricular function and thin rim pericardial effusion: (A) two-chamber SSFP slice at the level of the left cardiac cambers; LA & LV showing large central regurgitant jet at the LA (blue arrow). (B) Short axis SSFP at level of mitral valve (MV) shows mildly thickened valve (blue arrow), and thin rim pericardial effusion is seen. (C) Phase contrast at same level as (B) shows small signal void regurgitant jet (blue arrow) due to reversal of flow. (D) Time flow curve at the level of the MV showing the following parameters: regurgitant volume ~31 mL and regurgitation fraction ~33%. On functional analysis of the LV volumes and function: EDV: 153 mL, ESV: 60 mL, SV: 93 mL, EF: 60.8%.

jet during systole make it difficult to measure Mr with phase contrast. SSFP sequence is utilized to measure LV stroke volume (SV) and phase-contrast imaging to calculate forward flow volume at the aortic (or pulmonary) valves to calculate Mr RVol and RF. This is simply performed by calculation of the total LV SV and subtracting this from the aortic forward flow volume. Peak velocities can also be underestimated by low temporal resolution or if the selected image plane is not perpendicular to the direction of blood flow. To date, no Mr severity thresholds for RVol/RF are available, yet guidelines encourage application of the same thresholds of ECHO: mild <30 mL, moderate $30-59$ mL, and severe ≥ 60 mL (Fig. 5.3) [7−10].

5.3.3 Right-sided valve assessment

5.3.3.1 Pulmonary valve

CMR has proved to be superior to echocardiography regarding assessment of tricuspid and pulmonary valves (which is poorly seen in transesophageal and/or transthoracic echocardiography) especially in congenital cases with distorted anatomy. On CMR, pulmonary valve is best evaluated in the en-face and right ventricular outflow tract (RVOT) views. RV volumetric studies composed of SSFP short axis or axial stacked images are more reliable as compared to 2D or 3D ECHO. Flow jets detected on SSFP or GRE RVOT cine imaged permits qualitative assessment of regurgitation or stenosis. The best method for pulmonic valve area calculation is to do pulmonic valve orifice planimetry using a slice taken directly perpendicular to valve in RVOT cine view. Noncontrast "dark blood" TSE imaging provides better anatomic assessment of the outflow tract [11,12].

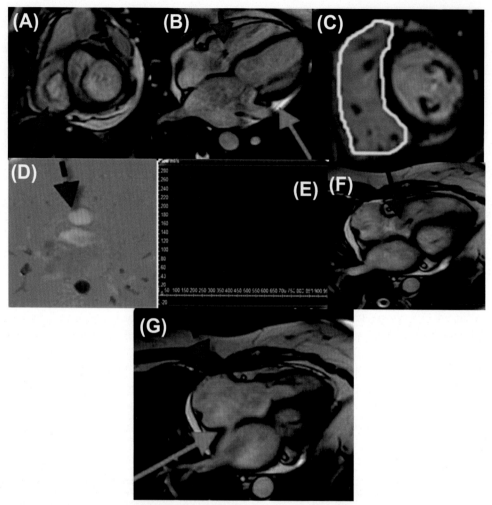

Figure 5.4 Mild tricuspid regurgitation with preserved ventricular function: (A) Short axis SSFP at level of the TV shows relatively thickened tricuspid valve cusps (leaflets) "blue arrows." (B) four-chamber SSFP image shows small central tricuspid regurgitant jet seen in the right atrium (blue arrow). The green arrow shows minimal pericardial effusion. (C) Short axis SSFP image at the level of RV & LV shows marking of the endocardial contour of the RV for functional analysis. (D) Phase-contrast image at level of the proximal pulmonary artery (Blue arrow) for functional analysis. (E) Time flow curve at level of the proximal main pulmonary artery showing that forward flow (stroke volume) = 44 mL. (F) Another 4-chamber SSFP image showing the signal void regurgitant jet in the right atrium (blue arrow). (G) 4-chamber SSFP image showing the four cardiac chambers with the right atrium mildly dilated (blue arrow). Evidence of accidentally discovered small secondum ASD ~8 mm with right-to-left shunt (green arrow). On functional analysis: RV volumes and function: EDV: 128 mL, ESV: 61 mL, SV: 67 mL, EF: 52.3%. Then by calculation: Regurgitant volume = 23 mL. Regurgitation fraction: 34%. LV volumes and function: EDV: 149 mL, ESV: 65 mL, SV: 84 mL, EF: 56.4%.

Qualitative evaluation of pulmonic stenosis (PS) utilizes the "through-plane" phase-contrast imaging adjusted at the level of maximal stenosis at level of the valve, supra or subvalvular. Peak velocity at the stenotic site is calculated via postprocessing software. On the other hand, pulmonic regurgitation (PR) can be measured by calculating the RF, which is considered severe if $\geq 40\%$. In cases of TOF repair, CMR-derived RV end-systolic and diastolic volume index prior to pulmonic valve replacement (PVR) best predict improvement in RV volumes regardless of the severity of PR. Limitations of CMR evaluation of PS and PR include high peak velocities in pulmonary stenosis that are difficult to be assessed, while PR jets are difficult to be recognized in SSFP images owing to less turbulent flow with less flow void [7].

5.3.3.2 Tricuspid valve

CMR shows the same pros and drawbacks as in assessment of Mr (Fig. 5.4). RV volumes and function assessment are a must and are performed in a similar way as in pulmonary valve disease [13–15].

5.4 Recent techniques

5.4.1 Four-dimensional flow MRI

Four-dimensional flow MRI or time-resolved 3D phase-contrast MRI enable noninvasive measurement of blood flow velocities in vivo in the major three orthogonal planes. It enables cardiac and vascular dynamic quantification of blood flow. Scan times range from 5–10 minutes with the use of advanced acceleration techniques, which require compensation of breathing movements by navigator gating [16,17].

5.4.2 Wall shear stress

Wall shear stress (WSS) is the frictional force of the blood on the endothelial cells with subsequent mural remodeling. A good example is seen in the ascending aorta of subjects with bicuspid aortic valve in whom excess extracellular matrix and degeneration of elastic fiber was proved histologically [18,19].

References

[1] Situ Y, Birch SCM, Moreyra C, et al. Cardiovascular magnetic resonance imaging for structural heart disease. Cardiovasc Diagn Ther 2020;10:361–75.
[2] Blanken CPS, Farag ES, Boekholdt SM, et al. Advanced cardiac MRI techniques for evaluation of left-sided valvular heart disease. J Magn Reson Imaging 2018;48:318–29.
[3] Mathew RC, Löffler AI, Salerno M. Role of cardiac magnetic resonance imaging in valvular heart disease: diagnosis, assessment, and management. Curr Cardiol Rep 2018;20:119.
[4] Gulsin GS, Singh A, McCann GP. Cardiovascular magnetic resonance in the evaluation of heart valve disease. BMC Med Imaging 2017;17:67.

[5] Cui C, Yin G, Lu M, et al. Retrospective electrocardiography-gated real-time cardiac cine MRI at 3T: comparison with conventional segmented cine MRI. Korean J Radiol 2019;20:114—25.

[6] Nayak KS, Nielsen JF, Bernstein MA, et al. Cardiovascular magnetic resonance phase contrast imaging. J Cardiovasc Magn Reson 2015;17:71.

[7] Zoghbi WA, Adams D, Bonow RO, et al. Recommendations for noninvasive evaluation of native valvular regurgitation: a report from the American Society of Echocardiography Developed in Collaboration with the Society for Cardiovascular Magnetic Resonance. J Am Soc Echocardiogr 2017;30:303—71.

[8] Kammerlander AA, Wiesinger M, Duca F, et al. Diagnostic and prognostic utility of cardiac magnetic resonance imaging in aortic regurgitation. JACC Cardiovasc Imaging 2019;12:1474—83.

[9] El Sabbagh A, Reddy YNV, Nishimura RA. Mitral valve regurgitation in the contemporary era: insights into diagnosis, management, and future directions. JACC Cardiovasc Imaging 2018;11:628—43.

[10] Uretsky S, Argulian E, Narula J, et al. Use of cardiac magnetic resonance imaging in assessing mitral regurgitation: current evidence. J Am Coll Cardiol 2018;71:547—63.

[11] Rajiah P, Nazarian J, Vogelius E, Gilkeson RC. CT and MRI of pulmonary valvular abnormalities. Clin Radiol 2014;69:630—8.

[12] Jonas SN, Kligerman SJ, Burke AP, et al. Pulmonary valve anatomy and abnormalities: a pictorial essay of radiography, computed tomography (CT), and magnetic resonance imaging (MRI). J Thorac Imaging 2016;31:W4—12.

[13] Qureshi MY, Sommer RJ, Cabalka AK. Tricuspid valve imaging and intervention in pediatric and adult patients with congenital heart disease. JACC Cardiovasc Imaging 2019;12:637—51.

[14] Khalique OK, Cavalcante JL, Shah D, et al. Multimodality imaging of the tricuspid valve and right heart anatomy. JACC Cardiovasc Imaging 2019;12:516—31.

[15] Hahn RT, Thomas JD, Khalique OK, et al. Imaging assessment of tricuspid regurgitation severity. JACC Cardiovasc Imaging 2019;12:469—90 106.

[16] Garcia J, Barker AJ, Markl M. The role of imaging of flow patterns by 4D flow MRI in aortic stenosis. JACC Cardiovasc Imaging 2019;12:252—66.

[17] Kamphuis VP, Westenberg JJM, van der Palen RLF, et al. Unravelling cardiovascular disease using four dimensional flow cardiovascular magnetic resonance. Int J Cardiovasc Imaging 2017;33:1069—81.

[18] Fatehi Hassanabad A, Garcia J, Verma S, et al. Utilizing wall shear stress as a clinical biomarker for bicuspid valve-associated aortopathy. Curr Opin Cardiol 2019;34:124—31.

[19] Bollache E, Guzzardi DG, Sattari S, et al. Aortic valve-mediated wall shear stress is heterogeneous and predicts regional aortic elastic fiber thinning in bicuspid aortic valve-associated aortopathy. J Thorac Cardiovasc Surg 2018;156:2112—20 e2.

CHAPTER 6

Software-based analysis for computed tomography coronary angiography: current status and future aspects

Kenji Fukushima[1] and Michinobu Nagao[2]
[1]Department of Nuclear Medicine (and Cardiology), Saitama Medical University International Medical Center, Hidaka, Saitama, Japan
[2]Department of Diagnostic Imaging and Nuclear Medicine, Tokyo Women's Medical University, Tokyo, Japan

6.1 Introduction

Coronary artery disease (CAD) is the leading cause of death in leading countries [1]. The disease progression of coronary atherosclerosis is known to be occult and lead to sudden onset with thrombosis or the development of symptoms due to plaque rapture or obstructive disease [2]. Thus the assessment of coronary atherosclerosis using noninvasive imaging is vital. Coronary computed tomography angiography (CTA) has been increasingly used in the diagnosis of CAD due to improved spatial and temporal resolution with high diagnostic value being reported when compared to invasive coronary angiography [3]. Although invasive coronary angiography still remains as the reference standard for the evaluation of CAD, multislice computed tomography (MSCT) coronary angiography has recently emerged as a first-line and noninvasive imaging modality [4].

The computed tomography (CT) scanner has rapidly evolved from single slice to multislice CT systems with wider detectors (up to 320 rows) in the last decade. With improved longitudinal volume coverage and faster gantry rotation speed, the newest CT scanners allow the acquisition of the whole heart image within a single heartbeat [5]. This technique also allows precise visualization of luminal narrowing as well as atherosclerotic changes within the coronary vessel wall with the help of submillimeter-level spatial resolution. Continuous improvements in CTA technology have also contributed to reduced radiation dose and contrast material [6,7]. The clinical usefulness including diagnostic accuracy and prognostic value have been demonstrated by several large multicenter clinical trials (i.e., CONFIRM, and PROMISE trials) [8,9]. The main components of CTA analysis are follows: coronary calcification, the assessment of organic stenosis and plaque deposition, and structural abnormality. Those assessments can be performed using image processing such as multiplanar reformation, maximum intensity projection, surface-shaded display, and volume-rendering techniques obtained from axial dicom data, and these reconstructed visualizations have made CTA an important component of medical imaging in daily clinical practice [10]. Unlike other chest CT images, software-based analysis is mandatory for the diagnosis of CAD using CTA. In this chapter, we address software-based CTA analysis in clinical routine and its future potential.

6.2 Coronary artery calcification measurement

The evaluation of coronary artery calcification plays a key role in cardiovascular risk stratification, surrogating a significant coronary atherosclerosis associated with the major adverse cardiovascular events [11]. Coronary artery calcium (CAC) was originally investigated using electron beam computed tomography, and later replaced by multislice computed tomography when introduced into clinical routine [12]. A key advantage of the calcium scan is to identify a high-risk candidate out of low-to-intermediate subjects without using contrast media, which is not recommended for patients with renal insufficiency or allergic status. As Agatston et al. initially reported, CAC grading shows a predictive value according to its severity; in other words, the absence of CAC can assure patients of significantly low risk of future event [11]. In a clinical routine setting, the evaluation of coronary calcium by CT is done on axial slices, with a thickness of 3 mm, without overlapping or gaps, limited to the cardiac region, acquired with prospective ECG gating usually in the mid-to-late diastole phase without the use of intravenous contrast medium. The radiation dose was recommended to be less that 1.5 mSv. Calcification is defined as areas of hyperattenuation over 1 mm^2- with >130 Hounsfield units (HU) [13]. The most common technique for the quantification of the calcium score are the Agatston method, which measures the volume of calcium and generates the calcium mass [13]. The calcified region was graded as density factor according to HU value; 130–199 HU as factor 1, 200–299 HU as 2, 300–399 HU as 3, and over 400 as 4. When the area of maximum attenuation over 400 HU occupies 10 mm^2, CAC score will be 40. Fig. 6.1 shows CAC analysis using automatic coronary calcium calculation software (Vincent, Fuji-film medical Inc. Tokyo, Japan). Most software is available for either automatic or manual region of interest (ROI) setting including naming the artery. The Agatston score can be calculated for either whole coronary artery, each vessel, or segment. However, CAC measurement is less useful if the candidate has already undergone coronary stenting, chest surgery including cardiac, or device implantation.

6.3 Software-based plaque analysis

One of the main roles of CTA is to evaluate coronary atherosclerosis. In general, atherosclerotic plaque is initiated by deposition of low-density lipoproteins in the vessel wall of coronary artery, and in the course of the disease progression, it leads to calcified plaque or inflammation with extracellular matrix alteration, so-called "vulnerable plaque" [14].

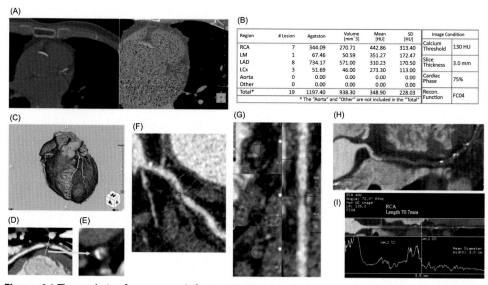

Region	# Lesion	Agatston	Volume [mm^3]	Mean [HU]	SD [HU]	Image Condition	
RCA	7	344.09	270.71	442.86	313.40	Calcium Threshold	130 HU
LM	1	67.46	50.59	351.27	172.47		
LAD	8	734.17	571.00	310.23	170.50	Slice Thickness	3.0 mm
LCx	3	51.69	46.00	273.30	113.00		
Aorta	0	0.00	0.00	0.00	0.00	Cardiac Phase	75%
Other	0	0.00	0.00	0.00	0.00		
Total*	19	1197.40	938.30	348.90	228.03	Recon. Function	FC04
* The "Aorta" and "Other" are not included in the "Total"							

Figure 6.1 The analysis of coronary calcification (CAC) using Agatston method is shown in upper panel (A and B). Region or volume of interest is automatically drawn using threshold of CT value (i.e., Houncefield unit > 130) from axial slices. (A) The purple colored indicates left coronary artery, and total Agatston score is generated as a sum of CAC of all coronary arteries. (B) shows output sheet for CAC calculation. Standardized analysis of coronary atherosclerosis is shown in C to E. First, a volume rendering image is useful for comprehension of the whole structural appearance of the heart (C) Curved planar reconstruction, and cross-sectional images are standard reformatting techniques to visualize coronary atherosclerosis such as luminal narrowing, plaques, and bifurcation stenosis. (D) shows significant vessel stenosis in mid-distal of left circumflex artery with calcified and noncalcified plaque. (E) shows a cross-sectional image for significant stenosis by eccentric deposition of low-attenuation plaque with extensive calcified plaque, which may consist of necrotic core indicating high-risk of plaque rupture, so-called "vulnerable plaque." (F,G) show quantitative measurement for lumina stenosis using dedicated software (Ziosoft). The mean luminal diameter of stenosis is calculated on a curved planar reconstruction image. (H,I) show the measurement of the lesion length for an occlusive coronary artery. (H) shows a reconstructed image of chronic total occlusion in the right coronary artery, and I shows lesion length on straight curved planar reconstruction.

Histopathologic findings of high-risk plaque demonstrate thin cap fibroatheromas, which can be defined by attenuated area in the vessel wall. Among established findings of vulnerable plaque, "napkin-ring sign" refers to an eccentric structure comprising circumferential low-attenuated plaque with mild luminal narrowing, which is hard to detect in conventional axial CT images. Napkin-ring should be visualized by cross-sectional image obtained from dedicated software or on-site workstation. Several investigations reported the usefulness of visual grading for coronary plaque severity [15]. The multisociety working group included the society of cardiovascular computed tomography, the American college of radiology, and north American society for cardiovascular imaging produced the Coronary Artery Disease Reporting & Data System (CAD-RADS), standardized CTA reporting including quantitative evaluation of coronary atherosclerosis [16]. In CAD-RADS, a segment involvement score or total plaque score represent the sum of semiquantitative scoring for atherosclerotic plaque burden in each coronary segment, which can be easily transparently communicated [16]. With well-controlled heart rate, coronary CTA is capable of visualizing the luminal stenosis, and the characteristics of the coronary wall, thus allowing noninvasive differentiation between lipid-rich and fibrotic tissue based on various CT attenuation values. To date, the mean Hounsfield Unit values can surrogate the different plaque components and lower value below 100 HU suggests lipid-rich plaque. Nevertheless, from *meta*-analysis or literature reviews, semiquantitative or truly quantitative plaque analysis such as low-attenuation plaque volume measurement can demonstrate advanced noninvasive coronary wall analysis and well correlate to histopathologic findings [14]. Intravascular ultrasound (IVUS) by invasive cardiac catherization is known as referential standards in vivo so far [17], and several investigators have validated the feasibility and detectability of the plaque by CT attenuation, and compared to IVUS findings [18]. Other investigations have suggested the usefulness of quantitative histogram analysis output [19]. Meta-analysis revealed that the usefulness of serial assessment of quantitative plaque volume progression and demonstrated the incremental prognostic value have been investigated [20,21]. Fig. 6.2 shows the automated plaque analysis using dedicated software (Intuition Terarecon Inc. Tokyo, Japan). The lesion was analyzed and colored according to HU value, the volume

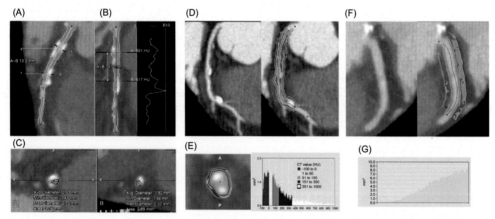

Figure 6.2 Software-based, quantitative analysis for coronary atherosclerosis and pericoronary adipose tissue is shown. (A,B) show curved planar reconstruction (CPR) for coronary arteries, and (C) show the luminal area and mean diameter. (D,E) show color mapping for plaque using the threshold of Houncefield units (HU) differentiating calcified, fibrotic, and lipid-rich plaque. (E) shows a histogram of the distribution for HU in plaque. (F) shows the quantitative measurement for pericoronary adipose tissue. Outlier of coronary wall analysis is expanded outside of the coronary wall (approximately 10–15 mm), and the volume of the low attenuated area using thresholds < 30 HU is measured. (G) shows a histogram of HU in pericoronary site.

Table 6.1 Clinical trials for software-based atherosclerosis analysis.

Study/author	Journal	year	number	CT specifications	Software (or Provider)	Study design/ referential standard	Diagnostic accuracy/ reference or prognosis
Zeb [57]	Atherosclerosis	2013	100	64DSCT	Vitrea	Noncalcified plaque volume	Serial scan with statin treatment
Dey [58]	Radiology	2010	20	64DSCT	AUTOPLAQ and Syngo. multimodality Workspace	Plaque analysis	Automated 3D analysis/ IVUS
Goller [47]	JAMA Cardiology	2018	35	64DSCT	AUTOPLAQ	Neighboring attenuated plaque	
Seifarth [59] Inoue [60]	Atherosclerosis JACC: Cardiovasc Imaging	2012 2010	7 32	64MSCT 64MSCT	na ZIO soft	Napkin-ring sign Low-attenuation plaque volume	Serial scan with statin treatment
Rajani [49]	J Cardiovasc Comput Tomogr	2013	1256	64DSCT	QFAT	Epicard-fat volume and plaque	
Najidri [61]	J Cardiovasc Comput Tomogr	2013	402	64MSCT	Original	Low-attenuation plaque volume	Prognosis of low attenuation plaque
Dey [62]	J Cardiovasc Comput Tomogr	2014	28	64DSCT	APQ	Low-attenuation plaque volume	Invasive CAG
Marwan [63]	Atherosclerosis	2011	40	64DSCT	ImageJ	Comparison to IVUS	

(Continued)

Table 6.1 (Continued)

Study/author	Journal	year	number	CT specifications	Software (or Provider)	Study design/ referential standard	Diagnostic accuracy/ reference or prognosis
Puchner [64]	Int J Cardiovasc Img	2013	9	64MSCT	Vitrea	Compare among reconstruction algorithms	
Nakazato [65]	Eur Radiology	2013	27	64DSCT	Advanced Workstation	Low-attenuation plaque volume	
Weber [66]	Eur J Rad	2020	350	16MSCT	QAngioCT	Low-attenuation plaque volume	Serial scan
Banberg [67]	Int J Cardiovasc Img	2012	412	64MSCT	Leonardo	Noncalcified plaque volume and hs-CRP	Subanalysis from ROMICAT
Oberoi [24]	Am J Rouent	2013	47	64MSCT	Aquerious, Vitrea, Circulation	Low-attenuation plaque volume	Comparison among multivendor
Diaz-Zamudio [68]	Radiology	2015	56	64MSCT or 320 row	AUTOPLAQ	Plaque analysis	
Ceponiene [69]	JACC: Cardiovasc Imaging	2018	211	64MSCT	QAngioCT	Plaque analysis, semiautomated	Serial scan
Conte [18]	Eur Heart J Cardiovasc Imaging	2020	59	64MSCT or 256 row	na	Plaque analysis	IVUS
Goeller [48]	J Cardiovasc Comput Tomogr	2018	456	4MSCT	QFAT	Pericoronary fat	noncontrast CT

Kwiecinski [50]	JACC: Cardiovasc Imaging	2019	41	64MSCT or 320 row	AUTOPLAQ	Pericoronary fat	combined with NaF-PET
Sugiyama T [70]	J Am Heart Assoc	2020	2474	320 row	Aquerious	Pericoronary fat	
CAPIRE [71]	JACC: Cardiovasc Imaging	2020	544	64DSCT or higher	CardiIQ	Plaque analysis	Prognosis of high-risk plaque
Discover-flow [36]	J Cardiovasc Comput Tomogr	2012	103	64DSCT or higher	ZIO Soft or Vital image	FFRct/Invasive FFR	

CT, computed tomography; *DSCT*, dual-source CT; *MSCT*, multislice CT; *CRP*, c-reactive protein; *CAG*, coronary angiography; *PET*, positron emission tomography; *FFR*, fractional flow reserve; *na*, not available.

measurement. A histogram analysis is also available to evaluate plaque distribution in target lesion (Fig. 6.2E). Various dedicated software packages including commercially available or in-house originally for coronary plaque analysis can be employed in clinical trials. The feasibility and reproducibility have been demonstrated by multiple studies (Table 6.1) [22,23]. Studies have employed the software without eccentric use. Oberoi et al. reported coronary plaque quantification was reproducible among different software packages [24].

6.4 Quantitative analysis for obstructive coronary artery

An obstructive coronary is usually visually interpreted and graded in clinical routine. Visual grading for organic stenosis was originally divided into four groups according to conventional coronary angiography (0% no stenosis, under 25% mild stenosis, 50% moderate or significant stenosis, 75% moderate to severe, over 90% severe stenosis) [15,16]. Recently, total atherosclerotic burden can be calculated as Segment Stenosis Score (SSS). The stenosis of multiple segments were visually graded on a 5-point scale (0—4) as stenosis 0%, 1%—29%, 30%—49%, 50%—69%, and over 70%, respectively [15,16,25]. The atherosclerosis in distal artery or side branch was not measured when the vessel diameter was below 2 mm. Total SSS was calculated by summing all 15 individual SSSs with a possible score ranging from 0 to 60. This visual scoring has been investigated to determine whether the score had incremental diagnostic value over grading for organic stenosis, and several studies have shown promising results. Most software vendors install the automatic calculation application for coronary stenosis. It mostly performs direct measurement for cross-sectional diameter of stenotic lesion, and calculates as %diameter stenosis for the physiologic gradient of diameter from proximal to distal site [26]. Fig. 6.1 shows representative case for significant organic stenosis. The vessel contour was automatically traced and manually corrected if necessary. In the vessel with total occlusion, the distance of occluded legion is crucial information for coronary intervention. Fig. 6.1F shows the measurement of region length for chronic total occlusion in proximal right coronary artery. The distance of occluded lesion is manually measured in straight CPR image because it is not available for the curved planar reconstruction. However, a visual or software-based quantification of coronary stenosis can limit the diagnostic accuracy for predicting flow-limiting disease because organic stenosis frequently comprises calcified plaque, which causes overestimation of the severity of luminal narrowing due to significant blooming artifact. Recently, the gradient of CT value in coronary artery from proximal site to distal branch was validated for the patients with intact coronary and threshold for abnormal value has been investigated. This technique is called Transluminal Attenuation Gradient (TAG). TAG may be significantly decreased when hemodynamically overt coronary stenosis is present. Several studies have reported the clinical usefulness of TAG for predicting hemodynamically significant coronary stenosis. The advantage of

TAG is to perform the analysis for routine CTA. However, recent studies have revealed that TAG is less useful to introduce in clinical routine as a relevant technique due to the difficulties of optimal scan timing or significantly less usability [27]. More recently, TAG analysis from dynamic CTA was reported and this analysis may draw scientists' attention. TAG analysis can be performed for each dynamic phase and change of the gradient [28].

6.5 Computational fluid dynamics

Recently, with the rapid innovation of image processing, software-based coronary analysis using computational fluid dynamics (CFD) has emerged as a promising technique in clinical routine [29,30]. The primal concept of CFD was initially established based on Navier-strokes equations in the late 1800s, and subsequently applied to various physiological modeling to simulate intraluminal flow dynamics and vascular resistance [31,32]. To date, several studies have shown that a fractional flow reserve (FFR) measurement during invasive coronary angiography is crucial to determining hemodynamically functional stenosis rather than visual estimation of luminal narrowing, and FFR guided intervention has significantly improved patients' outcome and the weakness of visual grading guided therapy for organic stenosis was confirmed [33]. FFRct has been developed to simulate invasive FFR using datasets obtained from routine CTA, and favorable results have been obtained from several prospective clinical trials such as DISCOVER-FLOW, DE FACTO, and NXT, and those trials have proved superior diagnostic accuracy of FFRct by comparing CTA alone to predict significant functional stenosis determined by invasive FFR as gold standard [29,34—36]. Among several methods under investigation in diagnostic research studies, currently the only vendor providing noninvasive FFR analysis is FFRCT (HeartFlow Inc. CA). However, the conditional datasets can be rejected during FFRCT analysis. In the ADVANCE registry, Fairbairn et al. found that the main reasons for scan rejection include calcium blooming artifact, motion artifacts, and clipped structures and image noise. The result of subanalysis from other studies also suggest optimal image quality of CTA is strictly required to maximize the diagnostic accuracy of FFRct [37]. Therefore the Society of Cardiovascular Computed Tomography (SCCT) suggest a guideline for required CT image in order to maintain the accuracy of results from FFRct analysis (i.e., multislice CT scanner with 64 or higher, adequate heart rate reduction, and nitrate administration). Another shortcoming of FFRct is that the CTA data should be transfered outside the hospital.

6.6 Anatomical 2D bull's eye display

The bull's eye map display from 3D data was initially established in the early 1980s, when the image interpretation by reading conventional hard-copy films was the main process. This technique was mainly employed for nuclear cardiology because the interpretation of 3D images in plane film has been difficult in a number of cases. The bull's eye map is known to be helpful in intuitive assessment for abnormal regions in whole 3D structures. Additionally, qualitative or semiquantitative assessment is available to detect and localize regional abnormality as well as interpret at a glance. A basic algorithm was established: count profile of oblique and circumferential are mapped onto a 2D plane [38]. This technique also enables the visual detection of abnormal region by comparing with normal bull's-eye database using American Heart Association 17 segment-model, which is used for universal segmental analysis of left ventricle [39]. Another strength of this technique is to create a map of any functional information such as wall motion, thickening, and phase as well as myocardial perfusion.

For other modalities such as CT, MRI, and echocardiography, several algorithms have been suggested for creating a bull's eye map from 3D volume data. Most of them are to simply divide LV into three to four levels to assign the segments (basal, mid, and apex). However, this rough assignment can be erroneous because the anatomical dominancy of the coronary artery is varied among individuals. Thus the converted 2D bull's eye map should be geographically corresponded to the original 3D spatial information. Most vendors have already introduced a basic algorithm for creating plane 2D display from 3D volume data. In clinical research, Nakahara et al. reported a method for generating a 2D bull's eye map of nuclear cardiology and CTA fusion from the 3D volume rendering SPECT-CTA image fusion data, which was originally reconstructed using dedicated commercially available software. 3D CTA was extracted to 540 images to create a panoramic image, and then converted to 2D bull's eye formation after definition of longitudinal axis using transparency tool. The coronary path is pasted on LV wall in advance for original 3D volume rendering image [40].

In our previous work, we reported the method of creating a 2D bull's eye map directly from the original 3D CTA image. The basic concept is to enable intuitive assessment of anatomical dominancy of coronary tree in 2D images on plane display such as picture archiving and communication system, which is not capable of displaying 3D objects in multiangle views. The conversion algorithm of this method is to morph the individual left ventricle wall and coronary path on cylind-spherical virtual phantom. As shown in Fig. 6.3 upper panel, the left ventricular apex was defined as 0 on the Z axis in virtual 3D coordinate system, and the LV wall was divided into 64 segments along the Z axis from apex to basal area, namely 64 rings with different radius reflecting the distance from apex are made. The X and Y axis are defined as transaxial and cephalocaudal directions. The location of the coronary path was translated to be the point on the ring, and the coordinate is defined as the angle from the arc on the corresponding point on the circumference of the circle. In other words, the path of coronary artery is defined as the coordinate on the Z axis and the angle from the X axis. However, similar to most vendors' algorithms,

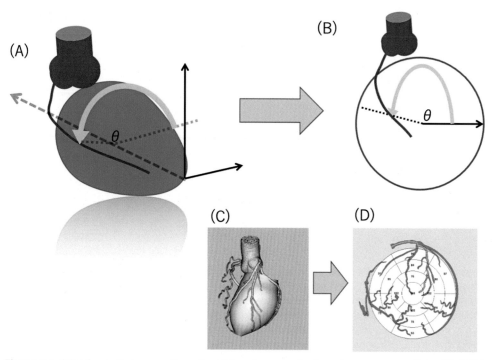

Figure 6.3 (A) schematic image of creating 2D polar map display of coronary tree from 3D CTA is shown. 3D coordinate setting is allotted for 3D CTA image. Apex was defined as 0 on Z axis in virtual 3D coordinate system (A), and the LV wall was divided into 64 segments along Z axis from apex to basal area, namely 64 rings with different radius reflecting the distance from apex are made. The X and Y axis are defined as transaxial and cephalocaudal direction. The location of coronary path was translated to be the point on the ring, and the coordinate is defined as the angle from the arc on the corresponding point on the circumference of circle (B) Patient-based coronary anatomy can be transported as 2D display map so that it can be transparently assessed in various output forms (i.e., electrical, medical chart, or paper).

this method keeps the right coronary artery (RCA) pasted on the left ventricular wall as well as left coronary artery, and this is not normal RCA course. RCA usually runs along the right basal edge of the right ventricle (RV) instead of the septal wall. Next, a fin-type of virtual right ventricular phantom was placed at 7−11 o'clock to create a physiological course of proximal RCA, which is supposed to run on the RV wall [41] (Fig. 6.4).

6.7 Territorial analysis with Voronoi diagram

The assessment of coronary anatomical distribution and vascular territory is crucial because they are closely associated with ischemic burden in CAD, and varied

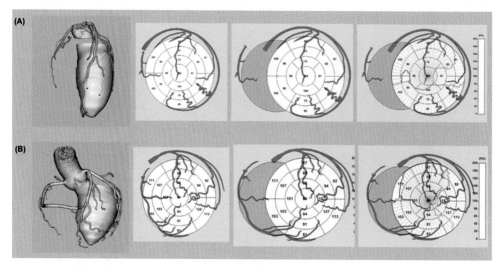

Figure 6.4 Patient-based coronary bull's eye displays for two typical anatomical variations are shown. (A) represents a large left coronary artery (LCA) dominant type with hypoplastic right coronary artery (RCA). Left circumflex artery (LCX) reaches the basal-inferior wall close to the right ventricular insertion point. (B) is a CTA of large RCA with relatively small LCX. RCA supplies are almost entirely inferior to apex in the left ventricle. Mid-right panels show the 2D bull's eye display with the right ventricle. Left panels are patient-based territorial segmentation with a voronoi diagram.

among individuals. Among several simulative methodology, a Voronoi diagram, which was initially used for geometrical analysis (i.e., path planning for marine vehicle, or identification of the most distant edges from the generator points). The basic algorithm of the Voronoi diagram is to divide a geometrical space according to the distribution of the objects present in the specific field. In the early application of coronary anatomical dominancy, the simulation of coronary dominancy was well correlated to that of postmortem analysis using animal models [42,43]. In clinical practice, Kurata et al. reported that the risk area of the culprit region was successfully evaluated using the Voronoi diagram [44]. Ide et al. validated the segmental analysis generating myocardial mass of the risk area supplied by culprit regions using the Voronoi diagram from the obtained 3D data of patients with normal coronary artery [42]. Fig. 6.4 shows typical cases of territorial simulation of coronary dominancy. The territorial dominancy of the perfused area corresponded to the simulated area by Voronoi diagram. The other feature of the Voronoi diagram is lower specification of computational processing making it feasible to introduce into clinical routine. Fig. 6.4 shows a typical 2D map display of coronary dominancy and distribution of coronary tree obtained from 3D images. Importantly, RCA runs on the surface of inferior LV wall from the distal site (level of segment no. 3), and mostly posterior descending artery (segment 4) runs through posterior intraventricular sulcus. Most hearts are right dominant, and posterior descending artery is supplied by the RCA, while inferior wall is not supplied by RCA when LCX is large enough.

6.8 Nobel analysis for computed tomography angiography

6.8.1 Pericardial and pericoronary fat measurement

Since metabolic disorders such as obesity and diabetes have become important public health issues, their link to cardiovascular complications has been frequently discussed. Pericardial adipose tissue (PAT), which is different from subcutaneous adipose tissue, has been known as a surrogate marker for various lifestyle-related diseases [45]. Pericoronary adipose tissue (PCAT), which is mainly found in the atrioventricular and interventricular grooves closely surrounding the coronary arteries, has been known to be linked to increased risk of major cardiovascular events. It has been well recognized that the adipose tissue is a source of various inflammatory mediators (e.g. adiponectin, leptin, resistin and visfatin, etc.), which is in direct contact with the vasculature. The primary effect of PCAT on coronary arteries has been hypothesized to be the release of inflammatory chemokines, which may directly effect coronary arterial endothelial cells [46]. Recently, the close relationship of coronary atherosclerosis and the amount of PCAT has been investigated [47]. Subanalysis from the Early Identification of Subclinical Atherosclerosis by Noninvasive Imaging Research (EISNER) registry has revealed the close relationship between epicardial fat deposition and coronary arterial calcification [48]. Several studies have also found that the epicardial fat volume is associated with impaired coronary microvascular response, suggesting the PCAT effects on vascular endothelial function and progress coronary atherosclerosis. Some other researchers have observed the epicardial fat volume measured in CTA, and reported the volume was strongly associated with early development of coronary atherosclerosis including nonstenotic and noncalcified plaques [49]. Measurement of PCAT can be a novel target for noninvasive imaging of coronary atherosclerosis because the magnitude and mount of PCAT can be evaluated qualitatively and quantitatively simultaneously using routine CTA in clinical practice. A clinical workflow of PCAT assessment using CTA is as follows. First, the wall of the coronary artery is traced and the contrast media in lumen or calcification is excluded: radially outwards area from coronary vessel wall in 3D image. This process is usually performed using standardized coronary plaque analysis software. Second, adipose tissue is defined as all voxels with Hounsfield Unit attenuation between -190 and -30. Measurements of mean attenuation and volume are obtained 10 mm from the coronary origin to 50 mm distal at a radial distance around 20 mm [46,50]. The proximal 10 mm of the vessel needs to be excluded to avoid interference from the aortic wall. Fig. 6.2F and G shows a representative image for measurement of PCAT. A curved planar reformatting image is useful to confirm the successful exclusion of aortic wall or heart chamber wall.

6.9 Computed tomography myocardial perfusion imaging

Although CTA is known as a first-line modality to triage high-risk CAD, several shortcomings should be noticed. First, the organic stenosis does not always indicate functionally flow limiting disease, which should be evaluated by functional or perfusion study such as nuclear cardiology or stress echocardiography. Second, there is substantial tendency to overestimate the severity of the coronary stenosis in high-risk patients due to the presence of calcified plaques. Thus the imaging technique for the detection of functional stenosis is required in CTA. Myocardial CT perfusion (CTP), combined conventional coronary CT angiography, can be an ideal imaging modality as a comprehensive tool that delivers the anatomical and functional assessment simultaneously [51]. CTP was initially reported using electron beam CT in the 1970s, but several technological limitations including limited field of view have prevented it from reaching clinical application [52]. In the 1990s the newest generation of scanners become available for single volume scan covering a whole heart chamber, and the concept of whole heart dynamic volume scan was designed. This technical innovation using more sensitive detectors promised advantages for rapid scan and minimal radiation exposure. Compared to MRI or nuclear cardiology, CTA is capable of visualizing atherosclerotic plaque burden and calcification, which have been recognized as strong indicators for cardiovascular events [53]. Of note, CT machines are usually accessible in most hospital compared to MRI or nuclear medicine, thus introducing stress CTP is relatively available for local hospitals compared to other costly modalities [54].

Rest then pharmacological stress (or vice versa) protocol is required to detect functional stenosis. The increase of the contrast enhancement during stress directly indicates coronary vasomotor response, which can be represented as myocardial perfusion reserve: the ratio of myocardial HU for stress versus rest, while hypo or nonenhancement indicate perfusion defect [53]. The stress vasodilator agents used in stress CTP are similar to that of stress cardiac MRI and nuclear cardiology (i.e., adenosine, dipyridamole, dobutamine, or regadenoson). An optimal interval of 10−15 minutes is required to avoid the risk of contrast media contamination of earlier phase, optimal contrast wash-out between rest and stress scan. Generally, CTP protocol is combined with conventional CTA imaging including calcium scan to obtain anatomical information. There are two main acquisition protocols for CTP. First, static perfusion for one-single phase during the first-pass with monoenergetic or dual acquisition, namely, targeting maximal enhancement in the ascending aorta under both rest and pharmacological stress to obtain optimal scan timing for snapshot. Second, dynamic

CTP based on repeated acquisition of whole heart with multiphase to generate the animated cine images or the time-attenuation curves for the perfusion analysis. These imaging technique have been established using 64-slice CT, ideally wider detector CT (128 or 320 slices) with faster gantry rotation. Additionally, a third optional delayed-phase acquisition can be performed in cases where late contrast enhancement evaluation for myocardial scar is desired when myocardial infarction or damage is suspected [55]. The latest generations of CT scanners and reconstruction algorithms can minimize radiation exposure. Recent technological developments in the latest generations of CT scanners and reconstruction algorithms have enabled reduced doses. Danad et al. estimated an average radiation exposure of 5.9 mSv (range 1.9−15.7) for snapshot CTP and 9.2 mSv (range 3.8−12.8) for dynamic CTP, and this can be further reduced when using low-kv protocol with advanced reconstruction algorithm [53].

6.10 The analysis of dynamic images by motion coherence technique

As described above, the latest MSCT with wide FOV enables serial dynamic study in addition to conventional volume scan. A 4D dynamic CT scan with multiphase can contribute to accurate interpretation of cardiac function and reginal motion. However, due to increasing radiation exposure, the scan phases and effective dose should be appropriately restricted. Motion coherence image processing (MCIP) (PhyZiodynamics; Ziosoft Inc., Tokyo, Japan) is a novel image processing technique that has been increasingly used in clinical setting. This imaging technique can multiply dynamic images throughout all phases by interpolating between one phase to another with deformable registration. For instance, if 10 phases or cycles of dynamic images are obtained, MCIP can generate from 20 up to 50 datasets by multiplying and interpolating between phases. The middle and lower panel in Fig. 6.5 show dynamic series of CT images multiplied by MCIP from original dynamic scan [56]. This imaging technique can also offer noise reduction and motion coherence improvement, which enable visual assessment of dynamic motion of cardiac chamber, coronary arteries, and vessels. This technique is also available for dynamic images with multiplanar reconstruction or 3D volume rendering. The other feature of MCIP by Ziosoft is it can track specific voxels throughout phases. When VOI is placed on coronary artery, an intracoronary flow dynamics can be measured. In ZIO Soft, a spherical volume of interest (VOI) in coronary arteries are automatically tracked and time-density curves. The VOI can be placed anywhere to track if sufficient change of CT value was obtained, and available to avoid calcification or metal, which may interrupt sufficient time density curves. One of the promising features of MCIP is to perform in routine clinical setting.

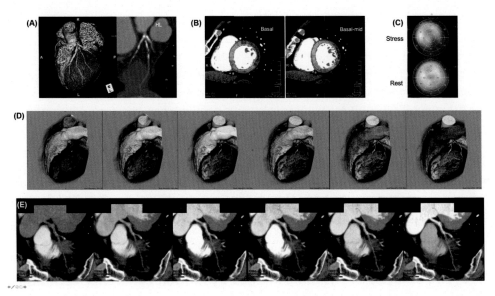

Figure 6.5 Dynamic CT studies are shown. The upper panels (A to C) are for rest-pharmacological stress static CT perfusion (CTP). (A) shows 3D CTA and curved planar reconstruction image for a patient with significant organic stenosis in hilateral branch (HL) in left coronary artery. Rest-adenosine stress static CTP demonstrated stress induced hypoattenuated region in lateral area, which indicates transient myocardial ischemia (B) Adenosine stress-rest nuclear myocardial perfusion imaging revealed significant transient ischemia in the lateral wall (C) upper stress; lower rest). Middle to lower panels (D and E) are for dynamic 4D CT angiography (4D-CTA). D shows 4D CTA cine-imaging using motion coherence image processing for volume rendering reconstruction. This technique is also available for curved planar reconstruction images (E) Using this technique, the intracoronary flow dynamics can be visualized, and the changes of the intracoronary CT attenuation are quantified.

6.11 Closing remarks

Software-based analysis is necessary for accurate diagnosis of coronary CTA. Continuous innovation in CTA for cardiovascular imaging can be achieved by collaboration with both hardware and software development. The iterative process of improvements can contribute to comprehension of the precise mechanism of coronary atherosclerosis.

References

[1] Virani SS, Alonso A, Benjamin EJ, Bittencourt MS, Callaway CW, Carson AP, et al. Heart disease and stroke statistics 2020 update: a report from the american heart association. Circulation. 2020;141 (9):e139−596.
[2] Libby P, Theroux P. Pathophysiology of coronary artery disease. Circulation. 2005;111(25):3481−8.
[3] Ahmadi A, Argulian E, Leipsic J, Newby DE, Narula J. From subclinical atherosclerosis to plaque progression and acute coronary'events. J Am Coll Cardiol 2019;74(12):1608−17.

[4] Knuuti J, Wijns W, Saraste A, Capodanno D, Barbato E, Funck-Brentano C, et al. 2019 ESC Guidelines for the diagnosis and management of chronic coronary syndromes. Eur Heart J 2020;41(3):407–77.

[5] Hsiao EM, Rybicki FJ, Steigner M. CT coronary angiography: 256-slice and 320-detector row scanners. Curr Cardiol Rep 2010;12(1):68–75.

[6] Chen MY, Shanbhag SM, Arai AE. Submillisievert median radiation dose for coronary angiography with a second-generation 320−detector row CT scanner in 107 consecutive patients. Radiology. 2013;267(1):76−85.

[7] de Graaf FR, Schuijf JD, van Velzen JE, Kroft LJ, de Roos A, Reiber JHC, et al. Diagnostic accuracy of 320-row multidetector computed tomography coronary angiography in the non-invasive evaluation of significant coronary artery disease. Eur Heart J 2010;31(15):1908−15.

[8] Cheruvu C, Precious B, Naoum C, Blanke P, Ahmadi A, Soon J, et al. Long term prognostic utility of coronary CT angiography in patients with no modifiable coronary artery disease risk factors: results from the 5 year follow-up of the CONFIRM International Multicenter Registry. J Cardiovasc Comput Tomogr 2016;10(1):22−7.

[9] Hoffmann U, Ferencik M, Udelson JE, Picard MH, Truong QA, Patel MR, et al. Prognostic value of noninvasive cardiovascular testing in patients with stable chest pain: insights from the PROMISE trial (Prospective Multicenter Imaging Study for Evaluation of Chest Pain). Circulation. 2017;135(24):2320−32.

[10] Commandeur F, Goeller M, Dey D. Cardiac CT: technological advances in hardware, software, and machine learning applications. Curr Cardiovasc Imaging Rep 2018;11(8):19.

[11] Budoff MJ, Mayrhofer T, Ferencik M, Bittner D, Lee KL, Lu MT, et al. Prognostic value of coronary artery calcium in the PROMISE study (Prospective Multicenter Imaging Study for Evaluation of Chest Pain). Circulation. 2017;136(21):1993−2005.

[12] Detrano RC, Anderson M, Nelson J, Wong ND, Carr JJ, McNitt-Gray M, et al. Coronary calcium measurements: effect of CT scanner type and calcium measure on rescan reproducibility—MESA study. Radiology. 2005;236(2):477−84.

[13] Hecht HS, Cronin P, Blaha MJ, Budoff MJ, Kazerooni EA, Narula J, et al. 2016 SCCT/STR guidelines for coronary artery calcium scoring of noncontrast noncardiac chest CT scans: a report of the Society of Cardiovascular Computed Tomography and Society of Thoracic Radiology. J Cardiovasc Comput Tomogr 2017;11(1):74−84.

[14] Narula J, Nakano M, Virmani R, Kolodgie FD, Petersen R, Newcomb R, et al. Histopathologic characteristics of atherosclerotic coronary disease and implications of the findings for the invasive and noninvasive detection of vulnerable plaques. J Am Coll Cardiol 2013;61(10):1041−51.

[15] Arbab-Zadeh A, Hoe J. Quantification of coronary arterial stenoses by multidetector CT angiography in comparison with conventional angiography: methods, caveats, and implications. JACC: Cardiovasc Imaging 2011;4(2):191−202.

[16] Cury RC, Abbara S, Achenbach S, Agatston A, Berman DS, Budoff MJ, et al. CAD-RADS™: Coronary artery disease - reporting and data system: an expert consensus document of the society of cardiovascular computed tomography (SCCT), the American College of Radiology (ACR) and the North American Society for Cardiovascular Imaging (NASCI). Endorsed by the American College of Cardiology. J Am Coll Radiol 2016;13(12 Pt A):1458−66 e9.

[17] Fujii K, Hao H, Shibuya M, Imanaka T, Fukunaga M, Miki K, et al. Accuracy of OCT, grayscale IVUS, and their combination for the diagnosis of coronary TCFA. JACC: Cardiovasc Imaging 2015;8(4):451−60.

[18] Conte E, Mushtaq S, Pontone G, Li Piani L, Ravagnani P, Galli S, et al. Plaque quantification by coronary computed tomography angiography using intravascular ultrasound as a reference standard: a comparison between standard and last generation computed tomography scanners. Eur Heart J Cardiovasc Imaging 2019;21(2):191−201.

[19] Schlett CL, Maurovich-Horvat P, Ferencik M, Alkadhi H, Stolzmann P, Scheffel H, et al. Histogram analysis of lipid-core plaques in coronary computed tomographic angiography: ex vivo validation against histology. Invest Radiol 2013;48(9):646−53.

[20] Andelius L, Mortensen MB, Nørgaard BL, Abdulla J. Impact of statin therapy on coronary plaque burden and composition assessed by coronary computed tomographic angiography: a systematic review and meta-analysis. Eur Heart J Cardiovasc Imaging 2018;19(8):850−8.

[21] Ayoub C, Erthal F, Abdelsalam MA, Murad MH, Wang Z, Erwin PJ, et al. Prognostic value of segment involvement score compared to other measures of coronary atherosclerosis by computed tomography: a systematic review and *meta*-analysis. J Cardiovasc Comput Tomogr 2017;11(4):258−67.

[22] de Knegt MC, Haugen M, Linde JJ, Kühl JT, Nordestgaard BG, Køber LV, et al. Reproducibility of quantitative coronary computed tomography angiography in asymptomatic individuals and patients with acute chest pain. PLoS One 2018;13(12):e0207980.

[23] Lee MS, Chun EJ, Kim KJ, Kim JA, Vembar M, Choi SI. Reproducibility in the assessment of non-calcified coronary plaque with 256-slice multi-detector CT and automated plaque analysis software. Int J Cardiovasc Imaging 2010;26(Suppl 2):237−44.

[24] Oberoi S, Meinel FG, Schoepf UJ, Nance JW, De Cecco CN, Gebregziabher M, et al. Reproducibility of noncalcified coronary artery plaque burden quantification from coronary CT angiography across different image analysis platforms. Am J Roentgenol 2013;202(1):W43−9.

[25] Pagali SR, Madaj P, Gupta M, Nair S, Hamirani YS, Min JK, et al. Interobserver variations of plaque severity score and segment stenosis score in coronary arteries using 64 slice multidetector computed tomography: A substudy of the ACCURACY trial. J Cardiovasc Comput Tomogr 2010;4(5):312−18.

[26] Plank F, Burghard P, Friedrich G, Dichtl W, Mayr A, Klauser A, et al. Quantitative coronary CT angiography: absolute lumen sizing rather than %stenosis predicts hemodynamically relevant stenosis. Eur Radiol 2016;26(11):3781−9.

[27] Bom MJ, Driessen RS, Stuijfzand WJ, Raijmakers PG, Van Kuijk CC, Lammertsma AA, et al. Diagnostic value of transluminal attenuation gradient for the presence of ischemia as defined by fractional flow reserve and quantitative positron emission tomography. JACC Cardiovasc Imaging 2019;12(2):323−33.

[28] Kojima T, Nagao M, Yabuuchi H, Yamasaki Y, Shirasaka T, Kawakubo M, et al. New transluminal attenuation gradient derived from dynamic coronary CT angiography: diagnostic ability of ischemia detected by (13)N-ammonia PET. Heart Vessel 2021;36(4):433−41.

[29] Min JK, Leipsic J, Pencina MJ, Berman DS, Koo BK, van Mieghem C, et al. Diagnostic accuracy of fractional flow reserve from anatomic CT angiography. JAMA. 2012;308(12):1237−45.

[30] Zarins CK, Taylor CA, Min JK. Computed fractional flow reserve (FFTCT) derived from coronary CT angiography. J Cardiovasc Transl Res 2013;6(5):708−14.

[31] Taylor CA, Fonte TA, Min JK. Computational fluid dynamics applied to cardiac computed tomography for noninvasive quantification of fractional flow reserve: scientific basis. J Am Coll Cardiol 2013;61(22):2233−41.

[32] Kim HJ, Vignon-Clementel IE, Coogan JS, Figueroa CA, Jansen KE, Taylor CA. Patient-specific modeling of blood flow and pressure in human coronary arteries. Ann Biomed Eng 2010;38(10):3195−209.

[33] Tonino PA, De Bruyne B, Pijls NH, Siebert U, Ikeno F, van' t Veer M, et al. Fractional flow reserve vs angiography for guiding percutaneous coronary intervention. N Engl J Med 2009;360(3):213−24.

[34] Nakazato R, Park HB, Berman DS, Gransar H, Koo BK, Erglis A, et al. Noninvasive fractional flow reserve derived from computed tomography angiography for coronary lesions of intermediate stenosis severity: results from the DeFACTO study. Circ Cardiovasc Imaging 2013;6(6):881−9.

[35] Gaur S, Achenbach S, Leipsic J, Mauri L, Bezerra HG, Jensen JM, et al. Rationale and design of the HeartFlowNXT (HeartFlow analysis of coronary blood flow using CT angiography: NeXt sTeps) study. J Cardiovasc Comput Tomogr 2013;7(5):279−88.

[36] Min JK, Koo BK, Erglis A, Doh JH, Daniels DV, Jegere S, et al. Effect of image quality on diagnostic accuracy of noninvasive fractional flow reserve: results from the prospective multicenter international DISCOVER-FLOW study. J Cardiovasc Comput Tomogr 2012;6(3):191−9.

[37] Fairbairn TA, Nieman K, Akasaka T, Nørgaard BL, Berman DS, Raff G, et al. Real-world clinical utility and impact on clinical decision-making of coronary computed tomography angiography-derived fractional flow reserve: lessons from the ADVANCE Registry. Eur Heart J 2018;39(41):3701−11.

[38] Garcia EV, Slomka P, Moody JB, Germano G, Ficaro EP. Quantitative clinical nuclear cardiology, Part 1: established applications. J Nucl Med 2019;60(11):1507−16.

[39] null n, Cerqueira MD, Weissman NJ, Dilsizian V, Jacobs AK, Kaul S, et al. Standardized myocardial segmentation and nomenclature for tomographic imaging of the heart. Circulation. 2002;105 (4):539—42.

[40] Nakahara T, Iwabuchi Y, Murakami K. Diagnostic performance of 3D bull's eye display of SPECT and coronary CTA fusion. JACC Cardiovasc Imaging 2016;9(6):703—11.

[41] Fukushima K, Matsuo Y, Nagao M, Sakai A, Kihara N, Onishi K, et al. Patient based bull's eye map display of coronary artery and ventricles from coronary computed tomography angiography. J Computer Assist Tomogr 2020;44(1).

[42] Ide S, Sumitsuji S, Yamaguchi O, Sakata Y. Cardiac computed tomography-derived myocardial mass at risk using the Voronoi-based segmentation algorithm: a histological validation study. J Cardiovasc Comput Tomogr 2017;11(3):179—82.

[43] Malkasian S, Hubbard L, Dertli B, Kwon J, Molloi S. Quantification of vessel-specific coronary perfusion territories using minimum-cost path assignment and computed tomography angiography: Validation in a swine model. J Cardiovasc Comput Tomogr 2018;12(5):425—35.

[44] Kurata A, Kono A, Sakamoto T, Kido T, Mochizuki T, Higashino H, et al. Quantification of the myocardial area at risk using coronary CT angiography and Voronoi algorithm-based myocardial segmentation. Eur Radiol 2015;25(1):49—57.

[45] Oikonomou EK, Antoniades C. The role of adipose tissue in cardiovascular health and disease. Nat Rev Cardiol 2019;16(2):83—99.

[46] Antonopoulos AS, Sanna F, Sabharwal N, Thomas S, Oikonomou EK, Herdman L, et al. Detecting human coronary inflammation by imaging perivascular fat. Sci Transl Med 2017;9(398) eaal2658.

[47] Goeller M, Achenbach S, Cadet S, Kwan AC, Commandeur F, Slomka PJ, et al. Pericoronary adipose tissue computed tomography attenuation and high-risk plaque characteristics in acute coronary syndrome compared with stable coronary artery disease. JAMA Cardiol 2018;3(9):858—63.

[48] Goeller M, Achenbach S, Marwan M, Doris MK, Cadet S, Commandeur F, et al. Epicardial adipose tissue density and volume are related to subclinical atherosclerosis, inflammation and major adverse cardiac events in asymptomatic subjects. J Cardiovasc Comput Tomogr 2018;12(1):67—73.

[49] Rajani R, Shmilovich H, Nakazato R, Nakanishi R, Otaki Y, Cheng VY, et al. Relationship of epicardial fat volume to coronary plaque, severe coronary stenosis, and high-risk coronary plaque features assessed by coronary CT angiography. J Cardiovasc Comput Tomogr 2013;7(2):125—32.

[50] Kwiecinski J, Dey D, Cadet S, Lee S-E, Otaki Y, Huynh PT, et al. Peri-coronary adipose tissue density is associated with ^{18}F-sodium fluoride coronary uptake in stable patients with high-risk plaques. JACC Cardiovasc Imaging 2019;12(10):2000—10.

[51] de Jong MC, Genders TSS, van Geuns R-J, Moelker A, Hunink MGM. Diagnostic performance of stress myocardial perfusion imaging for coronary artery disease: a systematic review and meta-analysis. Eur Radiol 2012;22(9):1881—95.

[52] Robb RA, Ritman EL. High speed synchronous volume computed tomography of the heart. Radiology. 1979;133(3):655—61.

[53] Danad I, Szymonifka J, Schulman-Marcus J, Min JK. Static and dynamic assessment of myocardial perfusion by computed tomography. Eur Heart J Cardiovasc Imaging 2016;17(8):836—44.

[54] Celeng C, Leiner T, Maurovich-Horvat P, Merkely B, de Jong P, Dankbaar JW, et al. Anatomical and functional computed tomography for diagnosing hemodynamically significant coronary artery disease: a meta-analysis. JACC Cardiovasc Imaging 2019;12:1316—25 (7, Part 2).

[55] Rodríguez-Granillo G. Delayed enhancement cardiac computed tomography for the assessment of myocardial infarction: From bench to bedside. Cardiovasc Diagn Ther 2017;7:159—70.

[56] Nagao M, Yamasaki Y, Kamitani T, Kawanami S, Sagiyama K, Yamanouchi T, et al. Quantification of coronary flow using dynamic angiography with 320-detector row CT and motion coherence image processing: detection of ischemia for intermediate coronary stenosis. Eur J Radiol 2016;85 (5):996—1003.

[57] Zeb I, Li D, Nasir K, Malpeso J, Batool A, Flores F, et al. Effect of statin treatment on coronary plaque progression — a serial coronary CT angiography study. Atherosclerosis 2013;231:198—204.

[58] Dey D, Schepis T, Marwan M, Slomka PJ, Berman DS, Achenbach S. Automated three-dimensional quantification of noncalcified coronary plaque from coronary CT angiography: comparison with intravascular US. Radiology 2010;257:516−22.

[59] Seifarth H, Schlett CL, Nakano M, Otsuka F, Károlyi M, Liew G, et al. Histopathological correlates of the napkin-ring sign plaque in coronary CT angiography. Atherosclerosis. 2012;224:90−6.

[60] Inoue K, Motoyama S, Sarai M, Sato T, Harigaya H, Hara T, et al. Serial coronary CT angiography−verified changes in plaque characteristics as an end point. JACC: Cardiovasc Imaging 2010;3:691−8.

[61] Nadjiri J, Hausleiter J, Jähnichen C, Will A, Hendrich E, Martinoff S, et al. Incremental prognostic value of quantitative plaque assessment in coronary CT angiography during 5 years of follow up. J Cardiovasc Comput Tomogr 2016;10:97−104.

[62] Dey D, Achenbach S, Schuhbaeck A, Pflederer T, Nakazato R, Slomka PJ, et al. Comparison of quantitative atherosclerotic plaque burden from coronary CT angiography in patients with first acute coronary syndrome and stable coronary artery disease. J Cardiovasc Comput Tomogr 2014; 8:368−74.

[63] Marwan M, Taher MA, El Meniawy K, Awadallah H, Pflederer T, Schuhbäck A, et al. In vivo CT detection of lipid-rich coronary artery atherosclerotic plaques using quantitative histogram analysis: a head to head comparison with IVUS. Atherosclerosis. 2011;215:110−15.

[64] Puchner SB, Ferencik M, Karolyi M, Do S, Maurovich-Horvat P, Kauczor H-U, et al. The effect of iterative image reconstruction algorithms on the feasibility of automated plaque assessment in coronary CT angiography. Int J Cardiovasc Imaging 2013;29:1879−88.

[65] Nakazato R, Shalev A, Doh J-H, Koo B-K, Dey D, Berman DS, et al. Quantification and characterisation of coronary artery plaque volume and adverse plaque features by coronary computed tomographic angiography: a direct comparison to intravascular ultrasound. Eur Radiol 2013;23:2109−17.

[66] Weber C, Deseive S, Brim G, Stocker TJ, Broersen A, Kitslaar P, et al. Coronary plaque volume and predictors for fast plaque progression assessed by serial coronary CT angiography—a single-center observational study. Eur J Radiol 2020;123:108805.

[67] Bamberg F, Truong QA, Koenig W, Schlett CL, Nasir K, Butler J, et al. Differential associations between blood biomarkers of inflammation, oxidation, and lipid metabolism with varying forms of coronary atherosclerotic plaque as quantified by coronary CT angiography. Int J Cardiovasc Imaging 2012;28:183−92.

[68] Diaz-Zamudio M, Dey D, Schuhbaeck A, Nakazato R, Gransar H, Slomka PJ, et al. Automated quantitative plaque burden from coronary CT angiography noninvasively predicts hemodynamic significance by using fractional flow reserve in intermediate coronary lesions. Radiology. 2015;276:408−15.

[69] Ceponiene I, Nakanishi R, Osawa K, Kanisawa M, Nezarat N, Rahmani S, et al. Coronary artery calcium progression is associated with coronary plaque volume progression. JACC: Cardiovasc Imaging 2018;11:1785−94.

[70] Sugiyama T, Kanaji Y, Hoshino M, Yamaguchi M, Hada M, Ohya H, et al. Determinants of pericoronary adipose tissue attenuation on computed tomography angiography in coronary artery disease. J Am Heart Assoc 2020;9:e016202.

[71] Andreini D, Magnoni M, Conte E, Masson S, Mushtaq S, Berti S, et al. Coronary plaque features on CTA can identify patients at increased risk of cardiovascular events. JACC: Cardiovasc Imaging 2020;13:1704−17.

Further reading

Mancio J, Azevedo D, Saraiva F, Azevedo AI, Pires-Morais G, Leite-Moreira A, et al. Epicardial adipose tissue volume assessed by computed tomography and coronary artery disease: a systematic review and meta-analysis. Eur Heart J Cardiovasc Imaging 2017;19:490−7.

CHAPTER 7

Medical image analysis for the early prediction of hypertension

Heba Kandil[1,2], Ahmed Soliman[1], Ali Mahmoud[1], Fatma Taher[3] and Ayman S. El-Baz[4,5]

[1]Bioimaging Lab, Bioengineering Department, University of Louisville, Louisville, KY, United States
[2]Faculty of Computer and Information Sciences, Mansoura University, Mansoura, ElDakahlia, Egypt
[3]College of Technological Innovation, Zayed University, Dubai, United Arab Emirates
[4]University of Louisville, Louisville, KY, United States
[5]University of Louisville at Alamein International University (UofL-AIU), New Alamein City, Egypt

7.1 Introduction

Medical imaging is a vital evolving technology that has been studied and used tremendously in the past few decades. Medical imaging techniques enable physicians to capture noninvasive images of structures inside the body (e.g., blood vessels, tissue, bones) as well as their function (e.g., brain activity). Medical images comprise massive amounts of information that are very useful for understanding the structures and functions of different body organs. Yet, these huge amounts of data are very difficult to be processed by radiologists' or physicians' eyes. Therefore computerized systems that could store, analyze, and make use of these data are of great importance. The most important value of medical images analysis is to help physicians in predicting, detecting, and diagnosing diseases. Continuing research and innovations in this field will expand noninvasive evaluation methods and enable correlation of these findings to new and emerging diseases and conditions. This will increase options for and improve diagnostic techniques, allowing for early detection of developing conditions and preventive treatments. Specifically, there are many progressive diseases that may take many years before they are discovered or diagnosed. While some of these diseases are asymptomatic, they usually start to affect internal human body organs by changing or damaging their structures and/or functionalities.

Hypertension is a progressive disease that may take a decade or two before it is discovered or diagnosed. It is considered a "silent killer" as it may not have any apparent symptoms. One in every three adults in the US is suffering from hypertension which is also considered the main cause of mortality in 516,955 individuals in the United States. There are various factors that contribute to hypertension development including renal dysfunction, obesity, chronic stress, and high sodium intake. Chronically elevated cerebral perfusion pressure (CPP) alters the brain's cerebrovasculature and disrupts its vasoregulation mechanisms. The cerebrovascular alterations have severe effects on different human body organs and may lead to further complications such as dementia, cognitive impairment, ischemic cerebral

Cardiovascular and Coronary Artery Imaging
DOI: https://doi.org/10.1016/B978-0-12-821983-6.00007-2

injury, brain lesions, and strokes. Reported correlations between changes in smaller cerebrovascular vessels and hypertension may be used to diagnose hypertension in its early stages, 10–15 years before the appearance of symptoms such as cognitive impairment and memory loss. Specifically, the clinical hypothesis suggested by recent studies assumed that cerebrovasculature and CPP changes occur prior to the systemic blood pressure elevation. Cerebrovascular structural changes in blood vessel diameters have been reported to be an early indication of vascular dysfunction from in vivo and clinical observations. Correlations between vascular changes in blood vessel diameters and tortuosity and hypertension development have been validated. Current blood pressure measurement tools such as sphygmomanometers can easily be used to measure repeated brachial artery pressure to detect hypertension after its onset. However, these tools are not able to detect these cerebrovascular changes that occur prior to the onset of the disease and may lead to adverse events. The early detection and quantification of the alterations in the cerebrovasculature can help in the prediction of patients who are at a high risk of developing hypertension as well as other cerebral complications. Thus enabling early and appropriate medical intervention before the systemic onset of the disease to mitigate potential vascular-initiated end–organ damage.

This study aims at developing a novel efficient noninvasive computer-aided diagnosis (CAD) system that can predict hypertension before its onset. The developed CAD system works by analyzing magnetic resonance angiography (MRA) images of human brains gathered over years to extract, quantify, and track cerebrovascular changes correlated with hypertension development. This CAD system can make decisions based on available data to help physicians on predicting potential hypertensive patients before the onset of the disease. Thus taking appropriate actions to stop the progress of the disease and mitigating adverse events.

7.2 Methodology

This section presents the details of the CAD system for the early prediction of hypertension. The CAD system comprises three main steps: the segmentation step, the feature extraction step, and the classification step. The first subsection presents the segmentation algorithm used to delineate the cerebral vascular tree from the human brains using a 3D local adaptive method. The next subsection presents the process of selecting cerebral vascular features that change over time in correlation with hypertension development. The third subsection will present the details of the classification process that will differentiate between normal and potential hypertensive patients based on the extracted cerebral vascular features.

7.2.1 Cerebrovascular segmentation

The segmentation process is a main step in almost all medical imaging analysis. While the accuracy of the segmentation process is a top concern, it is affected by different factors including scanning parameters and inherited noise artifacts, imaging modality, and application domain. Particularly, the process of segmenting blood vessels from MRA images is challenging due to the complex geometry of the cerebral vascular system, density of smaller vessels, wide range of intensities, scanning errors, and noise artifacts. Additionally, the high interperson variability of the cerebral vascular system, which makes it difficult to create a common atlas to be used for segmentation, as is the case for other human organs. Because of the aforementioned reasons, there is a lack in the number of segmentation algorithms that aims at delineating cerebral blood vessels efficiently and automatically.

The segmentation algorithm presented in this study is automatic, adaptive, and accurate in delineating cerebral vasculature. As shown in Fig. 7.1, the algorithm starts with a preprocessing step to eliminate noise artifacts such as acquisition errors and image biasing that might result from the magnetic field of the MRA scanner. In this step, a bias correction method was used for resolving data inconsistencies. Then, to enhance image homogeneity, the 3D Generalized Gauss-Markov Random Field (3D GGMRF) was employed. The 3D GGMRF model analyzes the spatial homogeneous pairwise interactions between each voxel and its 26-neighborhood to minimize the difference between the voxel and its neighboring voxels. A skull stripping approach was then applied on the enhanced images to remove cerebral fat tissues that usually look like cerebral blood vessels. This approach employs a Markov-Gibbs Random Field (MGRF) model and a geometric deformable (brain iso-surface) model to preserve the topology of the cerebral vasculature during the skull stripping.

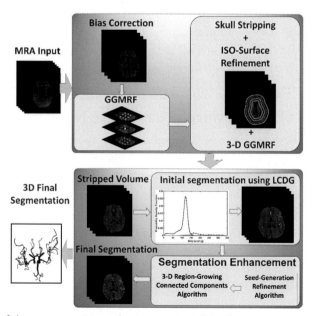

Figure 7.1 Steps of the preprocessing and segmentation algorithm.

After data preprocessing, the vasculature tree was delineated in two steps. First, a Linear Combination of Discrete Gaussians (LCDG) was used to produce the initial segmentation of the vascular tree by finding the marginal probability density of MRA voxels for brain vessels and other cerebral tissues. This initial segmentation, however, may miss some tiny blood vessels in the vascular tree. Therefore the second step in the segmentation process is very essential. In the second step, a 3D local adaptive segmentation algorithm was utilized to refine the initially segmented vasculature by finding any missing details, specifically the small vessels. This adaptive algorithm works by dividing each image into a set of connected components. Then, an adaptive search window is centralized over every connected component where a new threshold is calculated to separate blood vessels from other brain tissues. Cerebral segmentation using this algorithm achieved a sensitivity of 94.82%, a specificity of 99.00%, a dice similarity coefficient of 92.23%, and an average volume difference of 10.03% compared to state-of-the-art methodologies. Fig. 7.2 shows an output sample of the segmentation module. Additionally, this algorithm is fully automatic and thus resolves the associated problems of semiautomatic and automatic segmentation methods such as time-consuming and interobserver variability. Unlike most vascular segmentation algorithms in the literature, this algorithm has no constraints regarding the linearity or the circular cross-sections of blood vessels because it can segment both healthy and unhealthy blood vessels accurately and efficiently. The algorithm is also able to delineate even tiny blood vessels (≤ 1 mm), which makes it a very good fit in the proposed CAD system because it is clinically known that the impact of hypertension development mainly affects tiny blood vessels. In addition, the segmentation approach overcomes and handles the noise in the MRA (e.g., microscopic, or mesoscopic noisy disturbance) images through homogeneity enhancement using the 3D GGMRF model, which minimizes the energy between every voxel and its neighboring voxels to improve the homogeneity and remove any noise.

7.2.2 Extraction of cerebrovascular descriptive features

The change in cerebral vascular tree was quantified by the estimation of the changes in blood vessel diameter and tortuosity. The change in vascular diameter was estimated by calculating medians of the vascular radii. The cumulative distribution function (CDF) of the vascular radii was calculated using the cumulative distribution of the probability distribution function (PDF). A CDF value associated with each MRA volume defines the average of blood vessel diameters in that volume. It gives a probability estimate for vessels existing at or below a specific diameter value. Vascular tortuosity changes were quantified using two of the significant curvatures in the surface theory, namely, mean and Gaussian curvatures. Two curvatures metrics suffice to completely describe the curvature of a 2D manifold. These could be the principal curvatures or two independent functions thereof. Gaussian and mean curvatures are both traditional, which allows for easy comparison of our results with those

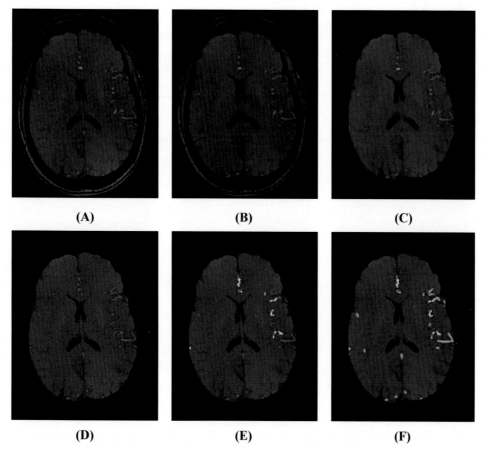

Figure 7.2 (A) Original 2D image. (B) Image after applying bias correction and homogeneity enhancement. (C) Image after applying skull-stripping. (D) Result of the initial LCDG-based global segmentation, (E) Effect after applying local adaptive segmentation from the same plane, (F) and preceding and succeeding planes.

obtained by other means, and intuitive, being the determinant and half-trace of the shape operator of the surface. Besides that, Gaussian curvature is significant as an intrinsic (scalar) metric of curvature that does not depend on the embedding. In contrast, mean curvature is an extrinsic measure that depends on the embedding. Using both extrinsic and intrinsic measures would provide a comprehensive means for quantifying the change in vascular tortuosity. Estimation of these curvatures was done across the entire cerebral vascular tree for each subject. Mean curvature is computed as the average of the principal curvatures $K1$, $K2$, while the Gaussian curvature is computed as the multiplication of $K1$, $K2$. Mean curvature $= (K1 + K2)/2$; Gaussian curvature $= K1^*K2$. As shown in Fig. 7.3, the estimated features for each subject in the dataset are used along with the blood pressure measurements to build the features vectors that will be used in the classification process.

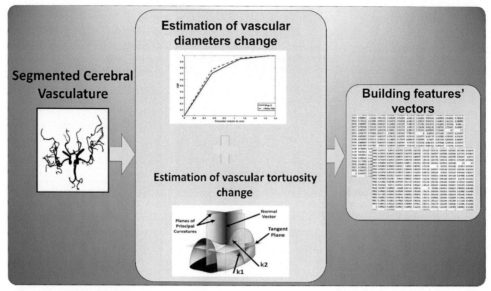

Figure 7.3 Steps in building feature vectors.

7.2.3 Classification

Today, the use of artificial neural networks (ANNs) in classification tasks is very common and efficient. Thus the classification step in the proposed CAD system has been performed using a feedforward neural network with two hidden layers of sizes 10 and 5. This ANN was used to classify the MRA data into two classes (normal and hypertensive classes) based on the estimated cerebrovascular features. We classified subjects based on these features for two reasons: (1) these features were clinically hypothesized to occur prior to the onset of hypertension, and (2) we wanted to prove the efficacy of using these features in predicting the disease prior to its systematic onset. In addition to the ANN, we also used the built-in MATLAB R2017a classification learner to test the CAD system using different classifiers with different parameters. Specifically, the classifiers that have been used during the classification task include the support vector machine (SVM) with polynomial (cubic) kernel, the ensemble bagged trees, and the linear discriminant. Moreover, all possible k-fold cross-validation scenarios have been tested during this step. MRA dataset was divided randomly into three subsets such that 70% of the dataset was used for training, 15% was used for validation (10-fold), and the remaining 15% was used for testing. The neural network has been trained using a scaled conjugate gradient backpropagation. Inputs for the neural network were the feature vectors created in the feature extraction step. Fig. 7.3 shows the steps used in creating feature vectors. Each feature vector corresponds to one subject in the dataset and is comprised of 15 values that quantify the alterations of the vascular diameter and tortuosity. The feature vector consists of 11 values (probability density function estimates) that represent the change of the blood vessels radii and four values (averages and medians of both mean curvature and Gaussian curvature) that represent the change in the vascular tortuosity. The purpose of the classification process was to show how effective the extracted cerebral features (vessel diameters and tortuosity) are in providing a discriminating measure for hypertension detection. The efficacy of these features can help clinicians in evaluating the cerebral structural changes as a sign for the development of severe diseases such as hypertension. This can potentially help clinicians in the diagnosis of prehypertension and in the treatment of potential patients with appropriate medical protocols.

7.3 Experimental results

7.3.1 Dataset description

To test the efficacy of the proposed CAD system, an MRA dataset of 66 subjects was used in the experiments. The dataset was balanced such that 33 subjects were normal and the other 33 subjects were prehypertensive or hypertensive patients. Subjects in the dataset were categorized as either normal, prehypertensive, or hypertensive according to the 2017 Guidelines for Hypertension Categorization. The guidelines define a normal individual by having a systolic blood pressure (BP) measurement <120 mmHg, and a diastolic blood pressure measurement of <80 mmHg. Similarly, elevated or prehypertension ($120-129/<80$ mmHg), hypertension stage 1 ($130-139$ mmHg systolic or $80-89$ mmHg diastolic), and hypertension stage 2 (≥ 140 mmHg systolic or ≥ 90 mmHg diastolic). Therefore in the experimentations of this study, a typical normal subject has a systolic BP of <120 mmHg and a diastolic BP of <80 mmHg, while a hypertensive subject has a systolic BP of >130 mmHg or a diastolic BP of >80 mmHg. Moreover, a prehypertensive subject is defined to have elevated blood pressure measurements of ($120-129$) mmHg systolic and <80 mmHg diastolic.

7.3.2 Classification results

Many experimental trials have been conducted with different classifiers, parameters, kernels, and validation scenarios. A summary of the classification results that recorded accuracy $>80\%$ are shown in Table 7.1. The best classification process recorded 95.6%, 90%, and 90% for training, validation, and testing, respectively. These results are evidence that the CAD system can successfully distinguish between normal and hypertensive subjects with promising accuracy percentage of about 91%, and this is done by studying the hypertension-correlated cerebral vascular structural changes that occur over time efficiently. The higher accuracy is also evidence of the efficacy and reliability of using the selected cerebral features to describe and quantify the vascular structural alterations that develop prior to hypertension onset. Thus these cerebral vascular features can be considered a diagnostic parameter that can be used for the early prediction of hypertension.

Table 7.1 Classification accuracy of the CAD (computer-aided diagnosis) system for the early prediction of hypertension.

Classifier	Accuracy (%)	Kernel (Metric)	Validation scenario
2 hidden-layer neural network	90.9	Feedforward	10-fold
SVM	87.5	Polynomial (cubic)	10-fold
Linear discriminant	84.8	Linear	33-fold
Ensemble	83.3	Bagged Trees	6-fold
SVM	80.3	Polynomial (cubic)	33-fold

7.4 Discussion

Cerebrovascular health and physiological changes, such as vascular remodeling, can provide important information about the risk for developing diseases like hypertension and dementia. It is estimated that roughly one-third of dementia cases could be prevented by treating the underlying cause, which is often hypertension. Chronic systemic hypertension can cause temporary or permanent disability, especially when left untreated. Hypertension causes damage especially to smaller blood vessels, and significantly increases the risk for end-organ damage, with greatest concern focused mainly on the heart (e.g., heart failure, LVH), kidneys (e.g., renal failure), eyes (visual impairment), brain (e.g., dementia, stroke), and the lungs (pulmonary hypertension). It also contributes to early mortality. The Center for Disease Control and Prevention (CDC) reports that in 2019, hypertension directly or indirectly affected the cause of death for 516,955 people in the United States. There are currently invasive and noninvasive methods for diagnosing hypertension and assessing its pathophysiological effects. The early stages of hypertension can cause left ventricular wall thickening and cerebrovascular remodeling, even while noninvasive blood pressure measurements are still within the normal range. However, these cerebrovascular changes are not easily detectable as current software programs are only capable of segmenting larger cerebrovascular structures in MRAs. Recently, there has been an increase in the usage of imaging technologies such as MRA, but there is a limitation in the number of the studies that investigates the alterations or remodeling of cerebral blood vessels' diameters and tortuosity changes and their correlation with elevated arterial pressure in human beings. This is because of the challenges associated with state-of-the-art segmentation algorithms. Current cerebrovascular segmentation algorithms are not able to delineate small blood vessels efficiently. The existence or nonexistence of these small blood vessels is usually a very important parameter in diagnosing many diseases. Additionally, the gold standard manual segmentation of blood vessels consumes so much time and is intensive and error prone. Manual segmentation is also subject to interobserver variability. Semiautomatic cerebral segmentation algorithms on the other hand usually requires further investigations, revisions, and/or evaluations by specialists. The automatic segmentation algorithm proposed in this study was able to overcome the inherited problems of the cerebrovascular segmentation algorithms and to efficiently extract cerebral vascular tree and detect even the smaller blood vessels accurately and automatically.

Moreover, several studies in literature have suggested that cerebrovascular remodeling and elevated CPP start to develop before the onset of hypertension in animals and humans. Importantly, cerebrovascular remodeling including the changes affecting the diameters of blood vessels and vascular tortuosity have been used to diagnose many severe diseases. In their 2016 published study, Warnert et al. confirmed the relationship between the changes in the cerebrovasculature and CPP and the development of hypertension. In their study, they investigated the higher prevalence of congenital cerebral vascular alterations in hypertension patients than normal individuals. The study showed that the cerebral changes resulted in an increase in the cerebral vascular resistance and the CPP. The authors observed that the cerebrovascular remodeling existed in patients with high-normal blood pressure (prehypertensive) with a family history of hypertension development. This could probably raise the assumption that these vascular changes were not caused by hypertension but may be a cause for hypertension development. This study suggested that hypertension can develop to maintain the balance in blood circulation of human brains to compensate for the imbalance caused by the cerebrovascular alterations. Kang et al. [1] used ultra-high-resolution MRAs of the lenticulostriate arteries (LSAs) to demonstrate the existence of a direct relationship between cerebral microvascular alterations and development of hypertension. Chen et al. investigated 3D TOF-MRA data and reported a significant decrease in the number of LSA stems in patients of hypertension compared to normal individuals. Additionally, several studies have reported the changes occurring in cerebral blood vessels' diameters as an early sign of cerebrovascular dysfunction from both in vivo and clinical observations. Additionally, vascular resistance associated with hypertension has resulted from the reduction of lumen size of smaller size arteries and arterioles as discussed inIntengan and Schiffrin [2]. Moreover, a study on rats has supported the link between chronic elevation of blood pressure and the diameter change in the carotid artery. Similarly, the relation between pulmonary hypertension and the diameter changes of the pulmonary artery in humans. On the other hand, excessive or abnormal tortuosity of blood vessels has been observed to correlate with the development of various severe diseases such as hypertension. Tortuosity is a term referring to how twisted—or tortuous—the curves and turns of the blood vessels are. It is a measure of how sharply a vessel is turning as it is traversing. Increased vascular tortuosity has been previously linked to hypertension, aging, genetic defects, diabetes mellitus, and atherosclerosis. Ophthalmologists have also used the tortuosity of retinal blood vessels as a diagnostic and disease assessment parameter. The increase of the coronary vessel tortuosity has been observed to correlate with patients with hypertension. Similarly, the study supported the relationship between the hemispheric white matter tortuosity and the severity of systemic hypertension and elevated CPP. These cerebrovascular changes can be bellwethers for the development or progression of problems such as cognitive impairment or memory loss. Early detection and quantification of cerebral blood vessel changes (alterations in vascular diameters and tortuosity) would potentially enable the diagnosis and treatment of hypertension at an early stage prior to disease onset and identify patients at risk of adverse events. Thus clinicians will be able to manage the appropriate medical treatment protocols and to recommend healthy lifestyles. In fact, timely information regarding vascular health can improve quality of life tremendously for patients and their families and reduce healthcare costs as well.

Current tools used by specialists are excellent at detecting disease and are very useful for identifying specific disease processes. However, most of them identify disease processes at later stages where most of the damage might not be reversed. While antihypertensive treatments can make the progression of the disease and its complications slower, detection and efforts to slow or halt its development earlier in the disease course are desired to reduce risk and improve patient quality of life. Thus there is a need for automatic computerized systems that can provide accurate screening and diagnoses for early detection of prehypertension for prolonging life and improving patients' quality of life. These automatic systems may help identify hypertension many years before its onset compared to current measurements methods. Screening and early diagnosis give patients, families, and providers the opportunity to take steps to prevent or delay the onset of the disease process, or to limit the severity of symptoms and sequelae, improving patient-oriented outcomes. One important seeming consequence of hypertension is the alterations in the cerebrovascular that include the loss of vessels as well as changes in their morphology. Such changes may relate to the now well-known impact of hypertension on cognitive function and risk of dementia.

7.5 Conclusion and future work

Usually, hypertensive patients are asymptomatic and may suffer no apparent symptoms even in advanced stages. This is why people consider the disease a silent killer. People also tend to neglect a high blood pressure measurement and consider it a temporary result due to may be stress or other factors rather than chronic hypertension. Common hypertension symptoms include nose bleedings, vomiting, headaches, shortness of breath, and dizziness. Hypertension prediction in early stages can help patients and clinicians in controlling the progression of the disease by following proactive and preventive medical protocols or lifestyles. In this study, a CAD system was developed for tracking changes in the cerebral vasculature and making decisions that can help clinicians in predicting the potentiality of developing hypertension before its onset. In the following, the main contributions of this study are highlighted:

Developing a 3D Local Adaptive Segmentation Algorithm: an automatic segmentation algorithm was developed and succeeded in accurately detecting and segmenting both large and small cerebral blood vessels (≤ 1 mm of diameter) and is applicable to either healthy or unhealthy vessels, unlike state-of-the-art segmentation algorithms that are suitable for only healthy vessels with assumptions of linearity and circular cross-section.

Finding and Estimating Descriptive and Discriminative Cerebral Vascular Features that are Correlated with Hypertension Development: cerebral features have been carefully selected (change in vascular diameters and change in vascular tortuosity) to describe and quantify the cerebral structural remodeling based on the state-of-the-art studies that support the relationships between the change of vascular diameter and tortuosity, and the development of hypertension. Efficient procedures have been developed to estimate and quantify these features.

Developing a CAD System for the Early Prediction of Hypertension: a CAD system was developed to help clinicians in the prediction process. This system can successfully distinguish between normal and hypertensive patients with an accuracy of $\sim 91\%$ by studying and tracking the hypertension-related alterations that affect cerebral vascular tree over time. The high accuracy of the system is evidence that the proposed cerebral features are effective and reliable enough to be used as a diagnostic parameter for predicting the potentiality of developing hypertension.

Future plans for this project include enhancing the accuracy of the CAD system by finding more cerebral vascular features that are correlated to hypertension and integrating them into the developed CAD system, which will increase the reliability of the CAD system as well. Secondly, testing the CAD system with more data collected over longer periods of time (more than 2 years) to ensure the effectiveness of the CAD system and update its functionality accordingly. Thirdly, there are plans to customize the developed CAD system to be applicable for predicting other cerebral-vascular-related diseases such as aneurysms, strokes, or stenosis. Additionally, the different algorithms and modules of the developed CAD system are built with flexibility for future chances to be tuned to fit in segmenting other vessels such as pulmonary artery, heart vessels, and retina blood vessels. Thus the functionality of the CAD system can also be extended to diagnose or predict diseases in the lung, in the heart, in the eye, etc.

References

[1] Kang C-K, Park C-A, Lee H, Kim S-H, Park C-W, Kim Y-B, et al. Hypertension correlates with lenticulostriate arteries visualized by 7t magnetic resonance angiography. Hypertension 2009;54 (5):1050−6.

[2] Intengan HD, Schiffrin EL. Structure and mechanical properties of resistance arteries in hypertension: role of adhesion molecules and extracellular matrix determinants. Hypertension 2000;36(3):312−18.

CHAPTER 8

Left ventricle segmentation and quantification using deep learning

Hisham Abdeltawab[1], Fahmi Khalifa[1], Fatma Taher[2], Mohammed Ghazal[3], Ali Mahmoud[4] and Ayman S. El-Baz[5,6]
[1]Bioengineering Department, University of Louisville, Louisville, KY, United States
[2]College of Technological Innovation, Zayed University, Dubai, United Arab Emirates
[3]Electrical, Computer and Biomedical Engineering, Abu Dhabi University, Abu Dhabi, United Arab Emirates
[4]Bioimaging Lab, Bioengineering Department, University of Louisville, Louisville, KY, United States
[5]University of Louisville, Louisville, KY, United States
[6]University of Louisville at Alamein International University (UofL–AIU), New Alamein City, Egypt

8.1 Heart: anatomy, function, and diseases

The heart is an important muscular organ that has two main functions: (1) the continuous collection of the blood from different parts of the body and the pumping of the blood to the pulmonary system and (2) the continuous collection of the blood from the pulmonary system and the pumping of the blood to all body's tissues. The heart lies at the center of the circulatory system. The circulatory system is composed of a complicated network of blood vessels, such as arteries, arterioles, capillaries, and veins. These vessels are responsible for carrying the blood to and from the tissues of the body [1].

An electrical system that is composed of electrical signals is responsible for giving the heart its contractile function. These electrical signals allow the heart to contract and pump the blood into the blood vessels. The heart contains valves that force the blood to move in the correct direction. The heart is crucial for the health of the human and his tissues. Without a working heart, the body loses the circulation of the blood to the tissues. In order to work and grow normally, the organs need oxygen and nutrients carried and delivered by the blood. Carbon dioxide and waste products are also carried by the blood to the lungs where the body gets ride of them into the air. A certain amount of blood at a certain rate is required to be pumped by the heart to different body parts in order to maintain a healthy status. If there is a disease or an injury in the heart, the body tissues will not receive a sufficient amount of blood for normal working [1].

8.1.1 Location, size, and shape of the heart

The heart is located in the protective thorax and occupies the area between lungs in a compartment called the mediastinum [2]. The mediastinum is the area inside the membrane enclosing the heart, the pericardium. The heart is located posterior to the sternum and costal

Cardiovascular and Coronary Artery Imaging
DOI: https://doi.org/10.1016/B978-0-12-821983-6.00008-4

113

cartilages and above the surface of the diaphragm at the fifth or the sixth rib. It has an oblique position in the chest and its two-thirds lies in the left of the midline. Fig. 8.1 shows the location of the heart in the thorax. The heart is roughly the size of the fist of the man and weigh about 250–350 g [3]. The heart has the shape of an inverted cone. The apex of the heart is the narrow end and is located above the diaphragm. While the base of the heart is the broad end that is located at the level of the second rib.

The pericardium is a double-layered fibrous sac that encloses the heart and contains the roots of the great vessels (Superior vena cava, Inferior vena cava, Pulmonary arteries, Pulmonary veins, Aorta). It has two layers: the outer layer called fibrous pericardium and the inner layer called serous pericardium.

The serous pericardium in turn consists of two layers: the parietal and visceral pericardium. There is a cavity in the pericardium called pericardial cavity that contains pericardial fluid. The fluid is a serous fluid secreted by the serous pericardium into the cavity. Fig. 8.2 describes the structure of the pericardium. The pericardium has multiple functions. It places the heart into its position in the thorax. The fluid forms as a lubricant to the outer wall of the heart. Therefore the heart beats without friction. Also, the pericardial sac prevents infections and overexpanding to the heart.

The heart wall consists of three layers: epicardium (visceral pericardium), myocardium, and endocardium, as shown in Fig. 8.2. The epicardium is the outer layer in the heart wall. The epicardium is known also as the visceral pericardium (the inner

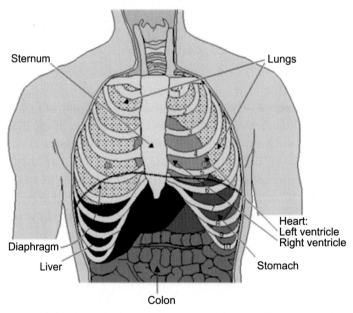

Figure 8.1 Location of the heart in the chest. Its boundaries are the sternum, lungs, diaphragm, and esophagus [1].

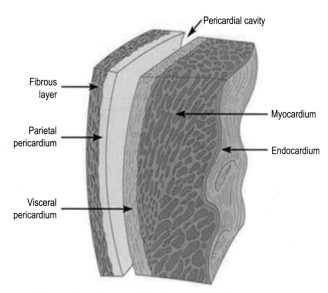

Figure 8.2 Structure of the pericardium and the heart wall [1].

surface of the pericardium). The epicardium has two tissue layers: the outer surface made of simple squamous tissue that secretes a fluid for lubrication into the pericardial cavity, and the inner surface made of areolar tissue.

The myocardium is the thick layer that lies at the center of the heart wall. It is composed of abundant cardiac muscle fibers that envelope the heart wall. When the myocardium contracts, the aorta and the pulmonary arteries receive the pumped blood from the heart.

The endocardium covers the inner surface of the heart wall and it also lines the heart valves and tendons. It meets the endothelium that covers the blood vessels that linked to the heart. Like the epicardium, simple squamous and areolar tissues constitute the composition of the endocardium

8.1.2 Anatomy of the heart and circulation system

The heart contains four chambers that consist of cardiac muscle or myocardium. At the upper level there are two chambers: the right atrium (RA) and the left atrium (LA), as shown in Fig. 8.3. The function of the atria is to collect the blood. At the lower level, there are another two chambers: the right ventricle (RV) and the left ventricle (LV). The function of the ventricle is to pump the blood [2]. The function of the right atrium and right ventricle is the collection of the blood from body parts and pumping it to the pulmonary system. The function of the left atrium and left ventricle is the collection of the blood from the pulmonary system and pumping it into the tissues of the body. A set of four valves are used to maintain a one-direction of blood movement throughout the heart. The tricuspid and bicuspid valves (atrioventricular valves) assure that the blood

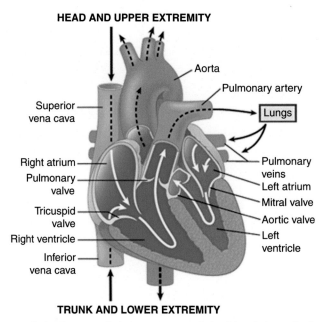

Figure 8.3 Anatomy of the heart and the movement of the blood through the heart chambers, valves, and arteries [1].

moves only from the atria to the ventricles. The pulmonary and semilunar valves assure that the blood moves from the ventricle to the great arteries.

Despite the fact that the heart contains a high amount of blood, the heart gives a small amount of blood to its tissues. The heart tissues receive the blood by an independent vessel supply. From the aorta arise the left and the right coronary arteries that supply the heart with nourishment and oxygen. Cardiac veins receive the deoxygenated blood from the heart tissues and return it to the right atrium.

The superior vena cava and inferior vena cava transport deoxygenated blood systemic circulation to the right atrium. Deoxygenated blood from the head and upper extremities is transported via superior vena cava while deoxygenated blood from lower extremities, abdomen, and thorax are transported via inferior vena cava. The blood moves from right atrium to the right ventricle through tricuspid valve. The blood leaves the right ventricle through pulmonary artery that forks into the right and left pulmonary arteries that transport deoxygenated blood to the lungs. Then, gas exchange happens in the lung. The oxygenated blood from the right pulmonary vein and left pulmonary vein moves to the left atrium. The blood travels from the left atrium to the left ventricle through the bicuspid valve. The left ventricle pumps the oxygenated blood to the circulatory system through the aorta.

8.1.3 Cardiac cycle

The events of the heart that happen from the start of one heartbeat to the start of the next are referred as the cardiac cycle. The action potential of the sinus node initiates spontaneously the cardiac cycle. The action potential moves through the right and left atrium and then in the A-V bundle to the ventricles. The cardiac cycle is composed of two periods: diastole and systole. The diastole is a relaxation period in which the blood fills the heart. The systole is a contraction period in which the heart pumps the blood. The heart rate (HR) is the reciprocals of the cardiac cycle (sum of the diastole and systole periods). The normal heart rate is 72 beats/min, where the cardiac cycle is 0.833 second/beat [1]. The function of the heart depends greatly on the performance of the left ventricle. The performance of the left ventricle is assessed mainly by some volumetric parameters. Let us dene some volumetric measures related to the left ventricle.

1. End Diastolic Volume (EDV): The volume of the LV at the end of the diastole. Normal values are 142 mL ($\pm$ 21 mL) [4].
2. End Systolic Volume (ESV): The volume of the LV at the end of the systole. Normal values are 47 mL ($\pm$ 10 mL) [4].
3. Stroke Volume (SV): The volume of blood pumped by the LV per minute. SV = EDV − ESV. Normal values are 95 mL ($\pm$ 14 mL) [4].
4. Cardiac Output (CO): The volume of the blood pumped by the left ventri-cle per unit time. It is the product of the HR and SV, that is, CO = HR*SV. Normal values are 4.0−8.0 L/min [4].
5. Ejection Fraction (EF): The volumetric fraction pumped from the LV with each heartbeat. EF = $\frac{EDV - ESV}{EDV}$ 100. Normal values are 67% ($\pm$ 4.6%) [4].

8.1.4 Cardiovascular diseases

Cardiovascular diseases (CVDs) are a group of diseases associated with the heart and blood vessels. Each disease has its own mechanism. Here, we will mention some of the most common CVDs.

- Coronary Artery Disease: It is known as ischemic heart disease [5]. This disease is caused due to the reduction of the blood supply to the cardiac muscle when there is a build-up of plaque (atherosclerosis) in the heart arteries. The types of this disease are:
  - Angina: Pressure or chest pain due to insufficient blood supply to the heart.
  - Myocardial Infarction: It is known as heart attack. It is a damage to the heart muscle that happens when the blood supply decreases or stops to an area of the heart. The symptoms of this type include chest pain that might traverse to the arm, neck, or back.
  - Cardiac Arrest: Sudden loss of blood supply caused by the inability of the heart to pump normally. Symptoms involve the loss of consciousness and breathing. If the treatment is not delivered in minutes, it leads to death.

- Heart Failure: It happens when the heart is unable to pump sufficient blood to meet the body needs. It can happen after myocardial infarction that reduces the heart performance to pump blood. Symptoms involve short breath, intense tiredness, and leg swelling. Heart failure causes a reduction in the EF. The European Society of Cardiology posted guidelines for the diagnosis and treatment of acute and chronic heart failure [6]. These guidelines defined the categories of the heart failure based on the value of the EF as follows:
  - Normal ejection fraction: $EF \geq 50\%$.
  - Moderately reduced ejection fraction: $40\% \geq EF \leq 49\%$.
  - Reduced ejection fraction: $EF < 40\%$.

In the United States a threshold of 30% for EF is used by the authorities to present disability benefits to patients.

8.2 Left ventricle segmentation and quantification

CVDs are dangerous health issues as they are responsible for the highest rate of mortality worldwide [7]. About 836,546 patients in the United States die each year because of CVDs [8]. A noninvasive quantitative evaluation for the heart functionality can be available for the cardiologist from cardiac magnetic resonance (CMR), which is an important imaging technique. The cardiologist can get functional heart indexes from performing segmentation for the LV in CMR short-axis view cine images [9]. These indexes are ESV, EDV, EF, wall mass, and regional indexes (e.g., wall thickening), which are essential for heart diagnosis and treatment. However, to estimate these parameters, accurate delineation of myocardial walls is required. Manual segmentation of LV in CMR short-axis view images requires significant effort and time. Furthermore, manual segmentation is prone to inter and intraoperator variability [10]. Therefore an alternative technique to manual segmentation is needed to perform automated segmentation for the LV cavity and myocardium. Furthermore, this technique should be accurate to obtain left ventricular functional metrics with high accuracy.

Currently, deep learning has achieved great success over conventional image processing methods in many medical imaging analysis domains [11,12]. Deep learning is a subdomain in ML that has the power of automated representation learning from the raw data itself without the need for manually crafting the appropriate features from the data. Convolutional neural network (CNN) is a deep learning algorithm that is widely used for processing image data and has demonstrated great success in computer vision tasks [13,14]. Researchers initially used CNNs to classify images by assigning the whole image to a specific class. On the other hand, CNNs are now redesigned to perform image segmentation. The new design is the fully convolutional neural network (FCN) that replaces the fully connected layers in the CNN by convolution layers. In a FCN algorithm, we perform dense classification in the image domain where each pixel is assigned to a certain class with the highest predicted probability. The need for accurate and automated estimation of LV parameters, and the success of the CNNs motivated us to build a framework for the automated functional assessment of the heart. This framework should segment and quantify the LV with a comparable accuracy to the human operator. In this chapter, we propose a novel fully automated framework that can segment and quantify the LV from CMR cine images. We performed segmentation to the LV cavity and myocardium to estimate the heart physiological parameters. Our main achievement is the accurate quantification of the LV indexes and reaching a lower error compared to other previous techniques applied on the same dataset. Our framework that is based on FCN has the following contributions:

- We propose an efficient method that is based of FCN to extract a region-of-interest (ROI) that contains the LV from CMR cine images. We perform this extraction process in the beginning to alleviate the class-imbalance problem and reduce the memory and computational requirements.
- After ROI extraction, we use a novel FCN model for cardiac segmentation. The architecture of this novel model is inspired from the U-net (i.e., the input is passed to a contracting path followed by an expanding path). The addition to the conventional model is the incorporation of multiple bottleneck layers that describe the input by multiple representations. The bottleneck layers are upsampled and combined to estimate the final segmentation. Our proposed model requires a fewer number of parameters than the state-of-the-art models such as U-net, yet it shows better performance.
- We propose a novel loss function that works on minimizing the difference between the ground truth LV contours and the predicted contours. We refer to the new loss by radial loss and we incorporate it with the cross-entropy loss.
- We evaluated the generalization strength of our proposed segmentation method by estimating the segmentation performance of our method when we use the ACDC 2017 data as a training set and a local dataset as a testing set. Our segmentation approach demonstrated good segmentation accuracy that is comparable to another model that uses only our local dataset.

8.3 Related work on left ventricle segmentation and quantification

Over the past years, considerable attention has been devoted to the problem of LV segmentation from CMR cine images. Firstly, semiautomatic segmentation methods have been proposed by researchers; see the review by Petitjean et al. [15]. These approaches such as presented in Refs. [16–19] used graph cut, active contours, dynamic programming, or atlas-based methods. On the other hand, significant user intervention is required in semiautomatic methods. Therefore they are not suitable when fast segmentation feature is required. To remedy that limitation, researchers have proposed fully automatic approaches for heart segmentation. Queiros et al. [20] and Liu et al. [21] proposed automatic approaches that are based on the level set. Despite the high accuracy they obtained from their approaches, level set is associated with initialization and is designed to delineate one anatomical structure only. Wang et al. [22] and Ringenberg et al. [23] proposed methods that are based on traditional image processing such as edge detection, thresholding, and morphology procession. However, when the prior assumptions of these methods are not satisfied, these methods do not work well. Furthermore, shape priors models have been added to the cardiac segmentation methods, such as the work of Refs. [24–26]. However, suboptimal segmentation is achieved when the prior information is imperfect. The shape prior may be restricted by certain assumptions that do not work well with the underlying testing image. On the other hand, we can obtain automatic representation learning from deep learning given sufficient training dataset. Therefore with the power of deep learning, we do not need shape prior information because automated segmentation for the test image can be directly obtained from the FCN.

Deep learning has been successfully applied on the problem of cardiac segmentation. Tran et al. [27] proposed the first application of FCN in cardiac image segmentation. They extracted an ROI that was centered at the LV cavity before segmentation. They assumed that the cavity center is at the image center which may lead to inaccurate results. A recurrent FCN was proposed by Poudel et al. [28]. Their network was a modified version of U-net. the spatial dependencies between slices were used during the segmentation of the left ventricular endocarduim. Linear regression using CNN was proposed by Tan et al. [29] to segment the LV. Their method was composed of two main stages: finding the left ventricular center followed by the calculation of the endocardial contour (EnC) radius and epicardial contour (EpC) radius in polar space. A regularized CNN was proposed by Oktay et al. [30]. The regularization is performed by the addition of anatomical prior. Their model is suitable for cardiac image analysis problems such as enhancement and segmentation. An iterative heart segmentation approach was proposed by Zheng et al. [31]. Their approach starts from the base of the LV to the apex. In each iteration, a new model of the U-net performs segmentation to the heart and the output is utilized for the prediction of the next slice and thus they maintain 3D consistency. An FCN that was inspired from VGG-16 [32] was proposed by Bai et al. [33] for the segmentation of the LV and right ventricle (RV) from CMR short-axis view, and right atrium and left atrium from CMR long-axis view. A novel computationally efficient DenseNet was proposed by Khened et al. [34]. Their model is based on FCN for heart segmentation. To build a system for cardiac disease classification, they calculated the clinical indexes from the segmentation maps. The U-net was employed in the work of Tao et al. [35]. Their work aimed at the calculation of LV parameters from CMR images. They evaluated the performance of their approach by a multivendor and multicenter cardiac data.

8.4 Methods

Our proposed framework for the automated segmentation and quantification of the LV is shown in Fig. 8.4. The quantification is performed by the calculation of LV functional parameters and mass. Our framework consists of four main steps: (1) ROI extraction using a FCN called FCN1, where the center of the ROI is at the center of left ventricular cavity; (2) Image cropping for all CMR images using the extracted ROI; (3) Segmentation of the left ventricular cavity and myocardium using a FCN called FCN2; and (4) Calculation of left ventricular functional parameters and mass. The following section explains our framework in detail.

8.4.1 Region-of-interest extraction

In CMR short-axis view image, the heart occupies a small proportion compared to the surrounding tissues that occupy a larger proportion. In this situation, deep learning models that make dense classification in the spatial domain of the image become biased towards the surrounding tissues, which is considered the majority class. Therefore it is a necessary processing step to extract an Region-of-interest (ROI) that encompasses the heart tissues before performing the final segmentation. Also, ROI extraction leads to a reduction in the computational load and boosts speed. In our framework, ROI extraction is performed using a bounding box of size 128×128 pixels. The center of the bounding box was at the center of the LV center point. We calculated the LV center point by a deep learning method that is based on a FCN, called FCN1, which is similar to the U-net. Fig. 8.5 depicts the ROI extraction process. We trained the network to segment the LV cavity from the original CMR cine images. Then, the center of mass of the segmented region is estimated. Then, we set the center of the ROI to this center of mass. Finally, the gray image is cropped to a 128×128 image using the estimated ROI center. The output of the model might suffer from the class imbalance problem that leads to a high number of false negative (FN) pixels. However, this network is not intended to segment the cavity ideally, but it is intended to provide an estimate for the

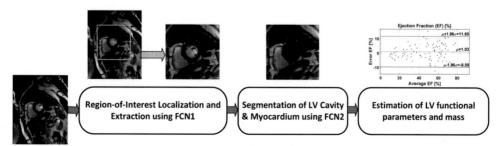

Figure 8.4 Illustration for the proposed framework for automated left ventricle (LV) segmentation and quantification (calculation of LV functional indexes and mass).

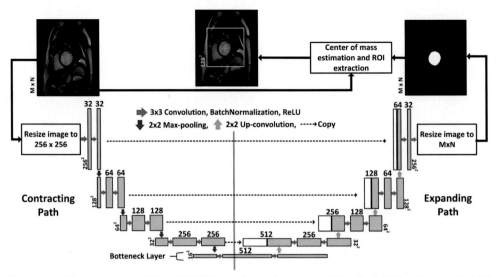

Figure 8.5 The extraction of the LV-ROI is performed using a FCN called FCN1. The original 2D CMR cine image is the input to the network. All images are resized to 256 × 256 pixels. The output of the network is a segmentation map for the LV cavity. The map is resized to the same spatial dimensions of the input image (M × N). The blue arrow refers to the successive operations of convolution (filter size 33), batch normalization, ReLU. For the convolution operation, the number of filters increases from 32 to 512 in the encoder path, and decreases from 512 to 1 in the decoder path. To maintain the same spatial dimension after convolution, we used zero padding. The red arrow indicates max-pooling operation that decreases spatial dimension by a factor of 2. The green arrow indicates upconvolution that increases the spatial dimension by a factor of 2. Finally, the contextual information is copied from the contracting path and is concatenated to the expanding path by the dashed arrows that are called skip connections.

LV center point. The left ventricular cavity in the apical slices occupies a very small part of the entire image. Therefore due to the high degree of the class imbalance, the model may fail to segment the cavity. To overcome this issue, we use the center of the cavity of the previous slice as a center for the slice that leads to a black map from FCN1. By adopting this strategy, the 3D consistency of the LV is maintained without negatively affecting the overall performance because the extracted ROIs that truly not associated with LV tissues will again lead to black maps from FCN2.

Despite the effort required to train a FCN and to tune its hyperparameters, the trained network takes little time to extract the LV-ROI. Our method is much faster than other approaches that use Hough Transform [34].

8.5 Cardiac segmentation

Fig. 8.6 shows our proposed model for the segmentation of LV cavity and myocardium. The model is inspired from the FCN that was employed for segmentation tasks

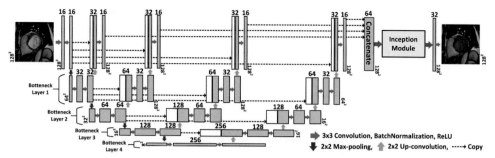

Figure 8.6 The proposed model for cardiac segmentation. The model is fed the extracted LV-ROI of size 128 × 128 pixels to produce an output that represent the segmentation map for the input ROI. In the map, red refers to LV cavity and green refers to the LV myocardium. The blue arrow refers to the successive operations of convolution (filter size 3 × 3), batch normalization, ReLU. For the convolution operation, the number of filters increases from 16 to 256 in the encoder path, and decreases from 256 to 1 in the decoder path. To maintain the same spatial dimension after convolution, we used zero padding. The red arrow indicates max-pooling operation that decreases spatial dimension by a factor of 2. The green arrow indicates upconvolution that increases the spatial dimension by a factor of 2. Finally, the contextual information is copied from the contracting path and is concatenated to the expanding path by the dashed arrows that are called skip connections.

[36]. By convention, the input of the FCN is passed through an encoder path followed by a decoder path. In the encoder path, we reduce the spatial dimensions progressively until we reach a bottleneck layer where the input is described by an abstract and dense representation. On the other hand, in the decoder path, we restore the original input dimensions from the bottleneck layer by applying transposed convolutions. The bottleneck layer is located between an encoder and decoder path, and it involves a representation for the input in a reduced dimensionality form [37]. Our proposed model has multiple encoder paths that restore the input dimensions from multiple bottlenecks with various representations to the input. Then, the output of each encoder path is concatenated into a single layer that is fed to an inception module that is based on Google research [38]. Fig. 8.7 depicts the used inception module. The learning of multiple-scales features can be obtained from the integration of the inception module that has filters with different sizes. Small cardiac regions are detected by filters with small sizes while larger cardiac areas are detected by the larger filter sizes. Also, filters with large sizes remove the false positive regions that are similar to the targeted cardiac areas. Finally, we process the output of the inception module with a convolution layer to get the segmentation map. We apply a sigmoid layer on the output of the network. Network FCN2 involves various versions of FCN1 with different depths. Typically, FCN2 has four versions of FCN1's architecture and they all have the same encoder path. We concatenated the output of each network into one layer to obtain the final segmentation. Fig. 8.8 demonstrates the relationship between FCN1 and FCN2.

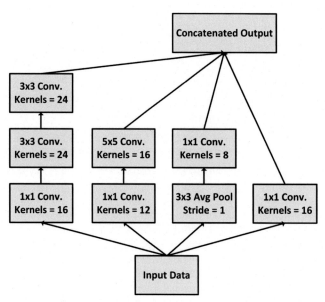

Figure 8.7 The structure of the employed inception module in FCN2 network. The module contains parallel processing paths with kernels of various sizes (i.e., 1×1, 3×3, and 5×5 convolutions), and average pooling operations with kernel of size 3×3. The feature maps obtained from these paths are then concatenated in the final layer.

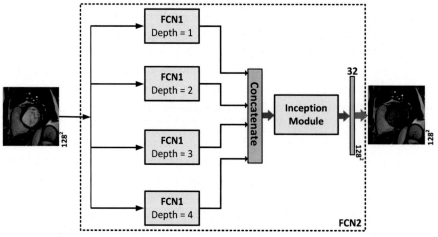

Figure 8.8 The relationship between model FCN1 and FCN2. Model FCN2 contains four FCN1s with different depths and the output of each model is concatenated to obtain the final segmentation.

8.5.1 Loss function

The class imbalance problem is mitigated by the extraction of a LV-ROI. Furthermore, the extraction of a ROI boosts the performance of the CE loss. We kept using CE loss for its advantages such as smooth training and we proposed a novel loss called the radial loss that gives us good segmentation for the left ventricular contours. Other loss functions have been proposed in deep learning literature and utilized segmentation metrics such as Dice loss [39]. However, these loss functions result in undersegmented areas with many false positives [39]. Therefore we excluded these functions from our analysis. Let θ indicates the parameters of the trained model, $X =$ {X1, X2,..., XN} indicates to the set of training images with size N, and Y = {Y1, Y2, ..., YN} indicates the set of ground truth segmentation labels. Then, the CE is given by the following equation:

$$LCE = -\log p(Yi|Xi, \theta) = \sum_{c=1}^{C} \sum_{p_j \in X_i} Y_{i,c,p_j} \log \widehat{Y_{i,c,p_j}} \tag{8.1}$$

where $p(Yi|Xi,\theta)$ refers to the probabilistic map predicted by the network after the sigmoid layer. Xi refers to the network's input. c indicates the class index. pj represents a pixel in image Xi. Y_{i,c,p_j} represents the true probability that pj in the class c, and $_j\log \widehat{Y_{i,c,p_j}}$ refers to the predicted probability that pj in the class c.

We exploited the fact that LV is associated with a radial shape to propose a new radial loss function. We define the radial distance (RD) at a specific angel by the distance between the center of mass of a segmented area to its surface at a specific direction. Thus if we have a ground truth surface G and a segmented area surface S, the error of the local radial distance d at an angle θ is demonstrated in Fig. 8.9 and is defined in Eq. (8.2):

$$d = s_\theta - g_\theta \tag{8.2}$$

where the RDs from the center of mass point to the surfaces G and S are described by g and s, respectively. Now, if we constructed an equispaced radial lines, we could

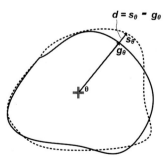

Figure 8.9 The solid line refers to the rue contour while the dashed line refers to the predicted contour in polar space. The local radial distance error at an angle θ is described by d.

calculate the RDs for the surfaces G and S, and save them in the same radial order in vectors g and s, respectively. We can define the RD loss as L2 penalty:

$$LRD = \frac{1}{M} \|s - g\|_2 \tag{8.3}$$

where M refers to the number of radial lines. By applying a Sobel filter on the ground truth Yi and the predicted probabilistic map Yi we can obtain the surfaces G and S, respectively, for an input image Xi. The loss function is an Euclidean norm. Thus it is differentiable by a deep learning library. The loss function LRD can be employed for both EnC and EpC of the LV as follows:

$$L_{RD} = \frac{1}{M} \|s_{EnC} - g_{EnC}\|_2 + \frac{1}{M} \|s_{EpC} - g_{EpC}\|_2 \tag{8.4}$$

We can define the final loss function as follows:

$$L = LCE + LRD \tag{8.5}$$

8.5.2 Network training settings

We used Pytorch deep learning framework to build both FCN1 and FCN2. Kaiming initialization [40] was used to initialize the weights of the convolutional layers. The variables that must be set before training the network are called the network's hyperparameters. These variables identify the architecture of the network such as the number of filters. They also determine network's training such as learning rate. The optimal values of the hyperparameters were calculated using a grid search approach when the segmentation accuracy is our criterion to optimize. The search space for the initial number of filters = {8, 16, 32}. We used Adam optimizer with a learning rate that has the search space = {0.01, 0.001, 0.0001} and the learning momentum = {0.9}. The search space of the batch size = {8, 16, 32}. The search space for the number of the epochs = 100:50:300. The size of the training set can be increased using the data augmentation approach. Data augmentation also helps in overcoming the problem of overfitting during a network's training. Thus a data augmentation strategy that was associated with random translations, scaling, and rotation was adopted.

8.6 Experimental results

8.6.1 Cardiac datasets

The LV segmentation and function quantification were performed on two different cardiac datasets. Namely, the ACDC cardiac dataset, which is publicly available from MICCAI 2017 challenge [41], and a locally acquired cardiac dataset.

ACDC-2017 Dataset: The dataset is composed of 150 exams for various patients. The patients are divided into five categories according to physiological heart parameters. The categories are (1) normal subjects, (2) patients with dilated cardiomyopathy, (3) patients with previous myocardial infarction, (4) patients with abnormal right ventricle, and (5) patients with hypertrophic cardiomyopathy. The data providers divided the dataset into two sets: (1) A set for training that is composed of 100 cases along with their ground truth manual segmentation at the ED and ES phases in all acquired heart slices; (2) A set for testing that is composed of 50 cases without annotation. The two sets have even arrangement of patient categories. The cardiac cine images were acquired in breath hold with a retrospective or prospective gating and with a SSFP sequence in short-axis orientation. The LV was covered entirely by the short-axis slices.

The imaging parameters were: slice thickness equals 5 or 8 mm, interslice gap equals 5 or 8 mm, and spatial resolution equals $1.37-1.68$ mm^2/pixel.

Locally acquired dataset: This dataset was utilized to answer the question of whether our segmentation method is generalizable by evaluating its performance on this dataset, which was not used in training. In this set, cross-sectional cardiac cine images were acquired from 11 patients with known history of myocardial infarction. The Institutional Review Board (IRB) approved our study. The dataset is composed of 26 cardiac scans that cover various heart sections. Twenty-five frames were captured at each section to cover the cardiac cycle. The sum of the 2D images was about 6000 images.

8.6.2 Framework training and validation

The ACDC dataset was used to analyze the performance of our novel framework for the automated left ventricular segmentation and quantification through the calculation of physiological heart indexes introduced in Section 8.3. The dataset is composed of 100 patients along with their ground truth manual annotation. A ten-fold cross-validation was adopted to train and validate FCN1 and FCN2. In each fold, we had an equal number of patients from the five introduced heart diagnoses. This was achieved by stratified sampling. We can reformulate our description of network evaluation by saying that we trained the networks ten times and in each time we used a training set of 90 cases (average of 1800 2D images) and a testing set of 10 cases (average of 200 2D images). Furthermore, the generalization of our segmentation approach was tested using the locally collected dataset.

A probabilistic map is the result of our segmentation network. This map is composed of pixels and each pixel is given a probability of belonging to the object. We applied Otsu thresholding [42] on the probabilistic map to get the final segmented binary mask. Additionally, To eliminate the false positive pixels, we looked for the connected components in the binary mask. Finally, morphological operations such as gap filling were applied on the resulted binary segmentation. We used segmentation metrics such as Dice score and Hausdorf distance (HD) to assess the segmentation accuracy of our approach.

8.6.3 Evaluation of LV-ROI extraction

To assess the performance of our novel approach of LV–ROI extraction, we trained and validated FCN1 by the ACDC dataset using a ten-fold cross-validation strategy. In each fold, we estimated the center of mass of the segmented LV cavity Ps for each image. Then, we used two mea–sures/metrics to evaluate the network performance; namely (1) the Euclidean distance between the center point of our predicted segmen-tation Ps and the center of mass of LV cavity from manually annotated segmentation Pm, and (2) the percentage of the images with ROI prediction that encompasses all pixels of LV cavity and myocardium. The statistics of the Euclidean distance between Pm and Ps is shown in Table 8.1. The statistics are for 1902 images from the ACDC dataset. Our method resulted in a good accuracy and surpassed the method in Ref. [34]. Our approach takes on average a 700 msec to extract the desired ROIs of one case at the phases of ED and ES. Furthermore, the resulted ROIs encompassed all the LV cavity and myocardium tissues.

8.6.4 Evaluation of the proposed loss function

After the extraction of the ROI, cardiac segmentation was performed using FCN2. We used LCE loss only in one time and the proposed loss LCE + LRD in another time. A comparison between the segmentation metrics resulting from the two loss functions is shown in Table 8.2. The table shows the segmentation for both LV cavity

Table 8.1 The statistics of difference in pixels between the predicted left ventricular center of mass point (Ps) and the center of mass resulted from manual annotation (Pm). The table compares our approach with the method of Ref. [34].

	Mean	STD	Max.
Hough transform [34]	4.00	3.83	36.24
Proposed (FCN1)	1.41	1.65	5.00

STD, standard deviation.

Table 8.2 The average segmentation accuracy of our segmentation approach when using two different loss functions in a ten-fold cross-validation strategy applied on the ACDC (Automated Cardiac Diagnosis Challenge) dataset.

Loss function	Dice coefficient		HD (mm)	
	LV Cavity	MYO	LV Cavity	MYO
LCE	0.93	0.86	9.52	11.41
LCE + LRD	0.94	0.89	6.71	7.13

LV, *left ventricle*; MYO, *myocardium*; HD, *Hausdorf distance*.

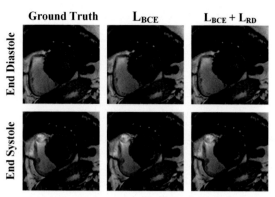

Figure 8.10 Comparison between the ground truth annotation of the LV in phases of ED and ES, the predicted LV delineation from FCN2 with LCE loss, and the predicted delineation from FCN2 with our loss (LCE + LRD). Green and red areas indicate the LV myocardium and cavity, respectively. The blue color indicates the segmentation error. We note the visual qualitative improvement for the delineation of our proposed loss function.

and myocardium (MYO). We can notice that when we used LCE alone, we obtained a good segmentation performance because the issue of class imbalance was mitigated by the ROI extraction step. While our proposed novel loss function resulted in a superior performance in terms of the used segmentation metrics. Furthermore, a better segmentation quality resulted from our proposed loss, as shown in Fig. 8.2. Thanks to the capability of the RD loss in which the distance between the predicted contours and the true contours is minimized (Fig. 8.10).

8.6.5 Evaluation of the proposed network model FCN2

To evaluate the performance of our proposed network FCN2, a comparison was made with two other methods: (1) the original model of the U-net [37] with four layers and initial convolutional layers that had 64 filters, and (2) the ConvDeconv model introduced in [43]. We trained all of the three networks with the same configurations as explained in Section 8.2 in a ten-fold cross-validation strategy. Table 8.3 shows a comparison in terms of the resultant segmentation accuracy between the proposed FCN2 model against the other models. The table also shows the number of the learnable parameters required by each model. This reflects the required computational cost by each model. As indicated, FCN2 resulted in the best segmentation performance for all segmented regions, while ConvDeconv model resulted in the lowest performance. The inferiority associated with the ConvDeconv net may be due to the lack of skip connections that works by adding high-resolution features to the expanding path. Furthermore, FCN2 works better than the original U-net model that starts with 64 filters. Therefore U-net with fewer filters were excluded with our

Table 8.3 A comparison between three different segmentation methods in terms of the segmentation metrics (Dice and HD). The values of the metrics are presented as the average values when we trained the model using a 10-fold cross-validation strategy. The number of learnable parameters are also shown.

Method	Dice coefficient				HD (mm)				No. of Params.
	LV Cavity		MYO		LV Cavity		MYO		
	ED	ES	ED	ES	ED	ES	ED	ES	
U-net [37]	0.94	0.90	0.83	0.85	8.22	10.53	9.81	11.51	31 M
ConvDeconv net [43]	0.92	0.88	0.80	0.83	9.14	11.34	10.81	11.95	252 M
FCN2 (proposed)	0.96	0.92	0.88	0.89	6.31	7.42	7.11	7.25	2.5 M

LV, *left ventricle*; MYO, *myocardium*; HD, *Hausdorf distance*.

comparison. Another advantage for our proposed FCN2 network is that it requires fewer parameters, and thus it requires less training time and GPU memory usage.

Segmentation results of FCN2 are shown in Fig. 8.11. The figure contains three different short-axis slices of a heart along with their ground truth segmentation at phases of ED and ES of the cardiac cycle. Overall, our method (FCN2) resulted in accurate segmentation with some errors at apical slices. After all of the described analysis, we decided to choose the segmentation results of FCN2 for the estimation of heart's physiological parameters.

8.6.6 Generalization evaluation

After obtaining good segmentation results from our approach applied on ACDC dataset only, we assess the generalization capability of our method. We have two models using our method:

1. Our method when we use the local dataset for both training and testing.
2. Our method when we use ACDC dataset for training and the local dataset for testing.

The segmentation performance of the two models is shown in Table 8.4. In the second model, although for training we used ACDC dataset that consists of about 1.4 K images acquired at the phases of ED and ES, we obtained good segmentation accuracy for the LV at all cardiac phases of the local dataset. In the first model, the same dataset distribution was used for training and testing. Therefore the results of the first model are

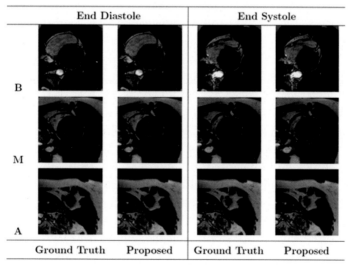

Figure 8.11 Left ventricular segmentation of FCN2 model at ED and ES phases of one case during the ten-fold cross-validation. Green and red regions refer to the LV myocardium and cavity, respectively. The basal, mid-cavity, and apical slices are indicated by the letters B, M, and A, respectively. LV, *left ventricle*.

Table 8.4 The segmentation performance of two models. In model A, the local dataset was used for training and testing. In model B, the ACDC (Automated Cardiac Diagnosis Challenge) dataset was used for training and the local dataset was used for testing. The estimates are mean values.

Model	Dice Coef.		HD (mm)	
	LV Cavity	MYO	LV Cavity	MYO
Model A	0.95	0.87	9.31	8.52
Model B	0.94	0.85	11.12	9.74

LV, *left ventricle*; MYO, *myocardium*; HD, *Hausdorf distance*.

slightly better than the second model that uses different distribution for training and testing. We can conclude that our approach generalizes well to different data. Furthermore, segmentation for the full cardiac cycle was obtained from our approach when trained only using a data that has annotation for the phases of ED and ES.

8.6.7 Physiological parameters estimation

After performing segmentation for the LV cavity and myocardium from the cardiac images, we estimated five functional parameters; namely the EDV, the ESV, the LVM, the SV, and the EF. These parameters were described in Section 8.3. To calculate the degree of agreement between the estimated values from the output segmentation and the estimated values from ground truth segmentation, we constructed Bland–Altman plots [44], as shown in Fig. 8.12. These figures demonstrate the bias μ (mean difference) and the 95% agreement limits (1.96 SD). In Bland–Altman plots, we must check the normality of the differences. Therefore Shapiro–Wilk test for normality was used with 5% significance level. The obtained P-values were .082, .052, .061, .154, and .787 for the EDV, the ESV, the LVM, the SV, and the EF, respectively. Given that the P-values are higher than .05, the test accepted normality. Our calculated parameters have a mean of only three outlying points, which is considered only 3% of the involved cases.

The error statistics are summarized in Table 8.5. The table shows the statistics for the EDV, the ESV, and the EF estimations of our approach and other approaches applied on the ACDC dataset. The lowest bias and standard deviation were obtained from the errors of the EDV and the ESV measures. Additionally, the error of the EF estimate has a lower standard deviation than the approach in Ref. [45]. Overall, our method resulted in acceptable differences that are comparable with intra- and intersubject variability associated with the manual calculation of functional parameters from cardiac images as reported in [46,47].

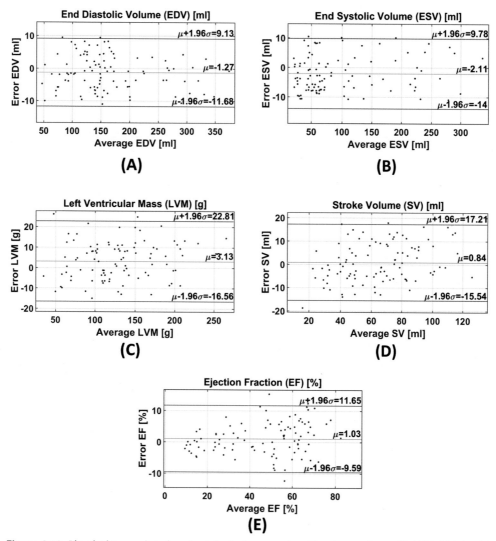

Figure 8.12 Bland-Altman plots for physiological parameters. The figure shows (A) EDV, (B) ESV, (C) LVM, (D) SV, and (E) EF. The bias of the calculated values from the ground truth is indicated by μ. 1.96 indicates the 95% confidence interval. To obtain a good agreement, the bias should be near the zero value and the error points should be within the confidence interval.

8.7 Discussion

In this chapter, we aimed at developing a deep learning based method for efficient and accurate segmentation to the LV myocardium and cavity. Our method is fully automated and provides accurate LV quantification through the estimation of LV

Table 8.5 A comparison between our approach and other methods that aim at the automated estimation of functional LV parameters. The values indicate the average (std.) of the differences between the automated and manual estimation.

Reference	EDV (mL)	ESV (mL)	EF (%)
Wofilterink et al. [45]	−1.57 (6.31)	−2.51 (7.66)	1.23 (4.99)
Grinias et al. [48]	1.43 (9.95)	2.61 (17.60)	−0.05 (8.61)
Proposed	−1.27 (5.31)	−2.11 (6.06)	1.03 (5.42)

functional parameters that are widely used for heart functional evaluation. Our framework features a novel network architecture and major contributions are explained below. Firstly, we introduced the idea of building an initial network (FCN1) for the task of automated ROI extraction from original CMR images. It turned out that this idea was successful in providing accurate estimates for LV center point.

This idea was also fast during detection. A comparison was made between our approach and another approach that has the same aim of LV localization and ROI extraction; however, it uses Hough transform. Table 8.1 demonstrates how our approach surpassed an approach that relies on Hough transform for ROI extraction. Additionally, the ROI of one patient at ED and ES were extracted by our method in only 700 msec. Our extracted ROIs contained all of the desired LV cavity and myocardium tissues. Thus our extraction method is fast, accurate, and reliable. We selected a suitable ROI size based on the minimum size that resulted in myocardial segmentation without clipping, assuring that there is no clipping for the LV necessary for further accurate calculation of heart physiological parameters. In our experiments, an ROI of size 128 × 128 was chosen because this size provided the smallest area that encompasses the LV tissues in our CMR dataset. Extracting an ROI of size 128x128 has two advantages: (1) it reduced the time and computational requirements during the training and inference of the network, and (2) it mitigated the class imbalance problem by discarding the unwanted surrounding tissues. However, our implementation can work with arbitrary ROI sizes.

Secondly, our proposed final segmentation is constructed by network FCN2 from various bottleneck layers. These bottleneck layers are different representations to the input image with different dimensionalities. Our network FCN2 resulted in accurate segmentation for the LV cavity and myocardium as demonstrated in Fig. 8.11. It also surpassed state-of-the-art models such as U-net and ConvDeconv networks in terms of the segmentation accuracy. Another advantage of our network is the efficient use of time and memory by requiring a fewer number of learnable parameters.

Moreover, we carefully chose the components of our deep learning model because this is essential for the overall success of the model. For instance, a novel loss function was implemented, and we called it radial loss, which is appropriate for LV segmentation because of the underlying radial shape of EpC and EnC. Our final loss function is the sum of both the baseline cross-entropy and 29 the radial loss. Cross-entropy is popular in the domain of deep learning segmentation because it is associated with the ability to provide smooth training and it has nice differentiable properties. Researchers consider cross-entropy as the standard loss in various applications, especially image segmentation. As demonstrated in Table 8.2 and Fig. 8.9, our loss provided a better segmentation performance when compared to cross-entropy alone. Our loss function showed superior performance due to the fact that radial loss minimizes the distances between the actual contours and the predicted contours of the LV. The problem of overfitting can be avoided by a smart way called data augmentation. Data augmentation also works on increasing the training samples which is useful in case of scarce annotated data. By adopting data augmentation, we reached good mean Dice and HD values for the delineation of LV cavity and myocardium.

Regarding Fig. 8.12, in the EDV and ESV measurements, there are small negative biases that mean that we slightly underestimated this measurement. We can also notice that EDV had a lower bias than the ESV and, consequently, the calculated EF had a positive bias. If there are points outside the confidence interval, we might have a wrong diagnosis for patients with CVD due to these errors. Therefore an accurate LV segmentation approach should not result in outlying points by reducing the segmentation errors that are transferred to the next step of functional parameters estimation.

Finally, a comparison has been made between our approach and other approaches that aimed at quantification of LV using the ACDC dataset to establish the merit of our method based on the reported errors of each approach. In general, our framework resulted in acceptable errors for the calculated parameters and surpassed the previous frameworks, as indicated in Table 8.5. Additionally, we would like to note that our framework is not limited to a specific dataset; we proved that our method can provide good results by using a different dataset, even with a network trained by a sparse data (ACDC-2017) and validated on a dense data that covers the whole cardiac cycle.

In addition the heart [49–69], this work could also be applied to various other applications in medical imaging, such as the prostate [70–74], the kidney [69], [75–94], the lung [95–144], the brain [145–167], the vascular system [168–178], the retina [179–191], the bladder [192–196], the liver [197], [198], the head and neck [199–201], and injury prediction [202] as well as several nonmedical applications [203–209].

References

[1] Hall JE, Hall ME. Textbook of medical physiology e-Book. Elsevier Health Sciences; 2020.
[2] Iaizzo PA. Handbook of cardiac anatomy, physiology, and devices. Springer Science & Business Media; 2009.
[3] Shah S, Gnanasegaran G, Sundberg-Cohon J, Buscombe JR. The heart: anatomy, physiology and exercise physiology. Integrating cardiology for nuclear medicine physicians. Springer; 2009. pp. 3(22).

[4] Maceira A, Prasad S, Khan M, Pennell D. Normalized left ventricular systolic and diastolic function by steady state free precession cardiovascular magnetic resonance. J Cardiovasc Magn Reson 2006;8 (3):417−26.

[5] Bhatia SK. Biomaterials for clinical applications. Springer Science & Business Media; 2010.

[6] Ponikowski P, Voors AA, Anker SD, Bueno H, Cleland JG, Coats AJ, et al. Esc guidelines for the diagnosis and treatment of acute and chronic heart failure. Eur Heart J 2016;37(27):2129−200 2016.

[7] WHO, Cardiovascular diseases (cvds); 2017. Available from: https://www.who.int/en/news-room/fact-sheets/detail/cardiovascular-diseases-(cvds)

[8] A. H. Association, Heart disease and stroke statistics 2018 at-a-glance; 2018. Available from: https://www.heart.org/-/media/data-import/downloadables/heart-disease-and-stroke-statistics-2018|at-a-glance-ucm498848:pdf.

[9] Frangi AF, Niessen WJ, Viergever MA. Three-dimensional modeling for functional analysis of cardiac images, a review. IEEE Trans Med Imaging 2001;20(1):2−5. Available from: https://doi.org/10.1109/42.906421.

[10] Souto M, Masip LR, Couto M, Suarez-Cuenca JJ, Martnez A, Tahoces PG, et al. Quantification of right and left ventricular function in cardiac mr imaging: comparison of semiautomatic and manual seg-mentation algorithms. Diagnostics (Basel, Switzerland) 2013;3(2):271−82. Available from: https://doi.org/10.3390/diagnostics3020271.

[11] Litjens G, Kooi T, Bejnordi BE, Setio AAA, Ciompi F, Ghafoorian M, et al. A survey on deep learning in medical image analysis. Med Image Anal 2017;42:60−88. Available from: https://doi.org/10.1016/j.media.2017.07.005.

[12] Abdeltawab H, Shehata M, Shalaby A, Khalifa F, Mahmoud A, El-Ghar MA, et al. A novel cnn-based cad system for early assessment of transplanted kidney dysfunction. Sci Rep 2019;9(1):5948.

[13] Krizhevsky A, Sutskever I, Hinton GE. Imagenet classification with deep convolutional neural networks. Part of Advances in Neural Information Processing Systems 25 (NIPS 2012) 2012;1097−105.

[14] Herath S, Harandi M, Porikli F. Going deeper into action recognition: a survey. Image Vis Comput 2017;60:4−21.

[15] Petitjean C, Dacher J-N. A review of segmentation methods in short axis cardiac mr images. Med Image Anal 2011;15(2):169−84.

[16] Auger DA, Zhong X, Epstein FH, Meintjes EM, Spottiswoode BS. Semi-automated left ventricular segmentation based on a guide point model approach for 3d cine dense cardiovascular magnetic resonance. J Cardiovasc Magn Reson 2014;16(1):8.

[17] Grosgeorge D, Petitjean C, Dacher J-N, Ruan S. Graph cut segmentation with a statistical shape model in cardiac mri. Comput Vis Image Underst 2013;117(9):1027−35.

[18] Peng P, Lekadir K, Gooya A, Shao L, Petersen SE, Frangi AF. A review of heart chamber segmentation for structural and functional analysis using cardiac magnetic resonance imaging. Magn Reson Mater Phys Biol Med 2016;29(2):155−95.

[19] Ayed IB, Chen H-M, Punithakumar K, Ross I, Li S. Max-ow segmentation of the left ventricle by recovering subject-specic distributions via a bound of the bhattacharyya measure. Med Image Anal 2012;16(1):87−100.

[20] Queiros S, Barbosa D, Heyde B, Morais P, Vilaca JL, Friboulet D, et al. Fast automatic myocardial segmentation in 4d cine CMR datasets. Med Image Anal 2014;18(7):1115−31.

[21] Liu Y, Captur G, Moon JC, Guo S, Yang X, Zhang S, et al. Distance regularized two level sets for segmentation of left and right ventricles from cine- mri. Magn Reson Imaging 2016;34(5):699−706.

[22] Wang L, Pei M, Codella NC, Kochar M, Weinsaft JW, Li J, et al. Left ventricle: fully automated segmentation based on spatiotempo- ral continuity and myocardium information in cine cardiac magnetic resonance imaging (lv-fast). BioMed Res Int 2015;2015:367583.

[23] Ringenberg J, Deo M, Devabhaktuni V, Berenfeld O, Boyers P, Gold J. Fast, accurate, and fully automatic segmentation of the right ventricle in short- axis cardiac mri. Comput Med Imaging Graph 2014;38(3):190−201.

[24] Woo J, Slomka PJ, Kuo C-CJ, Hong B-W. Multiphase segmentation using an implicit dual shape prior: application to detection of left ventricle in cardiac MRI. Comput Vis Image Underst 2013;117(9):1084−94.

[25] Wu Y, Wang Y, Jia Y. Segmentation of the left ventricle in cardiac cine mri using a shape-constrained snake model. Comput Vis Image Underst 2013;117(9):990—1003.

[26] Bai W, Shi W, Ledig C, Rueckert D. Multi-atlas segmentation with aug- mented features for cardiac mr images. Med Image Anal 2015;19(1):98—109.

[27] Tran P.V. A fully convolutional neural network for cardiac segmentation in short-axis MRI, arXiv preprint arXiv:1604.00494.

[28] Poudel RP, Lamata P, Montana G. Recurrent fully convolutional neural networks for multi-slice mri cardiac segmentation. Reconstruction, segmentation, and analysis of medical images. Springer; 2016. p. 83—94.

[29] Tan LK, Liew YM, Lim E, McLaughlin RA. Convolutional neural network regression for short-axis left ventricle segmentation in cardiac cine MR sequences. Med Image Anal 2017;39:78—86.

[30] Oktay O, Ferrante E, Kamnitsas K, Heinrich M, Bai W, Caballero J, et al. Anatomically constrained neural networks (acnns): application to cardiac image enhancement and segmen-tation. IEEE Trans Med Imaging 2018;37(2):384—95.

[31] Zheng Q, Delingette H, Duchateau N, Ayache N. 3-d consistent and robust segmentation of cardiac images by deep learning with spatial propagation. IEEE Trans Med Imaging 2018;37(9):2137—48.

[32] Simonyan K, Zisserman A. Very deep convolutional networks for large-scale image recognition, arXiv preprint arXiv:1409.1556.

[33] Bai W, Sinclair M, Tarroni G, Oktay O, Rajchl M, Vaillant G, et al. Automated cardiovascu- lar magnetic resonance image analysis with fully convolutional networks. J Cardiovasc Magn Reson 2018;20(1):65. Available from: https://doi.org/10.1186/s12968-018-0471-x.

[34] Khened M, Kollerathu VA, Krishnamurthi G. Fully convolutional multi-scale residual densenets for cardiac segmentation and automated cardiac diagnosis using ensemble of classiers. Med Image Anal 2019;51:21—45.

[35] Tao Q, Yan W, Wang Y, Paiman EH, Shamonin DP, Garg P, et al. Deep learning—based method for fully automatic quantification of left ventricle function from cine mr images: a mul-tivendor, multicenter study. Radiology 2019;290(1):81—8.

[36] Long J, Shelhamer E, Darrell T. Fully convolutional networks for semantic segmentation. In: Proceedings of the IEEE conference on computer vision and pattern recognition; 2015, p. 3431—40.

[37] Ronneberger O, Fischer P, Brox T. U-net: convolutional networks for biomedical image segmenta-tion. In: Proceedings of the international conference on medical image computing and computer-assisted intervention, Springer; 2015, p. 234—41.

[38] Szegedy C, Vanhoucke V, Ioe S, Shlens J, Wojna Z. Rethinking the inception architecture for computer vision. In: Proceedings of the IEEE conference on computer vision and pattern recogni-tion; 2016, p. 2818—26.

[39] Kamnitsas K, Bai W, Ferrante E, McDonagh S, Sinclair M, Pawlowski N, et al. Ensembles of multi-ple models and architectures for robust brain tumour segmentation. In: Crimi A, Bakas S, Kuijf H, Menze B, Reyes M, editors. Brainlesion: glioma, multiple sclerosis, stroke and traumatic brain injuries. Springer International Publishing; 2018. p. 450—62.

[40] He K, Zhang X, Ren S, Sun J. Delving deep into rectiers: surpassing human-level performance on imagenet classification. In: Proceedings of the IEEE International conference on computer vision; 2015, p. 1026—34.

[41] Bernard O, Lalande A, Zotti C, Cervenansky F, Yang X, Heng P, et al. Deep learning techniques for automatic MRI cardiac multi-structures segmentation and diagnosis: is the problem solved? IEEE Trans Med Imaging 2018;37(11):2514—25. Available from: https://doi.org/10.1109/TMI.2018.2837502.

[42] Otsu N. A threshold selection method from gray-level histograms. IEEE Trans Syst Man Cyber 1979;9(1):62—6. Available from: https://doi.org/10.1109/TSMC.1979.4310076.

[43] Noh H, Hong S, Han B. Learning deconvolution network for semantic segmentation. In: Proceedings of the IEEE international conference on computer vision; 2015, p. 1520—28.

[44] Bland JM, Altman D. Statistical methods for assessing agreement between two methods of clinical measurement. The Lancet 1986;327(8476):307—10.

[45] Wofilterink JM, Leiner T, Viergever MA, Isgum I. Automatic segmentation and disease classification using cardiac cine mr images. International workshop on statistical atlases and computational models of the heart. Springer; 2017. p. 101—10.

[46] Sardanelli F, Quarenghi M, Di Leo G, Boccaccini L, Schiavi A. Segmentation of cardiac cine mr images of left and right ventricles: interactive semiautomated methods and manual contouring by two readers with different education and experience. J Magn Reson Imaging 2008;27(4):785—92.

[47] Suinesiaputra A, Sanghvi MM, Aung N, Paiva JM, Zemrak F, Fung K, et al. Fully-automated left ventricular mass and volume mri analysis in the uk biobank population cohort: evaluation of initial results. Int J Cardiovasc Imaging 2018;34(2):281—91. Available from: https://doi.org/10.1007/s10554-017-1225-9.

[48] Grinias E, Tziritas G. Fast fully-automatic cardiac segmentation in mri using mrf model optimization, substructures tracking and b-spline smoothing. International workshop on statistical atlases and computational models of the heart. Springer; 2017. p. 91—100.

[49] Hammouda K, Khalifa F, Abdeltawab H, Elnakib A, Giridharan G, Zhu M, et al. A new framework for performing cardiac strain analysis from cine MRI imaging in mice. Sci Rep 2020;10(1):1—15.

[50] Abdeltawab H, Khalifa F, Hammouda K, Miller JM, Meki MM, Ou Q, et al. Artificial intelligence based framework to quantify the cardiomyocyte structural integrity in heart slices. Cardiovasc Eng Technol 2021;1—11.

[51] Khalifa F, Beache GM, Elnakib A, Sliman H, Gimel'farb G, Welch KC, et al. A new shape-based framework for the left ventricle wall segmentation from cardiac first-pass perfusion MRI. In Proceedings of IEEE International Symposium on Biomedical Imaging: From Nano to Macro, (ISBI'13), San Francisco, CA, April 7—11; 2013, p. 41—44.

[52] Khalifa F, Beache GM, Elnakib A, Sliman H, Gimel'farb G, Welch KC, et al. A new nonrigid registration framework for improved visualization of transmural perfusion gradients on cardiac first—pass perfusion MRI. In: Proceedings of IEEE International Symposium on Biomedical Imaging: From Nano to Macro, (ISBI'12), Barcelona, Spain, May 2—5; 2012, p. 828—31.

[53] Khalifa F, Beache GM, Firjani A, Welch KC, Gimel'farb G, and El-Baz A. A new nonrigid registration approach for motion correction of cardiac first-pass perfusion MRI. In: Proceedings of IEEE International Conference on Image Processing, (ICIP'12), Lake Buena Vista, Florida, September 30—October 3; 2012, p. 1665—8.

[54] Khalifa F, Beache GM, Gimel'farb G, and El-Baz A. A novel CAD system for analyzing cardiac first-pass MR images. In: Proceedings of IAPR International Conference on Pattern Recognition (ICPR'12), Tsukuba Science City, Japan, November 11—15; 2012, p. 77—80.

[55] Khalifa F, Beache GM, Gimel'farb G, and El-Baz A. A novel approach for accurate estimation of left ventricle global indexes from short-axis cine MRI, In: Proceedings of IEEE International Conference on Image Processing, (ICIP'11), Brussels, Belgium, September 11—14; 2011, p. 2645—49.

[56] Khalifa F, Beache GM, Gimel'farb G, Giridharan GA, El-Baz A. A new image-based framework for analyzing cine images. In: El-Baz A, Acharya UR, Mirmedhdi M, Suri JS, editors. Handbook of multi modality state-of-the-art medical image segmentation and registration methodologies, 2. New York: Springer; 2011. p. 69—98. ch. 3.

[57] Khalifa F, Beache GM, Gimel'farb G, Giridharan GA, El-Baz A. Accurate automatic analysis of cardiac cine images. IEEE Trans Biomed Eng 2012;59(2):445—55.

[58] Khalifa F, Beache GM, Nitzken M, Gimel'farb G, Giridharan GA, and El-Baz A. Automatic analysis of left ventricle wall thickness using short-axis cine CMR images. In: Proceedings of IEEE International Symposium on Biomedical Imaging: From Nano to Macro, (ISBI'11), Chicago, Illinois, March 30—April 2; 2011, p. 1306—9.

[59] Nitzken M, Beache G, Elnakib A, Khalifa F, Gimel'farb G, and El-Baz A. Accurate modeling of tagged CMR 3D image appearance characteristics to improve cardiac cycle strain estimation. In: 2012 19th IEEE International Conference on Image Processing (ICIP), Orlando, Florida, USA: IEEE, Sep; 2012, p. 521—4.

[60] Nitzken M, Beache G, Elnakib A, Khalifa F, Gimel'farb G, and El-Baz A. Improving full-cardiac cycle strain estimation from tagged cmr by accurate modeling of 3D image appearance characteristics. In: 2012 9th IEEE International Symposium on Biomedical Imaging (ISBI), Barcelona, Spain: IEEE, May; 2012, p. 462–5, (Selected for oral presentation).

[61] Nitzken MJ, El-Baz AS, Beache GM. Markov-gibbs random field model for improved full-cardiac cycle strain estimation from tagged cmr. J Cardiovasc Magn Reson 2012;14(1):1–2.

[62] Sliman H, Elnakib A, Beache G, Elmaghraby A, El-Baz A. Assessment of myocardial function from cine cardiac MRI using a novel 4D tracking approach. J Comput Sci Syst Biol 2014;7:169–73.

[63] Sliman H, Elnakib A, Beache GM, Soliman A, Khalifa F, Gimel'farb G, et al. A novel 4D PDE-based approach for accurate assessment of myocardium function using cine cardiac magnetic resonance images. In: Proceedings of IEEE International Conference on Image Processing (ICIP'14), Paris, France, October 27–30; 2014, p. 3537–41.

[64] Sliman H, Khalifa F, Elnakib A, Beache GM, Elmaghraby A, and El-Baz A. A new segmentation-based tracking framework for extracting the left ventricle cavity from cine cardiac MRI. In: Proceedings of IEEE International Conference on Image Processing, (ICIP'13), Melbourne, Australia, September 15–18; 2013, p. 685–9.

[65] Sliman H, Khalifa F, Elnakib A, Soliman A, Beache GM, Elmaghraby A, et al. Myocardial borders segmentation from cine MR images using bi-directional coupled parametric deformable models. Med Phys 2013;40(9):1–13.

[66] Sliman H, Khalifa F, Elnakib A, Soliman A, Beache GM, Gimel'farb G, et al. Accurate segmentation framework for the left ventricle wall from cardiac cine MRI. In: Proceedings of International Symposium on Computational Models for Life Science, (CMLS'13), 1559, Sydney, Australia, November 27–29; 2013, p. 287–96.

[67] Abdeltawab H, Khalifa F, Taher F, Alghamdi NS, Ghazal M, Beache G, et al. A deep learning-based approach for automatic segmentation and quantification of the left ventricle from cardiac cine mr images. Comput Med Imaging Graph 2020;81:101717.

[68] Abdeltawab H, Khalifa F, Taher F, Beache G, Mohamed T, Elmaghraby A, et al. Automatic segmentation and functional assessment of the left ventricle using u-net fully convolutional network. In: 2019 IEEE International Conference on Imaging Systems and Techniques (IST). IEEE; 2019, p. 1–6.

[69] Abdeltawab H, Shehata M, Shalaby A, Khalifa F, Mahmoud A, El-Ghar MA, et al. A novel cnn-based cad system for early assessment of transplanted kidney dysfunction. Sci Rep 2019;9(1):5948.

[70] Reda I, Ghazal M, Shalaby A, Elmogy M, AbouEl-Fetouh A, Ayinde BO, et al. A novel adcs-based cnn classification system for precise diagnosis of prostate cancer. In: 2018 24th International Conference on Pattern Recognition (ICPR). IEEE; 2018, p. 3923–28.

[71] Reda I, Khalil A, Elmogy M, Abou El-Fetouh A, Shalaby A, Abou El-Ghar M, et al. Deep learning role in early diagnosis of prostate cancer. Technol Cancer Res Treat 2018;17 1533034618775530.

[72] Reda I, Ayinde BO, Elmogy M, Shalaby A, El-Melegy M, El-Ghar MA, et al. A new cnn-based system for early diagnosis of prostate cancer. In: IEEE 2018 15th International Symposium on Biomedical Imaging (ISBI 2018). IEEE; 2018, p. 207–10.

[73] Ayyad SM, Badawy MA, Shehata M, Alksas A, Mahmoud A, Abou El-Ghar M, et al. A new framework for precise identification of prostatic adenocarcinoma Sensors 2022;22:5[Online]. Available. Available from: https://www.mdpi.com/1424-8220/22/5/1848.

[74] Hammouda K, Khalifa F, El-Melegy M, Ghazal M, Darwish HE, El-Ghar MA, et al. A deep learning pipeline for grade groups classification using digitized prostate biopsy specimens. Sensors 2021;21(20):6708.

[75] Abdeltawab HA, Khalifa FA, Ghazal MA, Cheng L, El-Baz AS, Gondim DD. A deep learning framework for automated classification of histopathological kidney whole-slide images. J Pathol Inform 2022;13:100093.

[76] Abdeltawab H, Khalifa F, Ghazal M, Cheng L, Gondim D, El-Baz A. A pyramidal deep learning pipeline for kidney whole-slide histology images classification. Sci Rep 2021;11(1):1–9.

[77] Shehata M, Shalaby A, Switala AE, El-Baz M, Ghazal M, Fraiwan L, et al. A multimodal computer-aided diagnostic system for precise identification of renal allograft rejection: preliminary results. Med Phys 2020;47(6):2427–40.

[78] Shehata M, Khalifa F, Soliman A, Ghazal M, Taher F, Abou El-Ghar M, et al. Computer-aided diagnostic system for early detection of acute renal transplant rejection using diffusion-weighted MRI. IEEE Trans Biomed Eng 2018;66(2):539−52.

[79] Hollis E, Shehata M, Abou El-Ghar M, Ghazal M, El-Diasty T, Merchant M, et al. Statistical analysis of adcs and clinical biomarkers in detecting acute renal transplant rejection. Br J Radiol 2017;90 (1080):20170125.

[80] Shehata M, Alksas A, Abouelkheir RT, Elmahdy A, Shaffie A, Soliman A, et al. A comprehensive computer-assisted diagnosis system for early assessment of renal cancer tumors. Sensors 2021;21(14):4928.

[81] Khalifa F, Beache GM, El-Ghar MA, El-Diasty T, Gimel'farb G, Kong M, et al. Dynamic contrast-enhanced MRI- based early detection of acute renal transplant rejection. IEEE Trans Med Imaging 2013;32(10):1910−27.

[82] Khalifa F, El-Ghar MA, Abdollahi B, Frieboes H, El-Diasty T, El-Baz A. A comprehensive non-invasive framework for automated evaluation of acute renal transplant rejection using DCE-MRI. NMR Biomed 2013;26(11):1460−70.

[83] Khalifa F, Elnakib A, Beache GM, Gimel'farb G, El-Ghar MA, Sokhadze G, et al. 3D kidney segmentation from CT images using a level set approach guided by a novel stochastic speed function. In: Proceedings of International Conference Medical Image Computing and Computer-Assisted Intervention, (MICCAI'11), Toronto, Canada, September 18−22; 2011, p. 587−94.

[84] Shehata M, Khalifa F, Hollis E, Soliman A, Hosseini-Asl E, El-Ghar MA, et al. A new non-invasive approach for early classification of renal rejection types using diffusion-weighted MRI. In: 2016 IEEE International Conference on Image Processing (ICIP). IEEE; 2016, p. 136−40.

[85] Khalifa F, Soliman A, Takieldeen A, Shehata M, Mostapha M, Shaffie A, et al. Kidney segmentation from CT images using a 3D NMF-guided active contour model. In: 2016 IEEE 13th International Symposium on Biomedical Imaging (ISBI). IEEE; 2016, p. 432−35.

[86] Shehata M, Khalifa F, Soliman A, Takieldeen A, El-Ghar MA, Shaffie A, et al. 3D diffusion mri-based cad system for early diagnosis of acute renal rejection. In: 2016 IEEE 13th International Symposium on Biomedical Imaging (ISBI). IEEE; 2016, p. 1177−80.

[87] Shehata M, Khalifa F, Soliman A, Alrefai R, El-Ghar MA, Dwyer AC, et al. A level set-based framework for 3d kidney segmentation from diffusion MR images. In: 2015 IEEE International Conference on Image Processing (ICIP). IEEE; 2015, p. 4441−5.

[88] Shehata M, Khalifa F, Soliman A, El-Ghar MA, Dwyer AC, Gimel'farb G, et al. A promising non-invasive cad system for kidney function assessment. In: International Conference on Medical Image Computing and Computer-Assisted Intervention. Springer; 2016, p. 613−21.

[89] Khalifa F, Soliman A, Elmaghraby A, Gimel'farb G, El-Baz A. 3d kidney segmentation from abdominal images using spatial-appearance models. Comput Math Methods Med 2017;2017:1−10.

[90] Hollis E, Shehata M, Khalifa F, El-Ghar MA, El-Diasty T, El-Baz A. Towards non-invasive diagnostic techniques for early detection of acute renal transplant rejection: a review. Egypt J Radiol Nucl Med 2016;48(1):257−69.

[91] Shehata M, Khalifa F, Soliman A, El-Ghar MA, Dwyer AC, and El-Baz A. Assessment of renal transplant using image and clinical-based biomarkers. In: Proceedings of 13th Annual Scientific Meeting of American Society for Diagnostics and Interventional Nephrology (ASDIN'17), New Orleans, LA, USA, February 10−12; 2017.

[92] Shehata M, Khalifa F, Soliman A, El-Ghar MA, Dwyer AC, and El-Baz A. Early assessment of acute renal rejection. In: Proceedings of 12th Annual Scientific Meeting of American Society for Diagnostics and Interventional Nephrology (ASDIN'16), Pheonix, AZ, USA, February 19−21; 2016.

[93] Eltanboly A, Ghazal M, Hajjdiab H, Shalaby A, Switala A, Mahmoud A, et al. Level sets-based image segmentation approach using statistical shape priors. Appl Math Comput 2019;340:164−79.

[94] Shehata M, Mahmoud A, Soliman A, Khalifa F, Ghazal M, El-Ghar MA, et al. 3d kidney segmentation from abdominal diffusion mri using an appearance-guided deformable boundary. PLoS One 2018;13(7):e0200082.

[95] Sharafeldeen A, Elsharkawy M, Alghamdi NS, Soliman A, El-Baz A. Precise segmentation of covid-19 infected lung from ct images based on adaptive first-order appearance model with morphological/anatomical constraints. Sensors 2021;21(16):5482.

[96] Elsharkawy M, Sharafeldeen A, Taher F, Shalaby A, Soliman A, Mahmoud A, et al. Early assessment of lung function in coronavirus patients using invariant markers from chest x-rays images. Sci Rep 2021;11(1):1−11.

[97] Abdollahi B, Civelek AC, Li X-F, Suri J, El-Baz A. PET/CT nodule segmentation and diagnosis: a survey. In: Saba L, Suri JS, editors. Multi detector CT imaging. Taylor, Francis; 2014. p. 639−51. ch. 30.

[98] Abdollahi B, El-Baz A, and Amini A.A. A multi-scale non-linear vessel enhancement technique. In: 2011 Annual International Conference of the IEEE Engineering in Medicine and Biology Society, EMBC. IEEE; 2011, p. 3925−9.

[99] Abdollahi B, Soliman A, Civelek A, Li X.-F., Gimel'farb G, and El-Baz A. A novel gaussian scale space-based joint MGRF framework for precise lung segmentation. In: Proceedings of IEEE International Conference on Image Processing, (ICIP'12). IEEE; 2012, p. 2029−32.

[100] Abdollahi B, Soliman A, Civelek A, Li X-F, Gimel'farb G, El-Baz A. A novel 3D joint MGRF framework for precise lung segmentation. Machine learning in medical imaging. Springer; 2012. p. 86−93.

[101] Ali AM, El-Baz AS, and Farag A.A. A novel framework for accurate lung segmentation using graph cuts. In: Proceedings of IEEE International Symposium on Biomedical Imaging: From Nano to Macro, (ISBI'07). IEEE; 2007, p. 908−11.

[102] El-Baz A, Beache GM, Gimel'farb G, Suzuki K, Okada K. Lung imaging data analysis. Int J Biomed Imaging 2013;2013:1−2.

[103] El-Baz A, Beache GM, Gimel'farb G, Suzuki K, Okada K, Elnakib A, et al. Computer-aided diagnosis systems for lung cancer: challenges and methodologies. Int J Biomed Imaging 2013;2013:1−46.

[104] El-Baz A, Elnakib A, Abou El-Ghar M, Gimel'farb G, Falk R, Farag A. Automatic detection of 2D and 3D lung nodules in chest spiral CT scans. Int J Biomed Imaging 2013;2013:1−11.

[105] El-Baz A, Farag AA, Falk R, La Rocca R. A unified approach for detection, visualization, and identification of lung abnormalities in chest spiral CT scans. International Congress Series, 1256. Elsevier; 2003. p. 998−1004.

[106] El-Baz A, Farag AA, Falk R, and La Rocca R. Detection, visualization and identification of lung abnormalities in chest spiral CT scan: Phase-I. In: Proceedings of International conference on Biomedical Engineering, Cairo, Egypt, 12, 1; 2002.

[107] El-Baz A, Farag A, Gimel'farb G, Falk R, El-Ghar MA, and Eldiasty T. A framework for automatic segmentation of lung nodules from low dose chest CT scans. In: Proceedings of International Conference on Pattern Recognition, (ICPR'06), 3. IEEE; 2006, p. 611−4.

[108] El-Baz A, Farag A, Gimel'farb G, Falk R, El-Ghar MA. A novel level set-based computer-aided detection system for automatic detection of lung nodules in low dose chest computed tomography scans. Lung Imaging and Computer Aided Diagnosis, 10. CRC Press; 2011.

[109] El-Baz A, Gimel'farb G, Abou El-Ghar M, and Falk R. Appearance-based diagnostic system for early assessment of malignant lung nodules. In: Proceedings of IEEE International Conference on Image Processing, (ICIP'12). IEEE; 2012, p. 533−6.

[110] El-Baz A, Gimel'farb G, Falk R. A novel 3D framework for automatic lung segmentation from low dose CT images. In: El-Baz A, Suri JS, editors. Lung imaging and computer aided diagnosis. Taylor, Francis; 2011. p. 1−16. ch. 1.

[111] El-Baz A, Gimel'farb G, Falk R, and El-Ghar M. Appearance analysis for diagnosing malignant lung nodules. In: Proceedings of IEEE International Symposium on Biomedical Imaging: From Nano to Macro (ISBI'10). IEEE; 2010, p. 193−6.

[112] El-Baz A, Gimel'farb G, Falk R, El-Ghar MA. A novel level set-based CAD system for automatic detection of lung nodules in low dose chest CT scans. In: El-Baz A, Suri JS, editors. Lung imaging and computer aided diagnosis, 1. Taylor, Francis; 2011. p. 221−38. ch. 10.

[113] El-Baz A, Gimel'farb G, Falk R, and El-Ghar M.A. A new approach for automatic analysis of 3D low dose CT images for accurate monitoring the detected lung nodules. In: Proceedings of International Conference on Pattern Recognition, (ICPR'08). IEEE; 2008, p. 1−4.

[114] El-Baz A, Gimel'farb G, Falk R, and El-Ghar M.A. A novel approach for automatic follow-up of detected lung nodules. In: Proceedings of IEEE International Conference on Image Processing, (ICIP'07), 5. IEEE; 2007, p. V−501.

[115] El-Baz A, Gimel'farb G, Falk R, and El-Ghar M.A. A new CAD system for early diagnosis of detected lung nodules. In: 2007 IEEE International Conference on Image Processing (ICIP 2007). 2. IEEE; 2007, p. II−461.

[116] El-Baz A, Gimel'farb G, Falk R, El-Ghar MA, and Refaie H. Promising results for early diagnosis of lung cancer. In: Proceedings of IEEE International Symposium on Biomedical Imaging: From Nano to Macro, (ISBI'08). IEEE; 2008, p. 1151−4.

[117] El-Baz A, Gimel'farb GL, Falk R, Abou El-Ghar M, Holland T, and Shaffer T. A new stochastic framework for accurate lung segmentation. In: Proceedings of Medical Image Computing and Computer-Assisted Intervention (MICCAI'08); 2008, p. 322−30.

[118] El-Baz A, Gimel'farb GL, Falk R, Heredis D, and Abou El-Ghar M. A novel approach for accurate estimation of the growth rate of the detected lung nodules. In: Proceedings of International Workshop on Pulmonary Image Analysis; 2008, p. 33−42.

[119] El-Baz A, Gimel'farb GL, Falk R, Holland T, and Shaffer T. A framework for unsupervised segmentation of lung tissues from low dose computed tomography images. In: Proceedings of British Machine Vision (BMVC'08); 2008, p. 1−10.

[120] El-Baz A, Gimel'farb G, Falk R, El-Ghar MA. 3D MGRF-based appearance modeling for robust segmentation of pulmonary nodules in 3D LDCT chest images chapter In: El-Baz A, Suri JS, editors. Lung imaging and computer aided diagnosis. Taylor, Francis; 2011. p. 51−63.

[121] El-Baz A, Gimel'farb G, Falk R, El-Ghar MA. Automatic analysis of 3D low dose CT images for early diagnosis of lung cancer. Pattern Recognit 2009;42(6):1041−51.

[122] El-Baz A, Gimel'farb G, Falk R, El-Ghar MA, Rainey S, Heredia D, et al. Toward early diagnosis of lung cancer. In: Proceedings of Medical Image Computing and Computer-Assisted Intervention (MICCAI'09). Springer; 2009, p. 682−9.

[123] El-Baz A, Gimel'farb G, Falk R, El-Ghar MA, Suri J. Appearance analysis for the early assessment of detected lung nodules chapter In: El-Baz A, Suri JS, editors. Lung imaging and computer aided diagnosis. Taylor, Francis; 2011. p. 395−404.

[124] El-Baz A, Khalifa F, Elnakib A, Nitkzen M, Soliman A, McClure P, et al. A novel approach for global lung registration using 3D Markov Gibbs appearance model. In: Proceedings of International Conference Medical Image Computing and Computer-Assisted Intervention (MICCAI'12), Nice, France, October 1−5; 2012, p. 114−21.

[125] El-Baz A, Nitzken M, Elnakib A, Khalifa F, Gimel'farb G, Falk R, et al. 3D shape analysis for early diagnosis of malignant lung nodules. In: Proceedings of International Conference Medical Image Computing and Computer-Assisted Intervention (MICCAI'11), Toronto, Canada, September 18−22; 2011, p. 175−82.

[126] El-Baz A, Nitzken M, Gimel'farb G, Van Bogaert E, Falk R, El-Ghar MA, et al. Three-dimensional shape analysis using spherical harmonics for early assessment of detected lung nodules chapter In: El-Baz A, Suri JS, editors. Lung imaging and computer aided diagnosis. Taylor, Francis; 2011. p. 421−38.

[127] El-Baz A, Nitzken M, Khalifa F, Elnakib A, Gimel'farb G, Falk R, et al. 3D shape analysis for early diagnosis of malignant lung nodules. In: Proceedings of International Conference on Information Processing in Medical Imaging (IPMI'11), Monastery Irsee, Germany (Bavaria), July 3−8; 2011, p. 772−83.

[128] El-Baz A, Nitzken M, Vanbogaert E, Gimel'farb G, Falk R, and Abo El-GharM. A novel shape-based diagnostic approach for early diagnosis of lung nodules. In: 2011 IEEE International Symposium on Biomedical Imaging: From Nano to Macro. IEEE; 2011, p. 137−40.

[129] El-Baz A, Sethu P, Gimel'farb G, Khalifa F, Elnakib A, Falk R, et al. Elastic phantoms generated by microfluidics technology: validation of an imaged-based approach for accurate measurement of the growth rate of lung nodules. Biotechnol J 2011;6(2):195−203.

[130] El-Baz A, Sethu P, Gimel'farb G, Khalifa F, Elnakib A, Falk R, et al. A new validation approach for the growth rate measurement using elastic phantoms generated by state-of-the-art microfluidics

technology. In: Proceedings of IEEE International Conference on Image Processing (ICIP'10), Hong Kong, September 26–29; 2010, p. 4381–83.

[131] El-Baz A, Sethu P, Gimel'farb G, Khalifa F, Elnakib A, Falk R, et al. Validation of a new imaged-based approach for the accurate estimating of the growth rate of detected lung nodules using real CT images and elastic phantoms generated by state-of-the-art microfluidics technology. In: El-Baz A, Suri JS, editors. Handbook of lung imaging and computer aided diagnosis, 1. New York: Taylor & Francis; 2011. p. 405–20. ch. 18.

[132] El-Baz A, Soliman A, McClure P, Gimel'farb G, El-Ghar MA, and Falk R. Early assessment of malignant lung nodules based on the spatial analysis of detected lung nodules. In: Proceedings of IEEE International Symposium on Biomedical Imaging: From Nano to Macro (ISBI'12). IEEE; 2012, p. 1463–66.

[133] El-Baz A, Yuksel SE, Elshazly S, and Farag A.A. Non-rigid registration techniques for automatic follow-up of lung nodules. In: Proceedings of Computer Assisted Radiology and Surgery (CARS'05), 1281. Elsevier; 2005, p. 1115–20.

[134] El-Baz AS, Suri JS. Lung imaging and computer aided diagnosis. CRC Press; 2011.

[135] Soliman A, Khalifa F, Dunlap N, Wang B, El-Ghar M, and El-Baz A. An iso-surfaces based local deformation handling framework of lung tissues. In: 2016 IEEE 13th International Symposium on Biomedical Imaging (ISBI). IEEE; 2016, p. 1253–59.

[136] Soliman A, Khalifa F, Shaffie A, Dunlap N, Wang B, Elmaghraby A, et al. Detection of lung injury using 4d-ct chest images. In: 2016 IEEE 13th International Symposium on Biomedical Imaging (ISBI). IEEE; 2016, p. 1274–77.

[137] SolimanA., Khalifa F, Shaffie A, Dunlap N, Wang B, Elmaghraby A, et al. A comprehensive framework for early assessment of lung injury. In: 2017 IEEE International Conference on Image Processing (ICIP). IEEE; 2017, p. 3275–79.

[138] Shaffie A, Soliman A, Ghazal M, Taher F, Dunlap N, Wang B, et al. A new framework for incorporating appearance and shape features of lung nodules for precise diagnosis of lung cancer. In: 2017 IEEE International Conference on Image Processing (ICIP). IEEE; 2017, p. 1372–76.

[139] Soliman A, Khalifa F, Shaffie A, Liu N, Dunlap N, Wang B, et al. Image-based cad system for accurate identification of lung injury. In: 2016 IEEE International Conference on Image Processing (ICIP). IEEE; 2016, p. 121–5.

[140] Soliman A, Shaffie A, Ghazal M, Gimel'farb G, Keynton R, and El-Baz A. A novel cnn segmentation framework based on using new shape and appearance features. In: 2018 25th IEEE International Conference on Image Processing (ICIP). IEEE; 2018, p. 3488–92.

[141] Shaffie A, Soliman A, Khalifeh HA, Ghazal M, Taher F, Keynton R, et al. On the integration of ct- derived features for accurate detection of lung cancer. In: 2018 IEEE International Symposium on Signal Processing and Information Technology (ISSPIT). IEEE; 2018, p. 435–40.

[142] Shaffie A, Soliman A, Khalifeh HA, Ghazal M, Taher F, Elmaghraby A, et al. Radiomic-based framework for early diagnosis of lung cancer. In 2019 IEEE 16th International Symposium on Biomedical Imaging (ISBI 2019). IEEE; 2019, p. 1293–7.

[143] Shaffie A, Soliman A, Ghazal M, Taher F, Dunlap N, Wang B, et al. A novel autoencoder-based diagnostic system for early assessment of lung cancer. In: 2018 25th IEEE International Conference on Image Processing (ICIP). IEEE; 2018, p. 1393–97.

[144] Shaffie A, Soliman A, Fraiwan L, Ghazal M, Taher F, Dunlap N, et al. A generalized deep learning-based diagnostic system for early diagnosis of various types of pulmonary nodules. Technol Cancer Res Treat 2018;17 pp. 1533033818798800.

[145] Abdel Razek AAK, Alksas A, Shehata M, AbdelKhalek A, Abdel Baky K, El-Baz A, et al. Clinical applications of artificial intelligence and radiomics in neuro-oncology imaging. Insights Imaging 2021;12(1):1–17.

[146] ElNakieb Y, Ali MT, Dekhil O, Khalefa ME, Soliman A, Shalaby A, et al. Towards accurate personalized autism diagnosis using different imaging modalities: SMRI, FMRI, and DTI. In: 2018 IEEE International Symposium on Signal Processing and Information Technology (ISSPIT). IEEE; 2018, p. 447–52.

[147] ElNakieb Y, Soliman A, Mahmoud A, Dekhil O, Shalaby A, Ghazal M, et al. Autism spectrum disorder diagnosis framework using diffusion tensor imaging. In: 2019 IEEE International Conference on Imaging Systems and Techniques (IST). IEEE; 2019, p. 1–5.

[148] Haweel R, Dekhil O, Shalaby A, Mahmoud A, Ghazal M, Keynton R, et al. A machine learning approach for grading autism severity levels using task-based functional MRI. In: 2019 IEEE International Conference on Imaging Systems and Techniques (IST). IEEE; 2019, p. 1–5.

[149] Dekhil O, Ali M, Haweel R, Elnakib Y, Ghazal M, Hajjdiab H, et al. A comprehensive framework for differentiating autism spectrum disorder from neurotypicals by fusing structural mri and resting state functional mri. Seminars in pediatric neurology. Elsevier; 2020. p. 100805.

[150] Haweel R, Dekhil O, Shalaby A, Mahmoud A, Ghazal M, Khalil A, et al. A novel framework for grading autism severity using task-based FMRI. In: 2020 IEEE 17th International Symposium on Biomedical Imaging (ISBI). IEEE; 2020, p. 1404–07.

[151] El-Baz A, Elnakib A, Khalifa F, El-Ghar MA, McClure P, Soliman A, et al. Precise segmentation of 3-D magnetic resonance angiography. IEEE Trans Biomed Eng 2012;59(7):2019–29.

[152] El-Baz A, Farag A, Elnakib A, Casanova MF, Gimel'farb G, Switala AE, et al. Accurate automated detection of autism related corpus callosum abnormalities. J Med Syst 2011;35(5):929–39.

[153] El-Baz A, Gimel'farb G, Falk R, El-Ghar MA, Kumar V, Heredia D. A novel 3D joint Markov-gibbs model for extracting blood vessels from PC–mra images. Medical image computing and computer-assisted intervention–MICCAI 2009, 5762. Springer; 2009. p. 943–50.

[154] Elnakib A, El-Baz A, Casanova MF, Gimel'farb G, and Switala A.E. Image-based detection of corpus callosum variability for more accurate discrimination between dyslexic and normal brains. In: Proceedings of IEEE International Symposium on Biomedical Imaging: From Nano to Macro (ISBI'2010). IEEE; 2010, p. 109–12.

[155] Elnakib A, Casanova MF, Gimel'farb G, Switala AE, and El-Baz A. Autism diagnostics by centerline-based shape analysis of the corpus callosum. In: Proceedings of IEEE International Symposium on Biomedical Imaging: From Nano to Macro (ISBI'2011). IEEE; 2011, p. 1843–46.

[156] Elnakib A, Nitzken M, Casanova M, Park H, Gimel'farb G, and El-BazA. Quantification of age-related brain cortex change using 3D shape analysis. In: 2012 21st International Conference on Pattern Recognition (ICPR). IEEE; 2012, pp. 41–4.

[157] Nitzken M, Casanova M, Gimel'farb G, Elnakib A, Khalifa F, Switala A, et al. 3D shape analysis of the brain cortex with application to dyslexia. In: 2011 18th IEEE International Conference on Image Processing (ICIP). Brussels, Belgium: IEEE, Sep; 2011, p. 2657–60, (Selected for oral presentation. Oral acceptance rate is 10 percent and the overall acceptance rate is 35 percent).

[158] El-Gamal F.E.-Z.A., Elmogy MM, Ghazal M, Atwan A, Barnes GN, Casanova MF, et al. A novel cad system for local and global early diagnosis of alzheimer's disease based on pib-pet scans. In: 2017 IEEE International Conference on Image Processing (ICIP). IEEE; 2017, p. 3270–74.

[159] Ismail MM, Keynton RS, Mostapha MM, ElTanboly AH, Casanova MF, Gimel'farb GL, et al. Studying autism spectrum disorder with structural and diffusion magnetic resonance imaging: a survey. Front Hum Neurosci 2016;10:211.

[160] Alansary A, Ismail M, Soliman A, Khalifa F, Nitzken M, Elnakib A, et al. Infant brain extraction in t1-weighted mr images using bet and refinement using lcdg and mgrf models. IEEE J Biomed Health Inform 2016;20(3):925–35.

[161] Asl EH, Ghazal M, Mahmoud A, Aslantas A, Shalaby A, Casanova M, et al. Alzheimer's disease diagnostics by a 3d deeply supervised adaptable convolutional network. Front Biosci (Landmark edition) 2018;23:584–96.

[162] Dekhil O, Ali M, El-Nakieb Y, Shalaby A, Soliman A, Switala A, et al. A personalized autism diagnosis cad system using a fusion of structural mri and resting-state functional mri data Front Psychiatry 2019;10:392[Online]. Available. Available from: https://www.frontiersin.org/article/10.3389/fpsyt.2019.00392.

[163] Dekhil O, Shalaby A, Soliman A, Mahmoud A, Kong M, Barnes G, et al. Identifying brain areas correlated with ados raw scores by studying altered dynamic functional connectivity patterns. Med Image Anal 2021;68:101899.

[164] Elnakieb YA, Ali MT, Soliman A, Mahmoud AH, Shalaby AM, Alghamdi NS, et al. Computer aided autism diagnosis using diffusion tensor imaging. IEEE Access 2020;8 pp. 191 298–191 308.

[165] Ali MT, Elnakieb YA, Shalaby A, Mahmoud A, Switala A, Ghazal M, et al. Autism classification using smri: a recursive features selection based on sampling from multi-level high dimensional spaces. In: 2021 IEEE 18th International Symposium on Biomedical Imaging (ISBI). IEEE; 2021, p. 267–70.

[166] Ali MT, ElNakieb Y, Elnakib A, Shalaby A, Mahmoud A, Ghazal M, et al. The role of structure mri in diagnosing autism. Diagnostics 2022;12(1):165.

[167] ElNakieb Y, Ali MT, Elnakib A, Shalaby A, Soliman A, Mahmoud A, et al. The role of diffusion tensor MR imaging (dti) of the brain in diagnosing autism spectrum disorder: Promising results. Sensors 2021;21(24):8171.

[168] Mahmoud A, El-Barkouky A, Farag H, Graham J, and Farag A. A non-invasive method for measuring blood flow rate in superficial veins from a single thermal image. In: Proceedings of the IEEE Conference on Computer Vision and Pattern Recognition Workshops; 2013, p. 354–9.

[169] Elsaid N, Saied A, Kandil H, Soliman A, Taher F, Hadi M, et al. Impact of stress and hypertension on the cerebrovasculature. Front Biosci (Landmark edition) 2021;26(12):1643.

[170] Taher F, Kandil H, Gebru Y, Mahmoud A, Shalaby A, El-Mashad S, et al. A novel mra-based framework for segmenting the cerebrovascular system and correlating cerebral vascular changes to mean arterial pressure. Appl Sci 2021;11(9):4022.

[171] Kandil H, Soliman A, Taher F, Ghazal M, Khalil A, Giridharan G, et al. A novel computer- aided diagnosis system for the early detection of hypertension based on cerebrovascular alterations. NeuroImage Clin 2020;25:102107.

[172] Kandil H, Soliman A, Ghazal M, Mahmoud A, Shalaby A, Keynton R, et al. A novel framework for early detection of hypertension using magnetic resonance angiography. Sci Rep 2019;9 (1):1–12.

[173] Gebru Y, Giridharan G, Ghazal M, Mahmoud A, Shalaby A, El-Baz A. Detection of cerebrovascular changes using magnetic resonance angiography. Cardiovascular imaging and image analysis. CRC Press; 2018. p. 1–22.

[174] Mahmoud A, Shalaby A, Taher F, El-Baz M, Suri JS, El-Baz A. Vascular tree segmentation from different image modalities. Cardiovascular imaging and image analysis. CRC Press; 2018. p. 43–70.

[175] Taher F, Mahmoud A, Shalaby A, and El-Baz A. A review on the cerebrovascular segmentation methods. In: 2018 IEEE International Symposium on Signal Processing and Information Technology (ISSPIT). IEEE; 2018, p. 359–64.

[176] Kandil H, Soliman A, Fraiwan L, Shalaby A, Mahmoud A, ElTanboly A, et al. A novel mra framework based on integrated global and local analysis for accurate segmentation of the cerebral vascular system. In: 2018 IEEE 15th International Symposium on Biomedical Imaging (ISBI 2018). IEEE, 2018, pp. 1365–8.

[177] Taher F, Soliman A, Kandil H, Mahmoud A, Shalaby A, Gimel'farb G, et al. Accurate segmentation of cerebrovasculature from tof-mra images using appearance descriptors. IEEE Access 2020;8:96139–49.

[178] Taher F, Soliman A, Kandil H, Mahmoud A, Shalaby A, Gimel'farb G, et al. Precise cerebrovascular segmentation. In: 2020 IEEE International Conference on Image Processing (ICIP). IEEE; 2020, p. 394–7.

[179] Haggag S, Khalifa F, Abdeltawab H, Elnakib A, Sandhu H, Ghazal M, et al. Automated cad system for intermediate uveitis grading using optical coherence tomography images. In: 2022 IEEE 19th International Symposium on Biomedical Imaging (ISBI). IEEE; 2022, p. 1–4.

[180] Yasser I, Khalifa F, Abdeltawab H, Ghazal M, Sandhu HS, El-Baz A. Automated diagnosis of optical coherence tomography angiography (octa) based on machine learning techniques. Sensors 2022;22(6):2342.

[181] Haggag S, Khalifa F, Abdeltawab H, Elnakib A, Ghazal M, Mohamed MA, et al. An automated cad system for accurate grading of uveitis using optical coherence tomography images. Sensors 2021;21(16):5457.

[182] Elsharkawy M, Sharafeldeen A, Soliman A, Khalifa F, Ghazal M, El-Daydamony E, et al. A novel computer-aided diagnostic system for early detection of diabetic retinopathy using 3d-oct higher-order spatial appearance model. Diagnostics 2022;12(2):461.

[183] Elsharkawy M, Elrazzaz M, Ghazal M, Alhalabi M, Soliman A, Mahmoud A, et al. Role of optical coherence tomography imaging in predicting progression of age-related macular disease: a survey. Diagnostics 2021;11(12):2313.

[184] Sandhu HS, Elmogy M, Sharafeldeen AT, Elsharkawy M, El-Adawy N, Eltanboly A, et al. Automated diagnosis of diabetic retinopathy using clinical biomarkers, optical coherence tomography, and optical coherence tomography angiography. Am J Ophthalmol 2020;216:201−6.

[185] Sharafeldeen A, Elsharkawy M, Khalifa F, Soliman A, Ghazal M, AlHalabi M, et al. Precise higher-order reflectivity and morphology models for early diagnosis of diabetic retinopathy using oct images. Sci Rep 2021;11(1):1−16.

[186] Sleman AA, Soliman A, Elsharkawy M, Giridharan G, Ghazal M, Sandhu H, et al. A novel 3d segmentation approach for extracting retinal layers from optical coherence tomography images. Med Phys 2021;48(4):1584−95.

[187] Sleman AA, Soliman A, Ghazal M, Sandhu H, Schaal S, Elmaghraby A, et al. Retinal layers oct scans 3-d segmentation. In 2019 IEEE International Conference on Imaging Systems and Techniques (IST). IEEE; 2019, p. 1−6.

[188] Eladawi N, Elmogy M, Ghazal M, Helmy O, Aboelfetouh A, Riad A, et al. Classification of retinal diseases based on oct images. Front Biosci (Landmark Ed) 2018;23:247−64.

[189] ElTanboly A, Ismail M, Shalaby A, Switala A, El-Baz A, Schaal S, et al. A computer-aided diagnostic system for detecting diabetic retinopathy in optical coherence tomography images. Med Phys 2017;44(3):914−23.

[190] Sandhu HS, El-Baz A, Seddon JM. Progress in automated deep learning for macular degeneration. JAMA ophthalmol 2018;.

[191] Ghazal M, Ali SS, Mahmoud AH, Shalaby AM, El-Baz A. Accurate detection of non-proliferative diabetic retinopathy in optical coherence tomography images using convolutional neural networks. IEEE Access 2020;8 pp. 34 387−34 397.

[192] Hammouda K, Khalifa F, Soliman A, Ghazal M, Abou El-Ghar M, Haddad A, et al. A cnn-based framework for bladder wall segmentation using MRI. In: 2019 Fifth International Conference on Advances in Biomedical Engineering (ICABME). IEEE; 2019, p. 1−4.

[193] Hammouda K, Khalifa F, Soliman A, Ghazal M, Abou El-Ghar M, Haddad A, et al. A deep learning-based approach for accurate segmentation of bladder wall using MR images. In: 2019 IEEE International Conference on Imaging Systems and Techniques (IST). IEEE; 2019, p. 1−6.

[194] Hammouda K, Khalifa F, Soliman A, Abdeltawab H, Ghazal M, Abou El-Ghar M, et al. A 3d cnn with a learnable adaptive shape prior for accurate segmentation of bladder wall using MR images. In: 2020 IEEE 17th International Symposium on Biomedical Imaging (ISBI). IEEE; 2020, p. 935−8.

[195] Hammouda K, Khalifa F, Soliman A, Ghazal M, Abou El-Ghar M, Badawy M, et al. A multiparametric mri-based cad system for accurate diagnosis of bladder cancer staging. Comput Med Imaging Graph 2021;90:101911.

[196] Hammouda K, Khalifa F, Soliman A, Ghazal M, Abou El-Ghar M, Badawy M, et al. A cad system for accurate diagnosis of bladder cancer staging using a multiparametric MRI. In: 2021 IEEE 18th International Symposium on Biomedical Imaging (ISBI). IEEE; 2021, p. 1718−21.

[197] Alksas A, Shehata M, Saleh GA, Shaffie A, Soliman A, Ghazal M, et al. A novel computer-aided diagnostic system for early assessment of hepatocellular carcinoma. In: 2020 25th International Conference on Pattern Recognition (ICPR). IEEE; 2021, p. 10375−82.

[198] Alksas A, Shehata M, Saleh GA, Shaffie A, Soliman A, Ghazal M, et al. A novel computer-aided diagnostic system for accurate detection and grading of liver tumors. Sci Rep 2021;11(1):1−18.

[199] Razek AAKA, Khaled R, Helmy E, Naglah A, AbdelKhalek A, El-Baz A. Artificial intelligence and deep learning of head and neck cancer. Magn Reson Imaging Clin 2022;30(1):81−94.

[200] Sharafeldeen A, Elsharkawy M, Khaled R, Shaffie A, Khalifa F, Soliman A, et al. Texture and shape analysis of diffusion-weighted imaging for thyroid nodules classification using machine learning. Med Phys 2022;49(2):988−99.

[201] Naglah A, Khalifa F, Khaled R, Abdel Razek AAK, Ghazal M, Giridharan G, et al. Novel mri-based cad system for early detection of thyroid cancer using multi-input cnn. Sensors 2021;21 (11):3878.

[202] Naglah A, Khalifa F, Mahmoud A, Ghazal M, Jones P, Murray T, et al. Athlete-customized injury prediction using training load statistical records and machine learning. In: 2018 IEEE International Symposium on Signal Processing and Information Technology (ISSPIT). IEEE; 2018, p. 459—64.

[203] Mahmoud A.H. Utilizing radiation for smart robotic applications using visible, thermal, and polarization images. PhD Dissertation, University of Louisville, 2014.

[204] Mahmoud A, El-Barkouky A, Graham J, and Farag A. Pedestrian detection using mixed partial derivative based his togram of oriented gradients. In: 2014 IEEE International Conference on Image Processing (ICIP). IEEE; 2014, p. 2334—37.

[205] El-Barkouky A, Mahmoud A, Graham J, and Farag A. An interactive educational drawing system using a humanoid robot and light polarization. In: 2013 IEEE International Conference on Image Processing. IEEE; 2013, p. 3407—11.

[206] Mahmoud AH, El-Melegy MT, and Farag A.A. Direct method for shape recovery from polarization and shading. In: 2012 19th IEEE International Conference on Image Processing. IEEE; 2012, p. 1769—72.

[207] Ghazal MA, Mahmoud A, Aslantas A, Soliman A, Shalaby A, Benediktsson JA, et al. Vegetation cover estimation using convolutional neural networks. IEEE Access 2019;7 pp. 132 563—132 576.

[208] Ghazal M, Mahmoud A, Shalaby A, El-Baz A. Automated framework for accurate segmentation of leaf images for plant health assessment. Environ Monit Assess 2019;191(8):491.

[209] Ghazal M, Mahmoud A, Shalaby A, Shaker S, Khelifi A, and El-Baz A. Precise statistical approach for leaf segmentation. In: 2020 IEEE International Conference on Image Processing (ICIP). IEEE; 2020, p. 2985—2989.

CHAPTER 9

Cardiac magnetic resonance imaging of cardiomyopathy

Ahmed Abdel Khalek Abdel Razek, Germeen Albair Ashmalla and Dalia Fahmy
Department of Diagnostic Radiology, Faculty of Medicine, Mansoura University, Mansoura, Egypt

9.1 Introduction

Nonischemic cardiomyopathies (NICM) consists of a large variety of pathologies involving the myocardium, whether primary (confined to the heart) or secondary to a systemic pathology involving the body. CMR provides images of high temporal and spatial temporal resolution to be taken in any desired plane that are not operator dependent and not affected by patient's size and body habitus. Accurate assessment of several chamber and vessel functional parameters can be done. CMR allows repeated and frequent examinations in young patients without fear of ionizing radiation. CMR is not only an initial diagnostic tool, but it provides data with great clinical impact regarding monitoring of therapy response, risk stratification, and prognosis determination.

9.2 Iron overload cardiomyopathy

Systemic iron (SI) overload due to hemosiderosis or transfusion-dependent anemias can lead to dilated or restrictive cardiomyopathy with progressive deterioration of diastolic and systolic function as well as dysrhythmias. Myocardial iron deposition in the form of ferritin and hemosiderin is well visualized on gradient-echo (GRE) images, as low SI at higher Echo time (TE) values. Utilizing GRE images at different TE levels, the absolute myocardial T2* can be calculated. The absolute myocardial T2* has proven to be a more accurate indicator of true myocardial iron content as compared to serum ferritin levels or liver iron (Fig. 9.1), as it can detect myocardial changes before the deterioration of LV ejection fraction. Myocardial T2* <20 Ms is a mark of significant iron deposition while <10 Ms is a mark of advanced iron deposition. A novel segmental T2* approach composed of analysis of different cardiac segments (not only the septum as in the traditional method) has been introduced as a more sensitive technique for measuring iron distribution [1–8].

CMR can monitor therapeutic response to chelation agents and predict clinical outcome as well. The American Heart Association (AHA) Consensus Statement noted

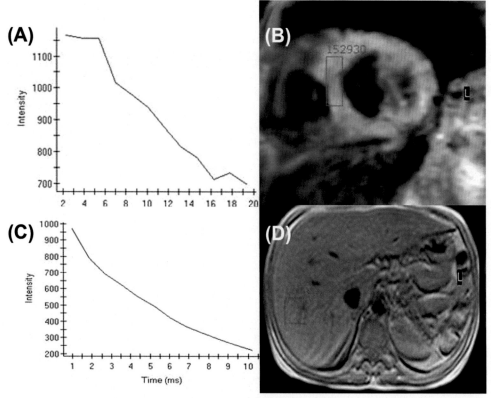

Figure 9.1 *Iron overload*: T2* decay and T2*-weighted image contrast of 10-year-old thalassemia patient: (A) Plot of signal intensity over Echo time for T2* weighted imaging of myocardium in (B): T2* value of myocardium 29.9Ms and MIC0.72 mg/g (no myocardial iron overload). (C) Plot of signal intensity over Echo time for T2* weighted imaging of liver in (D): T2* value of liver 6.5 Ms and LIC4.81 mg/g (light hepatic iron overload).

the crucial diagnostic tool of CMR in the clinical management of patients with iron overload cardiomyopathy. In the UK, there has been a noticeable reduction in mortality from cardiac iron overload in thalassemia patients owing to the widespread use of CMR [1–8].

9.3 Idiopathic dilated cardiomyopathy

Idiopathic dilated cardiomyopathy manifests by dilated left ventricle (LV) with diffuse systolic dysfunction. LGE classically shows a linear midmyocardial septal enhancement denoting fibrosis (Fig. 9.2). A study by McCrohon et al. found this peculiar pattern was noted in 28% of patients, with no enhancement in 59% of patients. On the other hand, a subendocardial pattern of enhancement was detected in 13% of these patients

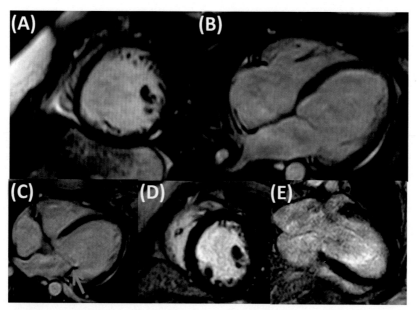

Figure 9.2 *Idiopathic dilated cardiomyopathy in 27-year-old female*: (A) Short-axis stack (end dia-stolic) shows dilated LV. (B, C) Four-chamber slice (end diastolic) shows dilated both ventricles and jet of mitral regurge. (D,E) LGE in short-axis and three-chamber view show no enhancement. *LV*, left ventricle.

despite normal coronary arteries in catheterization [9]. Several studies have shown that the presence of LGE (especially in midwall) is considered a significant risk factor for the development of arrhythmia and even sudden death and superior predictor as com-pared to other parameters such as decreased LVEF (less than 35%) even in asymptom-atic and minimally symptomatic patients [10−12].

9.4 Hypertrophic cardiomyopathy

Hypertrophic cardiomyopathy (HCM) is a one of the genetic heart diseases. It is hall-marked by increased LV wall thickness (end-diastolic LV wall thickness ≥15 mm or the equivalent relative to the body surface area in children) that is not caused by abnormal loading conditions. Yet in family members of a known case of HCM the diagnosis is confirmed with less wall thickness (13−14 mm). HCM is an autosomal dominant trait in up to 60% of adolescents and adults. It shows a variety of phenotypic expression with different progression that ranges from dyspnea and/or syncope to sudden cardiac death (SCD). HCM is marked as the leading cause of SCD in young athletes [11−14].

The phenotypic variability of HCM ranges from minor unnoticeable anomalies to LV remodeling that proceeds to heart failure (HF) similar to restrictive or dilated cardiomyopathy. Asymmetric septal hypertrophy (ASH) is commonly seen in clinical practice (Fig. 9.3); other varieties are apical, midventricular, concentric (Fig. 9.4), spiral, and mass-like. In ASH, there is hypertrophy of the basal septum. CMR detect and measure LVOT flow obstruction, in addition to flow velocity/gradient, which is present in about 70% of HCM with classic increased LV wall thickness. The systolic anterior motion of the mitral valve (SAM) represents the paradoxical movement of the anterior leaflet of mitral valve and/or chordae toward the interventricular septum during systole. MRI is helpful in the early recognition of papillary muscle morphological anomalies; anomalous insertion, double bifid morphology, antero-apical displacement, and hypermobile papillary muscles that may lead to LOV obstruction even before significant myocardial hypertrophy occurs [11–14].

Enhancement in LCE is present in 60% of HCM, and can be attributed to interstitial fibrosis, microfibrillar disarray, or microvascular obstruction. Classically it takes a midmyocardial patchy pattern at the RV insertion points but can involve the rest of

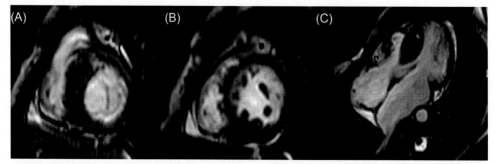

Figure 9.3 *Asymmetric septal HOCM*: (A, B) Short-axis, (C) four-chamber cine SSFP showing septal and infero-septal focal HOCM with systolic motion of the anterior mitral valve leaflet (SAM).

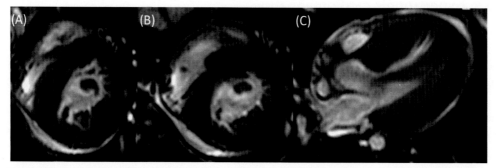

Figure 9.4 *Concentric diffuse HOCM*: (A,B) Short-axis, (C) four-chamber cine SSFP showing diffuse HOCM. (D) Maximum thickness of the interventricular septum (2.4 cm).

the myocardium regardless being hypertrophied or not. Presence of LGE is linked to lethal complications (e.g., malignant arrhythmia), and thus is used as an independent mortality predictor [11–14]. Currently, there is limited data regarding the actual role of CMR in monitoring different therapies of HCM [14].

9.5 Sarcoidosis

Sarcoidosis is a multisystem inflammatory disease. Cardiac involvement can be seen in up to 25% of disease-related mortality. Myocardial thickening and edema can be detected in the acute phase with midmyocardial or subepicardial distribution of LCE, while chronic disease is characterized by absence of edema. Severe end-stage sarcoidosis is manifested by transmural enhancement. LCE in sarcoidosis is a prognostic factor of adverse outcomes, which is stronger than other parameters including LVEF and presenting clinical symptoms. Several small studies found that CMR is effective in steroid therapy monitoring, as steroid therapy was associated with improved functional parameters (LVEF, LV end-diastolic volume index) and diminished LGE. Ise et al. found that treated patients with less extentsive LCE had significantly decreased LVEF and LV EDV. On the contrary, patients who had more extensive LCE had no significant change in LVEF or LV EDV and suffered worse clinical course of the disease [11,14,15].

9.6 Myocarditis

Acute myocarditis is hallmarked with myocardial edema that manifests in CMR as high SI in T2-WI and high values in T2 mapping. It showed enhancement in ECE and LCE with a mid- or subepicardial pattern. Other different enhancement patterns are noted in myocarditis according to the cause. Parvovirus B19 is characterized by basal inferolateral midmyocardial/subepicardial enhancement that resolves with no residual injury. On the contrary, human herpesvirus-6 showed septal linear midmyocardial enhancement that rapidly ends with heart failure [14]. Similar to other cardiomyopathies, the presence and persistence of LCE denotes the development of fibrosis and irreversible myocardial injury (Fig. 9.5).

The visualization of LCE in the ventricular septum was considered as the most reliable indicator for the development of chronic ventricular dysfunction/dilatation, while the absence of LCE was linked to much better clinical outcome [16]. Sarcoidosis was thought to be an acute, self-limiting disease, yet abnormal findings were still present in CMR after recovery from the acute phase. It is recommended to perform CMR 4 w post the initial symptoms of disease to recognize the complicated form of the disease [14].

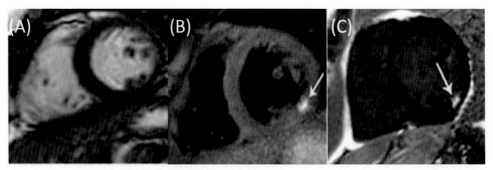

Figure 9.5 *Acute myocarditis*: (A) Short-axis T2W bright blood. (B) Short-axis T2W double IR dark blood image showing high SI in the midinferolateral wall of LV. (C) Short-axis LCE showing delayed enhancement at same location. *LV*, left ventricle.

9.7 Amyloidosis

Cardiac amyloidosis is manifested by diffuse subendocardial to transmural enhancement that may involve all cardiac chamber including both atria and both interventricular and interatrial septae. It is characterized by concentric myocardial thickening, thickening of the atrial walls and interatrial septum, and myocardium nulling preceding the blood pool (normally, the myocardium nulls after the blood pool) [11–14].

To date, there are a lot of conflicting data regarding the role of LCE as prognostic indicator; many studies reported significant association between LGE and adverse clinical outcome, yet others denied this association [17,18]. New emerging techniques such as T1 mapping and ECV estimation have shown promising results in the field of correlation with functional studies and risk assessment. CMR has also been used in differentiating light chain amyloid (AL) and transthyretin-related amyloidosis (ATTR) according to LV mass, location, and extent of LCE. Distinguishing cardiac amyloidosis subtypes is highly beneficial considering the presence of major differences in therapies and prognosis (worse survival in AL in comparison to ATTR) [1,19–21].

9.8 Left ventricle noncompaction

Left ventricular myocardial noncompaction (LVNC), sometimes termed spongy myocardium, is one of the primary genetic cardiomyopathies. It is hallmarked by prominent ventricular myocardial trabeculations and deep intertrabecular recesses. It can occur as a solitary disorder or in combination with other congenital heart or neuromuscular diseases. It is more prevalent in females (F: M = 8:1), and is attributed to familial inheritance pattern. Normally, the proportion of the trabeculations never exceeds the compacted layer, while the opposite occurs in LVNC (Fig. 9.6). Ventricular trabeculations are more prominent at the apical and midventricular

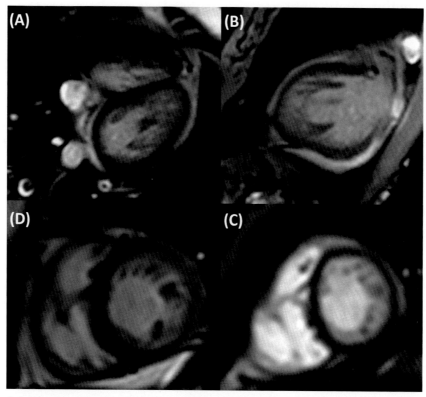

Figure 9.6 *LV noncompaction*: Cine Mr images in the axial (A), vertical long-axis (B) and short-axis vies (C, D) showing prominent myocardial trabeculations in the lateral wall with thinning of the adjacent compacted myocardium. *LV*, left ventricle.

myocardial segments of the LV. It is associated with deep intertrabecular recesses covered with endocardium and receives blood flow from the LV cavity [14].

LVNC has variable clinical manifestations according to proportion of trabeculations to compacted muscles, ranging from asymptomatic to severe HF, systemic embolism, and even SCD. CMR imaging with its 3D views enabled accurate examination of all cardiac segments. In comparison with Echo, CMR depicts subtle myocardial disease in asymptomatic family members [14].

The presence of pronounced trabeculae during routine assessment of CT or MRI is becoming relatively common today and is attributed mainly to high spatial resolution. Thus a segment is considered as noncompacted only if there are two visible myocardial layers with clearly different grades of compaction. It was proposed that a NC/C ratio of 2.3 in diastole distinguishes pathological noncompaction. Another more specific and sensitive method is to measure the ratio between LV trabecular mass and total LV mass in short-axis views, which is diagnostic for LVNC if >20% [14].

9.9 Arrhythmogenic right ventricular dysplasia/cardiomyopathy

Arrhythmogenic right ventricular dysplasia/cardiomyopathy (ARVD-C) is one of the inherited cardiomyopathies where the right ventricular wall is replaced by fibrofatty infiltration. Disease expression is variable and the spectrum of structural changes ranges from subtle basal RV involvement to diffuse biventricular involvement. The broad spectrum of phenotypic manifestations makes clinical diagnosis challenging. Many patients with ARVD-C are young, which necessitates recognition of cardiac structural abnormalities via noninvasive tools. The diagnosis is established upon fulfilling various clinical criteria suggested by an International Task Force [2,14].

CMR findings usually found in ARVD-C include thinned RV wall (Fig. 9.7), RV outflow tract (RVOT) dilatation, trabecular disarray, fibrofatty replacement, ventricular dilatation, and diffuse or focal systolic dysfunction. These abnormalities occur in typical sites; RV base and LV lateral wall. RV LCE was noted in up to 88% of ARVD patients, despite the difficult identification of enhancement in thin walled RV. LV involvement in ARVC is increasingly recognized; LV LCE was reported in up to 61% of cases. The presence of LCE implies an advanced stage of ARVD-C [2,14].

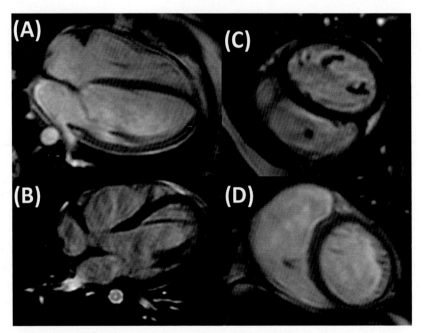

Figure 9.7 *ARVD*: (A, B) Four-chamber view and (C, D) short-axis cine steady state-free precession (SSFP) images showing aneurysmal dilation of the RV. There was also low EF (-35%), which is one major criterion of ARVD. *ARVD*, Arrhythmogenic right ventricular dysplasia.

9.10 Stress-induced (Takotsubo) cardiomyopathy

Stress-induced cardiomyopathy appears in CMR as a diffusely reduced systolic function and apical segmental abnormal wall motion combined with basal segmental normal/hyperkinesia. Myocardial edema may be present, but LCE is absent. Furthermore, CMR can identify existing valvular complications like mitral regurgitation (Mr). Additionally, CMR depicts RV involvement, which occurs in approximately one third of cases and is accompanied by longer hospitalization and worse LV function [14].

9.11 Fabry disease

Fabry disease is identified by concentric LV thickening that may mimic HCM. LCE occurs in midmyocardium or subepicardium of the basal inferolateral segment. LCE acts as prognostic indicator of ventricular arrhythmias and SCD. T1 mapping techniques have also been applied to the identification of Fabry's cardiomyopathy. T1 mapping identifies systolic and diastolic dysfunction before occurrence of structural changes through detection of low T1 values and reduced longitudinal strain early before the occurrence of LV hypertrophy [14].

9.12 Muscular dystrophy

On CMR, muscular dystrophy manifests as dilated ventricles and systolic dysfunction with midmyocardial/subepicardial enhancement in LCE. T1 mapping and ECV estimation are useful tools in evaluation of muscular dystrophy. Measurements of global ECV have been shown to correlate to LVEF and to the number of LGE-positive segments. Global ECV was also linked to the development of arrhythmic events. Lastly, myocardial strain analysis can show changes prior to changes in LVEF [22].

References

[1] Saeed M, Liu H, Liang CH, et al. Magnetic resonance imaging for characterizing myocardial diseases. Int J Cardiovasc Imaging 2017;33:1395—414.
[2] Situ Y, Birch SCM, Moreyra C, et al. Cardiovascular magnetic resonance imaging for structural heart disease. Cardiovasc Diagn Ther 2020;10:361—75.
[3] Seetharam K., Lerakis S. Cardiac magnetic resonance imaging: the future is bright. F1000Res 2019;8: F1000 Faculty Rev-1636.
[4] Messroghli DR, Moon JC, Ferreira VM, et al. Clinical recommendations for cardiovascular magnetic resonance mapping of T1, T2, T2* and extracellular volume: a consensus statement by the Society for Cardiovascular Magnetic Resonance (SCMR) endorsed by the European Association for Cardiovascular Imaging (EACVI). J Cardiovasc Magn Reson 2017;19:75.
[5] Kim PK, Hong YJ, Im DJ, et al. Myocardial T1 and T2 mapping: techniques and clinical applications. Korean J Radiol 2017;18:113—31.
[6] Baksi AJ, Pennell DJ. T2* imaging of the heart: methods, applications, and outcomes. Top Magn Reson Imaging 2014;23:13—20.

[7] Meloni A, Maggio A, Positano V, et al. CMR for myocardial iron overload quantification: calibration curve from the MIOT Network. Eur Radiol 2020;30:3217—25.

[8] Fernandes JL. MRI for iron overload in thalassemia. Hematol Oncol Clin North Am 2018; 32:277—95.

[9] McCrohon JA, Moon JC, Prasad SK, et al. Differentiation of heart failure related to dilated cardiomyopathy and coronary artery disease using gadolinium-enhanced cardiovascular magnetic resonance. Circulation 2003;108:54—9.

[10] Brown PF, Miller C, Di Marco A, et al. Towards cardiac MRI based risk stratification in idiopathic dilated cardiomyopathy. Heart 2019;105:270—5.

[11] Patel AR, Kramer CM. Role of cardiac magnetic resonance in the diagnosis and prognosis of nonischemic cardiomyopathy. JACC Cardiovasc Imaging 2017;10:1180—93.

[12] Jo Y, Kim J, Park CH, et al. Guideline for cardiovascular magnetic resonance imaging from the Korean Society of Cardiovascular imaging-part 1: standardized protocol. Korean J Radiol 2019;20: 1313—33.

[13] Hindieh W, Chan R, Rakowski H. Complementary role of echocardiography and cardiac magnetic resonance in hypertrophic cardiomyopathy. Curr Cardiol Rep 2017;19:81.

[14] Kalisz K, Rajiah P. Impact of cardiac magnetic resonance imaging in non-ischemic cardiomyopathies. World J Cardiol 2016;8:132—45.

[15] Hulten E, Aslam S, Osborne M, et al. Cardiac sarcoidosis-state of the art review. Cardiovasc Diagn Ther 2016;6:50—63.

[16] Gräni C, Eichhorn C, Bière L, et al. Comparison of myocardial fibrosis quantification methods by cardiovascular magnetic resonance imaging for risk stratification of patients with suspected myocarditis. J Cardiovasc Magn Reson 2019;21:14.

[17] Williams LK, Forero JF, Popovic ZB, et al. Patterns of CMR measured longitudinal strain and its association with late gadolinium enhancement in patients with cardiac amyloidosis and its mimics. J Cardiovasc Magn Reson 2017;19:61.

[18] Raina S, Lensing SY, Nairooz RS, et al. Prognostic value of late gadolinium enhancement CMR in systemic amyloidosis. JACC Cardiovasc Imaging 2016;9:1267—77.

[19] Lin L, Li X, Feng J, et al. The prognostic value of T1 mapping and late gadolinium enhancement cardiovascular magnetic resonance imaging in patients with light chain amyloidosis. J Cardiovasc Magn Reson 2018;20:2.

[20] van den Boomen M, Slart RHJA, Hulleman EV, et al. Native T_1 reference values for nonischemic cardiomyopathies and populations with increased cardiovascular risk: a systematic review and meta-analysis. J Magn Reson Imaging 2018;47:891—912.

[21] Robison S, Hong K, Kim D, et al. Evaluation of modified look-locker inversion recovery and arrhythmia-insensitive rapid cardiac T1 mapping pulse sequences in cardiomyopathy patients. J Comput Assist Tomogr 2018;42:732—8.

[22] Reindl M, Eitel I, Reinstadler SJ. Role of cardiac magnetic resonance to improve risk prediction following acute ST-elevation myocardial infarction. J Clin Med 2020;9:1041.

CHAPTER 10

Magnetic resonance imaging of pericardial diseases

Ahmed Abdel Khalek Abdel Razek, Germeen Albair Ashmalla and Dalia Fahmy
Department of Diagnostic Radiology, Faculty of Medicine, Mansoura University, Mansoura, Egypt

10.1 Introduction

Cardiac MRI is today considered an equivalent to Echo cardiography in the evaluation of pericardium. Mr can detect accurately pericardial thickening, masses, effusion, and even suggest type of effusion. Early and late postcontrast images provide advantages over Echo as it may show pericardial enhancement in cases of pericarditis even in absence of pericardial thickening, show infiltration and full extent of tumors, and give better anatomical delineation of exact origin of suspected cysts. In this chapter we will review different pericardial diseases with their MRI characteristics and discuss briefly extracardiac masses.

10.2 Normal pericardium

On cardiovascular magnetic resonance (CMR), the nondiseased pericardium is visualized as a thin curvilinear structure taking the same contour as the myocardium with epicardial fat surrounding it (Fig. 10.1). The pericardium is best assessed along with the RV. The average pericardial thickness is 1.9 ± 0.6 mm during systole in normal individuals, whereas pathological pericardium is >3 mm. Large and small pericardial sinuses and recesses are visualized in CMR (45% and 20% of cases, respectively), as linear (if not fluid filled) or band-like (if fluid filled); other varieties include; crescent, triangle, spindle, ovoid, hemisphere, or irregular shapes [1—5].

10.3 Pericarditis

Inflammation of the pericardium can be idiopathic in one third of cases or attributed to other pathologies including infections (viral, bacterial, fungal, tuberculosis); connective tissue diseases (systemic lupus erythematosus, rheumatoid arthritis, systemic sclerosis); radiation; uremia; and myocardial infarction (Dressler syndrome) [5—8].

Cardiovascular and Coronary Artery Imaging
DOI: https://doi.org/10.1016/B978-0-12-821983-6.00010-2

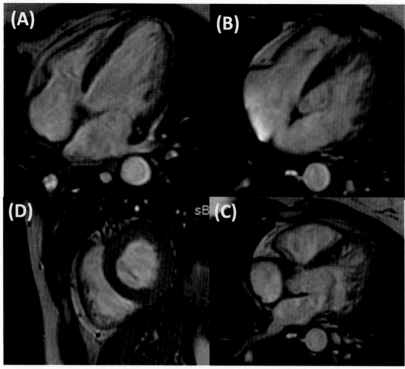

Figure 10.1 *Normal pericardium*: Four-chamber view (A, B, C) and short-axis view show normal pericardium as thin hypointense structure that follows the myocardium.

10.3.1 Chronic inflammatory pericarditis

Chronic inflammatory pericarditis is manifested on pathological examination by the accumulation of fibroblasts, collagen, and less fibrin deposition. On CMR irregular thick pericardium with mild effusion is noted with variable degree of enhancement. Sometimes exuberant epicardial fat is formed owing to chronic inflammatory response [3,5−9].

10.3.2 Chronic fibrosing pericarditis

Chronic fibrosing pericarditis is manifested in pathological examination by the presence of fibroblasts and collagen, which in late stages calcifies and ends with noncompliant pericardium. On CMR thick pericardium with low SI on all pulse sequences owing to fibrosis/calcification is noted. Pericardial effusion is either minimal or absent. Usually no enhancement can be detected apart from few cases with nonresolved inflammation. Signs of pericardial constriction could be present and should be assessed carefully [3,7,8].

10.4 Pericardial effusion

The term pericardial effusion is used to describe pericardial fluid exceeding normal limits. It could be attributed to various aetiologias including cardiac or renal failure, infection, neoplasm, trauma, radiation, and myocardial infarction. CMR has high sensitivity in visualization of minimal fluid; especially when loculated, fluid begins to accumulate around the posterolateral wall of LV or the inferolateral wall of RV, then the superior recess. Moderate effusion (100–500 mL) fills the anterior aspect of the RV (>5 mm) (Fig. 10.2). Large fluid accumulates anterior to the RA and RV, forming an asymmetric ring of fluid around the heart. The volume of pericardial fluid can be measured like ventricular volumes. Transudate displays low SI on T1 WI, high SI on T2 WI, fast spin echo (FSE) and steady-state free precession (SSFP) while complicated effusion (exudate/hemorrhage) attain high SI on T1WI and intermediate SI on T2WI. On SSFP, fibrin strands or coagulated blood can be visualized within the loculations. On double–inversion recovery (FSE), alterations of SI occur depending on the presence of flow within the collection. Free flow as in transudates show no signal, but complex collections with no flow display intermediate to high SI. However, a high SI can be seen on T1WI even in simple transudate owing to nonlinear motion of the fluid [3,5–9].

Sometimes, discriminating a small pericardial effusion from pericardial thickening may be difficult. Pericardial thickening appears gray/dark on T1WI, SSFP, and gradient-echo images with irregular or nodular margins and is not changed with changing the patient's decubitus [3,5–9].

10.5 Pericardial hematoma

This is a rare condition that is preceded by cardiac surgery, pericardiocentesis, chest trauma, or epicardial injury in almost all cases. At CMR, the SI depends on the age of

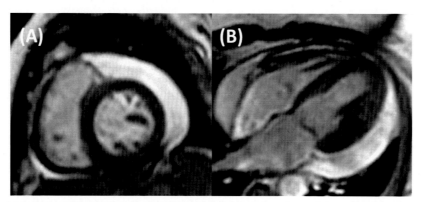

Figure 10.2 *Pericardial effusion*: (A-B) T2 bright blood, short-axis, and four-chamber views show moderate pericardial effusion displaying high SI.

the blood. In the subacute phase heterogeneous high SI on T1 & T2 WI, while in chronic phase low signal with a dark rim. No enhancement is seen. Large hematomas could lead to more adverse effects such as pericardial constriction, cardiac tamponade, or HF [3,9,10].

10.6 Cardiac tamponade

Cardiac tamponade is a life-threatening conditions that necessitates immediate intervention. Accumulation of fluid, blood, pus, or gas in the pericardial space with subsequent elevation of pericardial tension ends by compressing cardiac chambers, limiting diastolic filling with subsequent low of cardiac output (COP), followed by hypotension, tachycardia, and cardiogenic shock. Pericardial tamponade is usually diagnosed on clinical bases and confirmed mainly with echocardiography. CMR has a limited role in the initial diagnosis. Radiological signs include large pericardial effusion (or other contents such as air or blood), flattening or inversion of the right atrial or RV wall, with compression of RV and RA, inversion of the interventricular septum, dilatation of systemic veins (superior vena cava (SVC) & inferior vena cava (IVC)), restrictive diastolic filling of RV and LV, >25% fall in mitral inflow velocity and >40% increase in tricuspid velocity in the first beat after inspiration, and inversed changes in expiration. It must be discriminated from constrictive pericarditis; in the latter disease changes are attributed to nonfunctioning pericardium rather than compression by large pericardial contents [3,9,10].

10.7 Pericardial constriction

Constrictive pericarditis is characterized by thick, fibrotic, or calcified nonelastic pericardium hindering LV diastolic filling with subsequent increased systemic venous pressures and reduced COP. Previously, infection (especially TB) was the main cause of constrictive pericarditis but recently posttherapy (radiation, surgery) emerged as the most related cause. It could present as acute or chronic condition that may need up to 3–12 months to develop considerable clinical effect. It usually involves parietal pericardium, but in rare occasions could be limited to the visceral layer. CMR has limitations in showing pericardia calcifications; otherwise it is the best imaging tool to evaluate pericardial constriction. CMR is utilized to visualize the pericardium whether it is thick, inflamed, or nonthick but causing constriction and determines if the patient needs pericardial stripping or not. In the presence of clinical and radiological signs and symptoms of right-sided HF, pericardial thickening (>4 mm) is considered an indicator of constriction. Pericardial thickening is more evident along the RV and the anterior atrioventricular groove. Enhancing pericardium denotes underlying inflammation, while conical ventricular deformity denotes chronicity. Biatrial enlargement, narrow atrioventricular groove, dilated SVC, IVC, and hepatic veins, pleural effusion, and ascites are attributed to increased cardiac filling pressure. The SVC showed decreased, absent, or reversed systolic flow, while forward flow is significantly increased with increased late backflow in the diastole [9—12]. Another sign is reduced or absent pericardial motion during the cardiac cycle with tethering and limited ventricular expansion with overlying pericardial thickening. These findings can also be assessed using tagging. In patients with pericardial constriction, the tag lines are stretched and fail to break owing to limited motion between the pericardial layers [11].

Diastolic interventricular septal flattening (Fig. 10.3) is diagnostic for constrictive pericarditis of high sensitivity and specificity. Normally, there is a positive left-to-right trans-septal pressure gradient during the whole cardiac cycle with little variation during respiration. In constrictive pericarditis there is limited outward expansion of the RV during the early RV filling (which precedes LV filling) with subsequent elevated RV pressure, which is transmitted to the compliant septum causing flattening or even transient indentation to the left side ("diastolic septal bounce") in early diastolic filing [10—12].

In healthy individuals, during inspiration the negative intrathoracic pressure is transmitted to cardiac chambers causing a persistent driving pressure across the pulmonary veins into the left atrium and mitral valve. In patients with pericardial constriction, the fixed nonmobile pericardium breaks the link between intrathoracic and intracardiac pressures. So, during inspiration, the negative intrathoracic pressure increases venous return more toward the right side, which in combination with limited ventricular filling ends by septal flattening and paradoxical motion of the interventricular septum to the left. While during expiration, there is positive intrathoracic pressure with reduced systemic but increased pulmonary return, which causes septal bowing toward the right. This sign is well appreciated in real-time imaging sequence

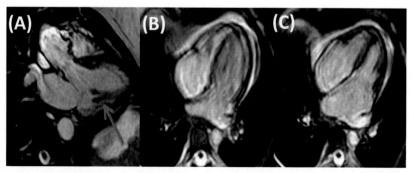

Figure 10.3 *Constrictive pericarditis*: Four-chamber cine views during end-diastole (A, B) and mid-systole (C) showing thickened pericardium, pericardial effusion, septal bouncing, and biatrial enlargement.

in the short-axis plane and is very useful in discrimination between constrictive pericarditis and restrictive cardiomyopathy [10–12].

10.8 Pericardial neoplasms

Pericardial tumors are not common, but secondaries are more commonly seen than primary neoplasms [5–7].

10.8.1 Pericardial metastasis

Pericardial metastasis occurs in 10% of oncology patients, especially those suffering from bronchogenic carcinoma, breast cancer, esophageal carcinoma, renal cell carcinoma, melanoma, leukemia, multiple myeloma, lymphoma, and thymoma. Malignant effusion is characterized by large volume, nodular pericardial thickening or mass-like displaying intermediate Si in T1 WI (part from melanoma which attains high SI on T1WI) and high SI in T2 WI with variable enhancement. Eventually heart failure occurs in about one-fourth of cases that may end by cardiac tamponade and death [5–7].

10.8.2 Primary benign pericardial neoplasm

Different benign neoplasms could arise from the pericardium, including lipoma, teratoma, fibroma, hemangioma, lymphangioma, neurofibroma, paraganglioma, and granular cell myoblastoma [3,12].

10.8.3 Primary pericardial malignant neoplasms

Malignant pericardial neoplasms include mesothelioma, sarcoma, lymphoma, malignant teratoma, and hemangioendothelioma. Mesothelioma is the most common primary pericardial malignancy. On CMR it presents by nodular thickening, pericardial mass, diffuse plaque-like thickening, or hemorrhagic effusion. Sarcoma occasionally arises from the pericardium; angiosarcoma, fibrosarcoma, malignant fibrous histiocytoma, or liposarcoma [3,12].

10.9 Pericardial cyst and diverticulum

Pericardial cyst is a developmental anomaly. It appears as a sharply delineated, encapsulated homogeneous unilocular cyst (rarely lobulated) with low SI on T1WI and high SI on T2 WI without any significant enhancement, and no detected nodules or internal septations. It may show bright SI in T1 WI if it has high protein content. Mostly it has direct attachment to the pericardium, and it is rare to have peduncular attachment. The most common location is the right cardio-phrenic angle (70% of cases), and less frequently the left cardio-phrenic angle (20% of cases) [3,12]. A pericardial diverticulum differs from pericardial cyst in possessing direct communication with the pericardial cavity [12].

10.10 Congenital absence of pericardium

Congenital absence of pericardium is one of the rare (0.002%−0.004%) developmental abnormalities. It is classically partial, but in rare occasions complete absences could occur. It is more prevalent in the left side (70%) than on the right side (17%) or inferior margins. It becomes symptomatic only if associated with complications. It could be associated other anomalies; atrial septal defect (ASD); tetralogy of Fallot (TOF); patent ductus arteriosus (PDA); mitral stenosis (Ms); and malformations of the lung, chest wall, and diaphragm. On CMR, nonvisualization of part or whole pericardium is associated with either mediastinal shift or focal bulge. It is also associated with cardiac displacement posteriorly and to the left (levorotation), interposition of lung tissue between the aorta and pulmonary artery and/or between the diaphragm and cardiac base. The axis of the pulmonary artery left atrial appendage may change in addition to enlarged pulmonary artery. Another characteristic sign is excessive mobilization of cardiac apex (15 mm instead of the normal 1.7 mm); this sign could be noticed in images taken with the patient in left and right lateral decubitus positions. Adverse complications occur when the left atrial appendage or left coronary artery herniates through the defect leading to strangulation and myocardial ischemia, respectively. There is elevated incidence of traumatic aortic dissection owing to hypermobility. Surgical pericardio-plasty is considered the appropriate therapy in patients with large hernial detects or strangulation [12−14].

10.11 Pericardial diaphragmatic hernia

The intrapericardial diaphragmatic hernia is a rare disorder where the stomach, bowel, or abdominal fat herniates into the pericardial sac. It might be congenital, traumatic, or iatrogenic, yet trauma accounts for the majority of cases. Congenital defects are due to failure of the septum transversum, while iatrogenic defects could occur postcoronary artery bypass graft (CABG) surgery, pericardial window, or pacemaker insertion via abdominal approach. It has variable clinical presentations and could be complicated by cardiac tamponade, bowel strangulation, or ischemia [13,14].

10.12 Extracardiac lesions

Numerous extracardiac structures are recognized during routine CMR. Findings are further divided into major findings, which require changes in treatment plan, additional

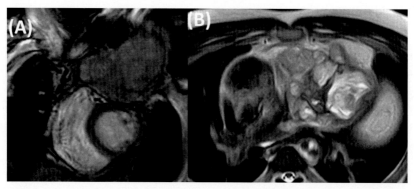

Figure 10.4 *Thymic carcinoma*: Coronal (A) and axial (B)True FISP images showing large anterior mediastinal mass compressing and displacing the main pulmonary artery; histopathological analysis proved thymic carcinoma.

intervention or follow-up, and minor findings that are benign and do not require any investigation or treatment. Most important major extracardiac lesions are newly discovered malignancies such as thymoma, mediastinal lymphoma, bronchogenic carcinoma, mediastinal vascular lesions, or breast cancer, and are followed by other causes of acute chest pain (pulmonary embolism and aortic dissection) and parenchymal lung disease (e.g., interstitial lung fibrosis). Recent Mr imaging such as diffusion-weighted Mr imaging may help in assessment and characterization of these mediastinal lesions (Fig. 10.4) [15−27].

References

[1] Situ Y, Birch SCM, Moreyra C, et al. Cardiovascular magnetic resonance imaging for structural heart disease. Cardiovasc Diagn Ther 2020;10:361−75.
[2] Dodd JD, Leipsic J. Cardiovascular C.T. and MRI in 2019: review of key articles. Radiology 2020;297:17−30. Available from: https://doi.org/10.1148/radiol.2020200605.
[3] Chetrit M, Xu B, Verma BR, et al. Multimodality imaging for the assessment of pericardial diseases. Curr Cardiol Rep 2019;21:41.
[4] Ozmen CA, Akpinar MG, Akay HO, et al. Evaluation of pericardial sinuses and recesses with 2-, 4-, 16-, and 64-row multidetector CT. Radiol Med 2010;115:1038−46.
[5] Razek AAKA, Samir S. Differentiation malignant from benign pericardial effusion with diffusion-weighted MRI. Clin Radiol 2019;74:325 e19-e325.e24.
[6] Kligerman S. Imaging of pericardial disease. Radiol Clin North Am 2019;57:179−99.
[7] Xu B, Kwon DH, Klein AL. Imaging of the pericardium: a multimodality cardiovascular imaging update. Cardiol Clin 2017;35:491−503.
[8] McNamara N, Ibrahim A, Satti Z, et al. Acute pericarditis: a review of current diagnostic and management guidelines. Future Cardiol 2019;15:119−26.
[9] Shabetai R, Oh JK. Pericardial effusion and compressive disorders of the heart: influence of new technology on unraveling its pathophysiology and hemodynamics. Cardiol Clin 2017;35:467−79.
[10] Azarbal A, LeWinter MM. Pericardial effusion. Cardiol Clin 2017;35:515−24.
[11] Chetrit M, Natalie Szpakowski N, Desai MY. Multimodality imaging for the diagnosis and treatment of constrictive pericarditis. Expert Rev Cardiovasc Ther 2019;17:663−72.
[12] Aldweib N, Farah V, Biederman RWW. Clinical utility of cardiac magnetic resonance imaging in pericardial diseases. Curr Cardiol Rev 2018;14:200−12.

[13] Chaturvedi A, Rajiah P, Croake A, et al. Imaging of thoracic hernias: types and complications. Insights Imaging 2018;9:989−1005.

[14] Shah AB, Kronzon I. Congenital defects of the pericardium: a review. Eur Heart J Cardiovasc Imaging 2015;16:821−7.

[15] Dunet V, Schwitter J, Meuli R, et al. Incidental extracardiac findings on cardiac MR: systematic review and meta-analysis. J Magn Reson Imaging 2016;43:929−39.

[16] Sokolowski FC, Karius P, Rodríguez A, et al. Extracardiac findings at cardiac MR imaging: a single-centre retrospective study over 14 years. Eur Radiol 2018;28:4102−10.

[17] Razek AA. Diffusion magnetic resonance imaging of chest tumors. Cancer Imaging 2012;12:452−63.

[18] Abdel Razek AA, Elkammary S, Elmorsy AS, et al. Characterization of mediastinal lymphadenopathy with diffusion-weighted imaging. Magn Reson Imaging 2011;29:167−72.

[19] Abdel Razek AA, Gaballa G, Elashry R, et al. Diffusion-weighted MR imaging of mediastinal lymphadenopathy in children. Jpn J Radiol 2015;33:449−54.

[20] Abdel Razek AA, Soliman N, Elashery R. Apparent diffusion coefficient values of mediastinal masses in children. Eur J Radiol 2012;81:1311−14.

[21] Razek AA, Fathy A, Gawad TA. Correlation of apparent diffusion coefficient value with prognostic parameters of lung cancer. J Comput Assist Tomogr 2011;35:248−52.

[22] Abdel Razek AA, Khairy M, Nada N. Diffusion-weighted M.R. imaging in thymic epithelial tumors: correlation with world health organization classification and clinical staging. Radiology 2014;273:268−75.

[23] Razek AA, Elmorsy A, Elshafey M, et al. Assessment of mediastinal tumors with diffusion-weighted single-shot echo-planar MRI. J Magn Reson Imaging 2009;30:535−40.

[24] Abdel Razek AA, Alvarez H, Bagg S, Refaat S, Castillo M. Imaging spectrum of CNS vasculitis. Radiographics 2014;34:873−94.

[25] Razek AA, Ashmalla GA. Prediction of venous malformations with localized intravascular coagulopathy with diffusion-weighted magnetic resonance imaging. Phlebology 2019;34:156−61.

[26] Abdel Razek AAK. Editorial for "Preliminary assessment of intravoxel incoherent motion diffusion-weighted MRI (IVIM-DWI) metrics in Alzheimer's disease.". J Magn Reson Imaging 2020;52:1827−8. Available from: https://doi.org/10.1002/jmri.27309.

[27] Razek A. Editorial for "Preoperative MRI-based radiomic machine-learning nomogram may accurately distinguish between benign and malignant soft tissue lesions: a two-center study. J Magn Reson Imaging 2020;52:883−4.

CHAPTER 11

Imaging modalities for congenital heart disease and genetic polymorphism associated with coronary artery and cardiovascular diseases

Gowtham Kumar Subbaraj[1], Santhosh Kumar Yasam[1,*], Langeswaran Kulanthaivel[2,*], Balamurugan Rangasamy[3,*], Priyanka Ganapathy[4,*], C. Kirubhanand[5,*], Selvaraj Jayaraman[6,*], Ponnulakshmi Rajagopal[7,*], Ramya Sekar[8,*], Vidhya Rekha Umapathy[9,*] and Shazia Fathima Jaffer Hussain[10,*]

[1]Faculty of Allied Health Sciences, Chettinad Hospital and Research Institute, Chettinad Academy of Research and Education (Deemed to be University), Kelambakkam, Tamil Nadu, India
[2]Department of Biotechnology, Science Campus, Alagappa University, Karaikudi, Tamil Nadu, India
[3]Viral Research and Diagnostic Laboratory (VRDL), Government Villupuram Medical College and Hospital, Mundiyampakkam, Villupuram, Tamil Nadu, India
[4]Department of Physiology, Sree Balaji Medical College and Hospital, Chromepet, Chennai, Tamil Nadu, India
[5]Department of Anatomy, All India Institute of Medical Sciences, Nagpur, Maharashtra, India
[6]Department of Biochemistry, Saveetha Dental College and Hospitals, Chennai, Tamil Nadu, India
[7]Department of Central Research Laboratory, Meenakshi Ammal Dental College and Hospitals, Chennai, Tamil Nadu, India
[8]Department of Oral Pathology, Meenakshi Ammal Dental College and Hospitals, Chennai, Tamil Nadu, India
[9]Department of Public Health Dentistry, Sree Balaji Dental College and Hospital, Chennai, Tamil Nadu, India
[10]Department of Oral and Maxillofacial Pathology, Ragas Dental College and Hospital, Chennai, Tamil Nadu, India

11.1 Introduction

Cardiovascular diseases (CVDs) are a group of heart and blood vessel abnormalities and the world's leading cause of mortality. CVDs claimed the lives of 17.9 million people worldwide accounting for 32% of all deaths [1]. A heart attack or stroke was the cause of 85% of these deaths. Low- and middle-income nations account for about three-quarters of CVD deaths. Peripheral artery disease, coronary artery disease (CAD), rheumatic heart disease, and congenital heart disease (CHD) are examples of CVD. A poor diet, physical inactivity, intolerance of glucose, tobacco consumption, alcohol abuse, high blood pressure, obesity, dyslipidemia, age, gender, and ethnicity are important risk factors for CVDs. The other risk factors for CVD are triglyceride (TG) and dyslipidemia (LDL-C) and with a low level of HDL-C. An active lifestyle

---

* Equal First Authors.

Cardiovascular and Coronary Artery Imaging
DOI: https://doi.org/10.1016/B978-0-12-821983-6.00019-9
169

can prevent most CVDs, including maintaining a healthy weight, eating a healthy diet, exercising regularly, not smoking, and not drinking excessively. A higher blood pressure, a high blood lipid level, a high blood glucose level, and obesity will all affect intermediate CVD risk factors. CVDs occur as a consequence of a complex interaction between an individual's genes and their environment, and with other diseases. Numerous investigations have established unequivocally that CVDs, such as CAD, have a hereditary component. CAD has an estimated heritability of 40%–50% [2]. Meanwhile, many disorders, such as sickle cell anemia, are known to be caused exclusively by genetics, with no influence from environmental variables [3]. The majority of diseases, though, are caused by the complex interactions between environment and genes, and lot of these interactions have not yet been fully understood. Over the last decade, research has been undertaken in attempt to reveal genes and genetic variations implicated in the pathogenesis of CVDs, as well as the specific processes by which they affect individuals. Since the 2007 Wellcome Trust Case Control Consortium Genome-Wide Association Study (GWAS) and hundreds of subsequent GWAS investigations, several single nucleotide polymorphisms (SNPs) have been linked to an increased risk of CVD. Patients with these conditions, such as high blood lipid levels, obesity, and high blood pressure, are at an increased risk of CVDs [4–6]. The risk of CVD for an individual can be evaluated by lifestyle factors, including physical activity levels and dietary habits. However, genetic susceptibility to CVD is not taken into account. It can be difficult to predict whether a person will develop CVDs when lifestyle variables are taken into consideration; this is where genotyping might be useful [7]. Furthermore, genetic information might be utilized to determine whether those with an increased risk of CVD would benefit from initial intervention [8]. A recent study by Khera et al. found that those who had a high genetic risk for CAD had a 91% higher risk of having a heart attack than those who had a low genetic risk for CAD. They had 46% less risk of heart attack when they lived a healthy lifestyle even though they had a genetic risk [9]. People who lived a healthy lifestyle even though they had a genetic risk had less risk than people who lived unhealthy lifestyles. They reported that genotyping for CVD risk can lower the number of cardiovascular problems. Thus asymptomatic individuals can affordably have their genotypes established in order to prevent CVD, which has a large financial impact on healthcare systems and individuals after it has progressed to the point of causing death [10]. People who have CVDs are more likely to get them and die from them if genetic testing isn't used in the medical setting.

GWAS also proved beneficial in the discovery of prospective novel medications for the treatment of CVDs. Proprotein Convertase Subtilisin/Kexin Type 9 (PCSK9) is encoded by the PCSK9 gene, and researchers have discovered a genetic variant in this gene that decreases the risk for CAD and myocardial infarction (MI) by lowering low-density lipoprotein (LDL) cholesterol levels [11]. Then they developed a monoclonal therapy for hyperlipidemia that selectively targets a protein, which has proven to be effective in individuals who are statin-resistant [12]. The identification of polymorphisms that make people more likely to get heart disease and those that make them more likely to respond to heart disease drugs will become more important as we move into the era of personalized medicine. CVDs kill more people around the world than any other disease, so it's important to find people who are at greater risk early. Specific medications can be administered, and lifestyle modifications can be implemented in this manner. The following literature focuses on the genetic markers involved in high-density lipoprotein (HDL), LDL, and TGs. It also focuses on the impact of genetics in determining an individual's vulnerability to CVDs including CAD, hypertension, and MI.

11.2 Sources of information and search

Generic markers were studied by reviewing and examining existent markers in research publications from numerous databases, including meta-analytic studies, GWAS, and database systems from the Medline, PubMed, Medline, and dbSNP. Due to the fact that some databases, such as EMBASE, require a fee to access, they were not included in the search approach. Each one of the diseases or genetic markers we were interested in led us to search for words that were linked to them.

When collecting data and preparing the publication, we searched several databases such as GWAS catalogs, dbSNP, PubMed as well as Science Direct and Google Scholar. Name of gene, rs number, condition or parameter (e.g., cholesterol levels, TGs, MI and CAD), and/or a SNP, risk, and/or susceptibility were some of the search phrases used in this study. Following a review of the search results, publications were selected for inclusion based on the following criteria: In this chapter, SNPs of interest, SNPs that are strongly linked to the parameter or condition of interest, and SNPs that raise the risk of CVD were included.

11.3 Study selection

The initial search was carried out by entering names of genes and/or desired markers into the databases specified above. The titles of the publications that were returned as a consequence of the search criteria were examined to exclude those that had a clear dissociation with the disease or marker of interest. No language restrictions were used throughout the searches. In the GWAS catalog search, articles with the highest number of associations were selected based on their number of associations with a trait or a gene and the number of SNPs they contained. Additional related SNPs were shortlisted for further evaluation and possible inclusion in the final report based on eligibility criteria. The reference lists for the papers that were chosen were looked at to see if there were any other sources that could be considered.

11.4 Diet and cardiovascular disease risk

Genetic biomarkers can predispose individuals to metabolize specific nutrients differently than others, which can have an influence on their risk of CVD. Numerous genetic biomarkers that were impact on the cholesterol and TG levels. All of these indicators were examined from the aspect of inhibiting the formation of atheromas, which is a significant predictor for CAD and other diseases. Cholesterol is any of a class of certain organic molecules called lipids are further divided. Excess cholesterol was removed by HDL from cells, including the linings of arteries, and transports it to the liver for further processing. HDL is produced by the liver. On the other hand, LDL is responsible for the delivery of cholesterol to cells and the build-up of lipids inside the blood vessels. This occurs when LDL passes through the barrier of endothelium and is oxidized before being taken up by macrophages. Damage to the endothelium, which can be induced by the amino acid homocysteine, a hazardous by product of abnormal folate metabolism, speeds up this process significantly. When macrophages differentiate into foam cells (lipid-laden macrophages), they release growth factors that cause smooth muscle cells to migrate into the affected region and exacerbate the inflammation. This formation, known as an atheroma, is composed of foam cells, necrotic debris, and lipids, and it is responsible for the narrowing of the artery, which is known as atherosclerosis.

11.5 High-density lipoprotein cholesterol

In people who have early atherosclerosis [13], the most common lipid abnormality is a low blood HDL cholesterol level. Polymorphisms in the following genes have been found to be associated with lower HDL cholesterol levels in multiple genome-wide studies and meta-analyses: CPTP, PTTC39R, BP4LIPC, HNF4A, GALNT2, ANGPTL4, ABCA1, FADS1, KCTD10, LCAT, LIPG, LPL, and PLTP [14–19]. Because these genes control a wide range of cell processes, including those that deal with lipid metabolism and transport, HDL cholesterol levels can be affected if their activity is different because of a polymorphism. The ABCA1 gene encodes a cellular ATP-binding cassette transporter that transports cellular cholesterol and phospholipids out of cells and into lipoproteins that develop into HDL particles. Polymorphisms in the ABCA1 gene cause sterols to build up in hepatocytes, intestinal cells, and tissue macrophages [20]. A person's lifestyle should be changed to increase HDL levels. Some medicines are available to raise HDL levels, such as niacin, gemfibrozil, simvastatin, and osuvastatin, which can raise HDL levels by up to 30% [21].

11.6 Low-density lipoprotein cholesterol

The higher the levels of LDL cholesterol, the higher the risk of coronary heart disease. Having underlying diseases such as type 2 diabetes and hypertension and your genetic makeup can contribute to having high levels of LDL cholesterol. The meta-analyses and genome-wide studies revealed that NCAN, HMGCR, HNF1A, LDL receptor (LDLR), MAFB, ABCG8, CELSR2, PCSK9, and polymorphisms have been associated with an increased risk of elevated LDL cholesterol [22–24]. People who have these genes are more likely to have high levels of LDL cholesterol in their blood, because they play a role in how lipids are made, packed, and transported [25]. The LDLR gene, which encodes for the LDLR, a critical component of receptor-mediated endocytosis, can remove the particles from circulation for further processing via receptor mediated endocytosis of LDL-C particles (LDLR). This gene has a variant that boosts the production of LDLR, which lowers the CAD risk [26–28].

11.7 Triglycerides

There are a variety of fats in the blood known as TGs, which are crucial energy sources for cells in the body and can be deposited as fat if not quickly used. Having high levels of total TGs is linked with an increased risk of CAD, regardless of HDL levels [29,30]. Certain gene polymorphisms have been associated with elevated TG levels it includes TRIB1, FADS1, GCKR, NCAN, ANGPTL3, PTLP, XKR6, and ZNF259; genes associated with lipid metabolism and transport are encoded by these proteins [31–35]. Transcriptional factors encoded by MLXIPL, for example, regulate genes involved in glucose use and storage as well as in the production of TGs, cholesterol, and LDL. As a result of polymorphisms in this gene, wild-type alleles of this gene are more efficient in using food, leading to weight gain and an increased risk of CAD [36]. Regardless of hereditary predisposition, the best way to lower TG levels is to adjust one's diet and lifestyle. Medications like statins, niacin, and gemfibrozil may be used if TG levels stay stable.

11.8 Inherited genetic susceptibility

11.8.1 Coronary artery disease

In the United States, heart attack is the most common reason of CAD-related mortality, accounting for an average of 846 fatalities each day. The coronary arteries get obstructed by the accumulation of cholesterol, lipids, calcium, and other elements. Chest pain (pain or discomfort), dyspnea, anxiety, agitation, dizziness, and weariness can all be symptoms of CAD [37]. According to research, the probability that a person may acquire CAD is strongly linked to hereditary factors. In a study using current genome-wide techniques, CAD heritability was estimated at 40%–50%. Several extensive meta-analyses and genome-wide association studies have demonstrated that the following genes' polymorphisms affect the risk of CAD: CDH13, MRAS, MTHFD1, CXCL12, MIA3, OR13G1, CDKN2B, and LPL [38,39]. Cadherin superfamily member

CDH13, in particular, protects vascular endothelial cells against necrosis and is related to atherosclerosis resistance. Heart gene polymorphism can lead to protein malfunction, which may raise the risk of CAD because arterial linings are more vulnerable to oxidative stress [40]. There are several metabolic processes that include cell development and differentiation that use the signal transducer protein MRAS to code for its own protein product. Mutations in the MRAS gene may make it more likely that someone will get CAD [41]. This is because adhesion signaling is very important in the atherosclerotic process. Maintaining a healthy lifestyle is essential to preventing CAD in those with hereditary risk factors. Aspirin may be good for people who are more likely to get a heart attack or stroke. Other drugs to lower LDL cholesterol, control blood pressure, or prevent blood clots may be good for people who are more at risk [42].

11.8.2 Hypertension

Having high blood pressure increases the risk of life-threatening conditions such as heart attacks and strokes if left untreated. Normal blood pressure is between 90/60 and 120/80 mmHg, and high blood pressure is above 140/90 mmHg [43]. Hypertension's heritability is estimated to range from 30% to 60%. An example of this genetic component is the BCAT1 gene polymorphism, which has been linked to an increased risk of hypertension in genome-wide studies [44,45]. The polymorphisms of BCAT1 gene have been linked to better salt tolerance and oxidative stress, but the reason for this is still unknown [46]. Maintaining a healthy lifestyle is essential to lowering the risk of having hypertension, and calcium channel blockers, or β-blockers, ACE inhibitors may be given to treat hypertension.

11.8.3 Myocardial infarction

The most prevalent cause of mortality from CAD is a heart attack, often known as a MI [47]. Nearly 200,000 people in the United States are hospitalized each year because of MI. It occurs when a thrombus forms in the coronary artery and blocks blood flow to the heart muscle, causing irreversible damage and eventually necrosis. MI is characterized by chest discomfort, breathlessness, fatigue, and dizziness, all of which are symptoms. MI can be caused by a wide range of environmental variables, but may also occur on its own if there are no other health conditions present. There is a genetic component to the risk of MI, since it has been demonstrated to be heritable. Genome-wide association and large meta-analyses studies show that SORT1, PCSK9, PHACTR1, MIA3, CXCL12, and intergenic areas on the chromosome increase the risk of MI [48–52]. The CXCL12 gene is one mechanism implicated in MI vulnerability. The CXC chemokine family member encoded by this gene is a CXCR4 receptor ligand. A number of processes, including embryonic development, hemopoiesis, and angiogenesis, have been related to this interaction; animal studies imply that

CXCL12 plays a role in vascular repair [53]. Early-onset MI and CAD have been reported to be enhanced by CXCL12 gene polymorphisms [54].

Hepatocytes express the PCSK9 gene, which makes an LDL receptor-binding protein that is released into the bloodstream and then degraded by lysosomes. As a result, there are fewer LDL receptors on the hepatocyte surface, so less LDL gets taken up from the circulation and deposited in the liver as a result. As a result of a loss of function, more LDL particles are eliminated from circulation, thereby lowering the risk of CAD. Although PCSK9 polymorphisms had a far bigger impact on the risk of MI than LDL levels [55], this suggests PCSK9 polymorphisms may provide protection through a distinct mechanism [56].

Worldwide, CAD, the most common cause of death among both men and women, is one of the leading causes of morbidity and disability [57,58]. Common diseases are associated with several clinical parameters that can be useful in expecting and preventing them. For example, lipid profiles have been well-recognized to have an association with several diseases of heart such as CAD and MI [59]. There has been a significant association found between LDL-C and CAD, and inverse association between HDL-C and CAD based on observational and experimental studies [60]. However, the significance of HDL-C in atherosclerosis development is still completely unknown [61−64]. There have been many epidemiological studies indicating that higher HDL-C is protective against CAD, such as the Framingham study [65]. In large randomized controlled trials, however, Torcetrapib and Dalcetrapib, two CETP inhibitors, tended to increase HDL-C circulating levels significantly, but did not benefit CAD patients [66,67]. A majority of these inconsistencies are thought to be affected by both environmental exposures and genetic aspects. The interaction between inherited factors and environmental factors may facilitate understanding of CAD pathology by exploring HDL-C metabolism regulation.

In the human body, CETP is an important regulator for levels of HDL. The cholesterol esters were transferred from HDL to LDL with the help of CETP, which is responsible for the conversion of VLDL cholesterol into rich lipoproteins of TGs [12]. The inverse relationship between activity of CETP and levels of HDL was reported by several studies in Ref. [68]. There have been a few GWAS studies suggesting that the locus of CETP is probably more strongly correlated with HDL-C levels than any other locus mapped to the human genome [37,69]. This polymorphism has been extensively investigated through the TaqIB gene polymorphism (rs708272) in intron 1 in the UCSC study [70,71]. A substantial association was found between gene polymorphism of TaqIB and modifiable circulating levels of HDL [72] as well as the activity of CETP promoter [73]. Specifically, higher HDL-C levels and lower CETP levels have been observed in B2 carriers compared to homozygotes of B1B1 [74,75]. Even so, the definitive association between the gene polymorphism of TaqIB and cognitive dysfunction has been controversial in several studies on genotype-disease associations [76−79], more likely because of smaller sizes of sample, ethnicity, classification of population, and environmental factors.

Common diseases are associated with several clinical parameters that can be useful in predicting and preventing them. For example, lipid profiles have been well-recognized to have an association with heart disease such as MI and CAD [80]. CAD is a prevalent complicated disease caused by both hereditary genetics and lifestyle. A considerable fraction of CAD is explained by risk scores based on age, gender, and modifiable risk variables such as blood lipid profile. Meanwhile, CAD is thought to be heritable in around 40%−50% of cases, and family history is a predictor of CAD [81]. Other than in the case of monogenic illness, genetic information has not been shown to produce statistically significant gains in prediction over nongenetic risk variables. Pharmacologic preventive therapies are intended for those who are at high risk of CAD over a 10-year period ($>$20% risk). In the context of risk scores, 15%−20% of MI patients would be considered from a significant population attributable fraction of CVD [82]. The results of GWAS have revealed a large number of genetic variants and chromosomal locations that are related with CAD [83−86]. The SMARCA4 gene encodes an ATP-dependent helicase BRG1 and belongs to SWI/SNF (switching defective/sucrose nonfermenting) complex [87]. SMARCA4 is one of the most often mutated subunits, according to prior studies, therefore knowing the processes by which SMARCA4 mutation causes cancer and the vulnerabilities it creates is critical for disease prevention [88]. Fujimaki et al. [89] conducted a case-control research in a Japanese population to determine the link between SMARCA4 genetic polymorphisms and CAD. Intron 30 of the SMARCA4 gene, which includes rs1122608, was linked to CAD in the Iranian population, according to Jamaldini et al. [90]. rs11879293, rs12232780, rs2072382, and rs1529729 variations have also been linked to lipid parameters and dyslipidemia-related disorders in previous research [37,91−95]. So a meta-analysis is needed to assess these associations with the risk of CAD. Thus the present meta-analysis aimed to evaluate the association of CETP and SMARCA4 gene polymorphism and the risk of CAD.

It is well known that regardless of geography and race that CHD is prevalent [96−98]. Due to advanced treatment options and palliative methods, imaging CHD has become increasingly important [99]. Evaluation of cardiac abnormalities continues to be centered on clinical examinations. Currently, many additional methods of evaluation are available, posing challenges to rational decision-making. Evaluation and follow-up of CVD are increasingly accomplished using noninvasive and radiation-free techniques [100−102]. This presentation is intended to provide a general practical view of imaging evaluation of cardiac disease. In addition to diagrammatic representations, cases are illustrated with plain radiography, echocardiography, computed tomography (CT), and magnetic resonance imaging (MRI) in varying combinations (Table 11.1).

Table 11.1 Imaging techniques used for diagnosing congenital heart disorders.

Congenital heart diseases	Common entities	Imaging technique
Mild	ASD, VSD, AVSD, PDA	MRI, Echocardiography
Moderate	Mod Pulmonary stenosis, Complex VSD or noncritical coarctations, Large ASD, Pulmonary regurgitation	MRI, Echo, MDCT
Severe	Hypoplastic right heart syndrome, TOF, Truncus, TAPVC, Pulmonary atresia, DORV, Single ventricle, Severe cases of shunts and valve stenosis	MDCT, MRI, Echo, Cath-Angiography

ASD, Atrial septal defect; *AVSD*, atrio, ventricular septal defect; *DORV*, double outlet right ventricle; *MDCT*, Multidetector Computed Tomography; *PDA*, patent ductus arteriosus; *PS*, pulmonary stenosis; *TAPVC*, total anomalous venous connection; *TOF*, tetrology of Falott; *VSD*, ventricular septal defect.

11.9 Imaging strategy and techniques

Cardiac abnormality analysis requires a specific approach. Evaluating the morphology, location, and connections of heart chambers is a crucial aspect of cardiac abnormality analysis. This procedure includes detecting the position of right- or left-sided morphological chambers. Identifying the relationship between systemic veins and atria, atria and ventricles, and ventricular outflow and the major vessels is the second step. Additionally, the morphology of the lungs and abdominal viscera contributes to the establishment of left and right sidedness. In the context of right sided chambers, the term concordant refers to the right atrium connecting to the right ventricle and the right ventricle connected to the pulmonary artery. Right atrium communicating with the left ventricle and right ventricle communicating with the aorta are examples of discordant relations. Thus there are several possible combinations, including bilateral duplication of one kind of atrium, termed as right or left atrial "isomerism." It is also possible for both the inflow and outflow valves to primarily link with one ventricle (a double-inlet or double-outlet ventricle) [99]. For identification and assessment of cardiac chambers in complicated CHD, a number of analytical techniques have been developed. Tynan et al. analyzed previous recommendations of a widely recognized sequential strategy and suggested adjustments [103,104]. Accordingly, he suggested that the most effective way to use the sequential approach is to adopt a technique demonstrating a synthesis of connections, morphology, and relationships at each junction of the cardiac segments. Consequently, connections, morphology, and relationships must be defined both at the junction of the atria and ventricles and between the chambers in the ventricular mass and the major arteries. This data serves as the foundation for analysis and interpretation.

11.10 Plain radiography

Evolution of newer imaging technology has led to limited use or underutilization of some of the older modalities. Plain radiography, generally a postero-anterior or antero-posterior frontal view, continues to be the initial examination at many cardiac centers. Inadequate training and incomplete information of the expected pathology has led to limited output from plain radiography. The basic tenets of cardiac evaluation on radiography are based on the assessment of cardiac size, position, outline, special features due to anomaly, and evaluation of the great vessels and the pulmonary vascular divisions [105,106]. The strength of plain radiography is in the assessment of the pulmonary vasculature and in the evaluation of specific cardiac contours. Increase or decrease in the size of pulmonary arterial structures can be easily perceived by comparing with adjacent end-on bronchus or by eyeballing the overall size and distribution of the vessels. Number of end-on vessels around the hilar area provides information about increased arterial vascularity (pulmonary plethora). In an adequately exposed radiograph, ability to trace the vessels to the peripheral lung indicates that pulmonary structure markings have increased. An interpretation of plain radiography requires adequate training, based on "pattern recognition" of normal and abnormal structures. Ventricular contours show the balance between right and left ventricular enlargement, RV enlargement leading to upturned apex (common in right ventricular outflow obstruction); LV enlargement leading to lateral and downward enlargement, as seen in chronic hypertension or aortic coarctation. Ebsteins anomaly leads to grossly exaggerate the right atrial contour due to right atrial enlargement. Left atrial enlargement is recognized by its retrocardiac double density, widening of subcarinal angle, and localized bulge in posterior cardiac contour. Another useful area to scrutinize in plain radiography is the location of the aortic arch that can be easily demonstrated by observing tracheal indentation on the side of the arch. Cardiac pedicle tends to be narrow with anomalies leading to single outflow or predominantly single vessel dominance. Demonstration of the location of the abdominal viscera is vital in the evaluation of a complex heart disease and various "heterotaxy syndromes." Occasionally there are specific cardiac anomalies like partial absence of the pericardium that can be detected on plain radiography by local contour changes. Evaluation of lung aeration and the anomalies of lung development are vital as they are associated with an anomalous pulmonary venous drainage. Anomalies of thoracic cage, ribs, and vertebrae are frequently noted in association of cardiac anomalies and observed on radiography.

11.11 Echocardiography

Radiologists who work in the field of cardiac imaging should be well-versed on the benefits and drawbacks of echocardiography. Before doing a more thorough cardiac imaging test, it is necessary to gather and analyze information from echocardiography about chamber location, size, valvular disease, and septal abnormalities. Echocardiography has become a major method for noninvasive cardiac evaluation due to high-resolution imaging with a small footprint probe [107,108].

Color Doppler and flow analysis are frequently used to augment the examination. The capacity to evaluate heart function with excellent temporal resolution is echocardiography's major strength.

For the demonstration of septal abnormalities, high-frequency probes give high-resolution pictures of cardiac architecture, ventricular and atrial septum. With the best available window, images can be acquired in different planes. Long- and short-axis views of heart chambers, outflow tracts, four-chamber views, unique views for aortic arch through suprasternal window, and subcostal view for right atrial evaluation are among the standard views. Echocardiography is also effective for evaluating the outflow of cardiac chambers, sequential assessment of chamber location, valve abnormality identification, wall motion abnormality detection, and septal defect evaluation. When possible, suprasternal windows are useful for assessing the aortic arch and major vessels. Transesophageal echocardiography is also useful for monitoring invasive intracardiac operations during surgery. By obtaining precise information for anatomical flaws and functional assessment, contrast aided Echo, 3D echocardiogram, and speckle trace echocardiography have brought new strengths. This modality is a vital aspect and modality of great value in pre- and postoperative evaluation of CHD due to its accessibility, cost, and ease of use, repeatability, noninvasive nature, and mobility.

11.12 Computed tomography

The volume of cardiac structures may be measured using contrast-enhanced Multidetector Computed Tomography (MDCT) at a specific period of the cardiac cycle. While non−ECG synchronized spiral CT scans can be used for diagnostic purposes, ECG synchronized CT scans can dramatically minimize cardiac motion artifacts and deliver superior findings. For homogenous contrast opacification, the injection dosage must be optimized and the injection rate must be modulated [109]. Following the contrast bolus can help with analysis by providing structural information as well as hints about chamber connections and flow dynamics. Images enable the examination of lung fields and the location of abnormal vascular drainage, in addition to providing good heart structural features. Normal cardiac architecture, typical preoperative and postoperative imaging findings, distinctive appearances associated to specific interventional procedures, and imaging findings of frequent problems are all required for interpretation of cardiac CT scan data. CT imaging's advantages include a quick assessment time and the capacity to offer information on the lungs, airways, and bony structures. Quantifying right and left ventricular volume, single breath-hold data capture, greater spatial and contrast resolutions, and easier and quicker data segmentation are all benefits of cardiac CT scanning over cardiac MRI [104]. Complications associated with iodinated contrast material and radiation dosage are two limitations of the CT technology. For newborns and young children who are likely to require MDCT cardiac examination, radiation dose reduction is a unique necessity. The radiation settings for CT scans should be tailored to the individual's body and weight. To reduce radiation exposure in pediatric patients, dose-reduction methods such as low tube voltage and tube current modulation should be used. Data processing for cardiac CT examinations need a sophisticated workstation capable of 2D and 3D analysis. Standard imaging planes (axial, coronal, and sagittal) are used to assess cardiac structures, as well as two-chamber, four-chamber, and short-axis views. A third technique for identifying septal abnormalities is to use an en-face image. Multiple imaging planes should be used to analyze great vessels and aberrant vascular structures throughout their long axes. The sagittal and oblique coronal imaging planes are aligned along the tracheal long axis to examine the airways. In order to measure vascular airway compression, curved multiplanar reformations along the major bronchi are effective. Three conventional orthogonal imaging planes are used to evaluate lung fields. The vascular and airway structures can be delineated using maximum and minimum intensity projections, as well as volume rendered approaches. Using maximum intensity projection to interrogate picture datasets with images of varied thickness gives significant clarity in understanding complicated anatomy.

11.12.1 Magnetic resonance imaging

Recently, MRI approaches have risen to prominence in cardiac examination [110,111]. MR images give functional information as well as chamber identification and high-quality structural information. Since it is a nonradiation approach, the examination can be repeated and used for patient follow-up. The capability of dynamic multiplanar imaging makes the MR approach versatile, accurate, and adaptable to any cardiac or extra-cardiac complicated condition. In CMR, the most often used sequences are spin echo and gradient echo. Spin-echo T1 weighted images give good structural details but create dark blood pictures owing to blood flow signal attenuation. Fast (turbo) spin echo (commercial names: TSE, Siemens; FSE, General Electric; TSE, Philips) and single-shot fast (turbo) spin echo are common versions of this technology (commercial names: HASTE, Siemens; SSFSE, General Electric; SSTSE, Philips) [15] Another significant imaging sequence in which moving blood looks bright is the gradient echo cine pulse sequence. Images captured with ECG-gating give several images throughout the cardiac cycle that may be shown in a cine loop to demonstrate motion. Breath-holding (preferred) or signal averaging can be used to reduce respiratory motion artifact. Gradient echo cine imaging can be accomplished with either a typical spoiled gradient echo pulse sequence or the SSFP sequence (commercial names: True FISP, Siemens; FIESTA, General Electric; balanced-FFE, Philips) [110]. SSFP imaging is more often utilized because it is quicker and gives better contrast between blood and myocardium than normal gradient echo imaging. The SSFP sequence is essentially unaffected by flow disruptions generated by stenosis or regurgitation jets [111]. In a short scan time, typically less than 30 seconds, contrast-enhanced magnetic resonance angiography (MRA) using intravenously administered Gadolinium-based contrast agents can produce a high-resolution, high-contrast, three-dimensional (3D) dataset of the cardiac chambers and entire chest vasculature. MRI delayed enhancement visualization offers information on myocardial vitality. MRA methods are widely used for repeat vascular examinations. Noncontrast bright blood methods are extremely beneficial in the postoperative monitoring of cardiac and vascular lesions. Standard imaging planes are defined, which roughly correspond to angiography and echocardiography imaging planes. Individual cardiac anomalies should be treated with their own methods. Compared to CT, MR examinations are often longer. Children require deeper sedation, which frequently necessitates the aid of an anesthesiologist or a pediatric intensivist. Cardiovascular pacemakers, older intracranial ferromagnetic clips, cochlear implants, and claustrophobia are all contraindications to MR scanning. Because of technological advancements, there has been a shift toward the use of MR compatible implants and clips. The measurement of quantitative flow information using phase contrast methods is an important component of the CMR evaluation. Cardiac output, pulmonary-to-systemic flow ratio (Qp/Qs), differential lung perfusion, valve regurgitation, aorto-pulmonary collateral flow, and pressure gradient measurement are all often monitored measures. Many cardiac centers now seek numerous evaluations for cardiac assessment. Plain radiography, echocardiography, MDCT, and/or MRI are done depending on availability, cost efficiency, and choice. Because of increased equipment availability, improved technology, and a higher number of experienced employees, there is a progressive trend toward MR imaging.

11.13 Methodology

11.13.1 Literature search

The literature search was further refined with the help of the advanced search builder. Search themes were combined by using the Boolean operators "AND" and "OR." Up to March 2022, formal computerized searches were conducted in electronic databases such as MEDLINE, PubMed, Embase, Science Direct, and Google scholar. This search used medical subheading terms and text words from the following list: SMARCA4 gene polymorphism, TaqIB or rs708272 or CETP gene polymorphism or cholesteryl ester transfer protein and myocardial infection or atherosclerosis or CAD.

In addition to screening reviews, new research articles, and previous meta-analyses, we also optimized the database by eliminating duplicates.

11.13.2 Selection criteria

The studies aiming to find associations between CAD risk with the TaqIB polymorphism and SMARCA4 gene polymorphism may be included. We have selected the articles based on the following criteria: (1) Articles about subjects of human (full texts or abstracts) without discrimination based on race, ethnicity, or language. (2) When multiple geographic or clinical subgroups are discussed in an article, they are considered separately. (3) When multiple studies were derived from the same population, to avoid data overlapping, studies that contain large sample size only were considered.

11.13.3 Extracted information

According to the inclusion criteria described above, the data was collected following a standard procedure. A consensus was reached after any disagreements were discussed. Each eligible study provided the following information: first author, publication year, country, ethnicity, study design, endpoints, and characteristics of clinical subjects.

11.13.4 Hardy-Weinberg equilibrium testing

Chi square test was used to determine whether SMARCA4 gene polymorphism and TaqIB polymorphisms were compatible with Hardy-Weinberg equilibrium (HWE) among controls in the studies. Sensitivity analysis was carried out by excluding studies to check deviations in the HWE. Effect of sizes was calculated for studies meeting the HWE and then for those that did not.

11.13.5 Statistical analysis

A 95% confidence interval with odds ratio was calculated to validate whether the gene polymorphism of TaqIB and SMARCA4 were associated with CAD risk or not. We used the following four genetic models: allele comparisons, recessive genetic regression, dominant genetic regressions, and overdominant genetic regression. In order to assess the possibility of heterogeneity, the Mantel-Haenszel model was used. The inconsistency index (I^2) was used to assess the consistency of findings across all studies, ranging from 0 to 100%. I^2 values of high proportions suggest that heterogeneity accounted for most of the variation between studies, whereas 0% signifies homogeneity. A Chi-square-based Q statistic test determined whether there was heterogeneity between the studies. Using the Z test, we calculated combined ORs that were significant at $P < .05$.

In order to identify those studies that likely brought about bias in the overall estimates, sensitivity analysis was carried out by sequentially removing them. For estimating publication bias, we used Egger's linear regression test and visual funnel plots. There can be a publication bias if there is an asymmetric plot, and *T*-test can be used for verification. Egger's test and I^2 statistics were considered significant if $P < .05$ was used. The review manager software version 5.4 was used to administer and analyze the data.

11.14 Results and discussion

The preliminary searches in Science Direct, PubMed, Google Scholar, and Embase resulted in the retrieval of 230 relevant articles. In the final analysis, 18 articles, comprising 20 studies assessing TaqIB polymorphisms and CAD risk, were considered (Fig. 11.1). The studies included in this review were all case-control studies. The studies that met the inclusion criteria were published between the year 1991 and 2022. A total of nine studies were carried out on Asian subjects [73,112−117], and eleven on Caucasian subjects [118−128]. The meta-analysis contains a total of 20 studies with controls and cases. Table 11.1 shows the genotype and allele frequencies for the TaqIB polymorphism. For all the eligible studies, we also list the results of the HWE among the controls. Each study was assessed for its association with CAD risk under different genetic models. According to the results, the CETP polymorphism was strongly associated with CAD risk in allelic, recessive, and overdominant contrast models ($P < .05$), while no association in the dominant model ($P > .05$) was found.

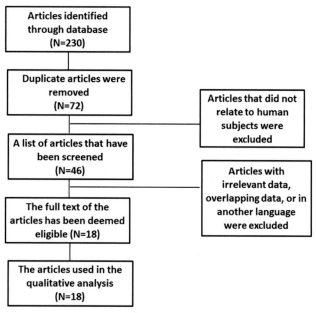

Figure 11.1 Flowchart of study design of CETP gene poly polymorphism with the risk of CAD. *CAD*, Coronary artery disease; *CETP*, cholesteryl ester transfer protein.

The subgroup analysis for heterogeneity was assessed and the results showed a strong association in allelic, recessive, and dominant contrast models ($P < .05$), while no association in the overdominant model ($P > .05$) was found (shown in Figs. 11.2–11.5). The subgroup analysis was carried out for heterogeneity based on ethnicity. The results revealed that Asian people showed higher CAD risk than caucasian people (Table 11.2).

The striking heterogeneity may be due to the number of studies deviating from HWE (five studies containing controls and cases). As a result, sensitivity analysis was conducted in order to determine the immediate effects as well as the extent of heterogeneity between studies before and after excluding studies that were HWE-deviating. Based on the results of each individual study, it was found that no single study had a significant effect on the overall outcome of the study (Fig. 11.6). The publication bias was carried out using funnel plot and Eggers test. All the results were constant, suggesting that the present study results were statistically stable (Fig. 11.7).

Meta-analysis is a formal, epidemiological, quantitative design that methodically assesses the outcomes of previous studies to determine the conclusions about that body of research. The meta-analysis report consists of a total of 16,449 cases, 12,771 controls through various databases. The CETP protein plays a vital role in regulating the metabolism of cholesterol. Several tissues express CETP, such as the spleen, liver, small intestine, adipose tissue, kidneys, adrenal glands, skeletal muscles, and heart.

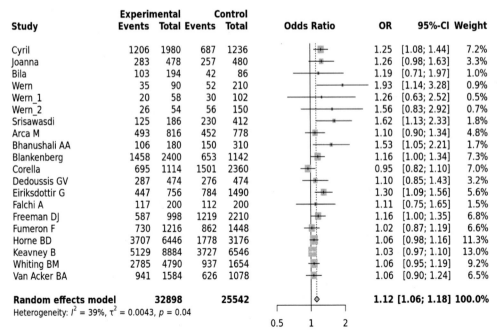

Study	Experimental Events	Total	Control Events	Total	Odds Ratio	OR	95%-CI	Weight
Cyril	1206	1980	687	1236		1.25	[1.08; 1.44]	7.2%
Joanna	283	478	257	480		1.26	[0.98; 1.63]	3.3%
Bila	103	194	42	86		1.19	[0.71; 1.97]	1.0%
Wern	35	90	52	210		1.93	[1.14; 3.28]	0.9%
Wern_1	20	58	30	102		1.26	[0.63; 2.52]	0.5%
Wern_2	26	54	56	150		1.56	[0.83; 2.92]	0.7%
Srisawasdi	125	186	230	412		1.62	[1.13; 2.33]	1.8%
Arca M	493	816	452	778		1.10	[0.90; 1.34]	4.8%
Bhanushali AA	106	180	150	310		1.53	[1.05; 2.21]	1.7%
Blankenberg	1458	2400	653	1142		1.16	[1.00; 1.34]	7.3%
Corella	695	1114	1501	2360		0.95	[0.82; 1.10]	7.0%
Dedoussis GV	287	474	276	474		1.10	[0.85; 1.43]	3.2%
Eiriksdottir G	447	756	784	1490		1.30	[1.09; 1.56]	5.6%
Falchi A	117	200	112	200		1.11	[0.75; 1.65]	1.5%
Freeman DJ	587	998	1219	2210		1.16	[1.00; 1.35]	6.8%
Fumeron F	730	1216	862	1448		1.02	[0.87; 1.19]	6.6%
Horne BD	3707	6446	1778	3176		1.06	[0.98; 1.16]	11.3%
Keavney B	5129	8884	3727	6546		1.03	[0.97; 1.10]	13.0%
Whiting BM	2785	4790	937	1654		1.06	[0.95; 1.19]	9.2%
Van Acker BA	941	1584	626	1078		1.06	[0.90; 1.24]	6.5%
Random effects model		**32898**		**25542**		**1.12**	**[1.06; 1.18]**	**100.0%**

Heterogeneity: $I^2 = 39\%$, $\tau^2 = 0.0043$, $p = 0.04$

0.5   1   2

Figure 11.2 Forest plot for the association of CETP gene polymorphism with CAD risk under allelic model. *CAD*, Coronary artery disease; *CETP*, cholesteryl ester transfer protein.

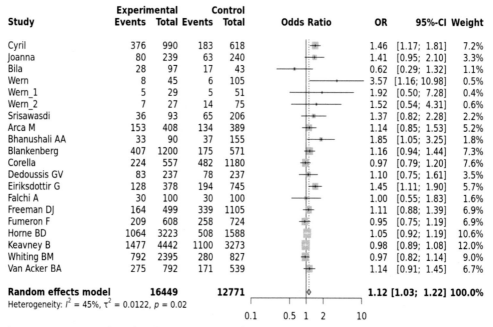

Figure 11.3 Forest plots for the association of CETP gene polymorphism with CAD risk under recessive model. *CAD*, Coronary artery disease; *CETP*, cholesteryl ester transfer protein.

Study	Experimental Events	Total	Control Events	Total	Odds Ratio	OR	95%-CI	Weight
Cyril	830	990	504	618		1.17	[0.90; 1.53]	7.2%
Joanna	203	239	194	240		1.34	[0.83; 2.16]	2.9%
Bila	75	97	25	43		2.45	[1.14; 5.30]	1.2%
Wern	27	45	46	105		1.92	[0.95; 3.91]	1.4%
Wern_1	15	29	25	51		1.11	[0.45; 2.77]	0.9%
Wern_2	19	27	42	75		1.87	[0.73; 4.79]	0.8%
Srisawasdi	89	93	165	206		5.53	[1.92; 15.93]	0.7%
Arca M	340	408	318	389		1.12	[0.77; 1.61]	4.5%
Bhanushali AA	73	90	113	155		1.60	[0.85; 3.01]	1.7%
Blankenberg	1051	1200	478	571		1.37	[1.04; 1.82]	6.6%
Corella	471	557	1019	1180		0.87	[0.65; 1.15]	6.5%
Dedoussis GV	204	237	198	237		1.22	[0.74; 2.01]	2.7%
Eiriksdottir G	319	378	590	745		1.42	[1.02; 1.97]	5.3%
Falchi A	87	100	82	100		1.47	[0.68; 3.19]	1.2%
Freeman DJ	423	499	880	1105		1.42	[1.07; 1.89]	6.5%
Fumeron F	521	608	604	724		1.19	[0.88; 1.61]	6.1%
Horne BD	2643	3223	1270	1588		1.14	[0.98; 1.33]	12.7%
Keavney B	3652	4442	2627	3273		1.14	[1.01; 1.28]	15.1%
Whiting BM	1993	2395	657	827		1.28	[1.05; 1.57]	9.9%
Van Acker BA	666	792	455	539		0.98	[0.72; 1.32]	6.0%
Random effects model		**16449**		**12771**		**1.23**	**[1.12; 1.34]**	**100.0%**

Heterogeneity: $I^2 = 30\%$, $\tau^2 = 0.0098$, $p = 0.10$

Figure 11.4 Forest plot for the association of CETP gene polymorphism with CAD risk under dominant model. *CAD*, Coronary artery disease; *CETP*, cholesteryl ester transfer protein.

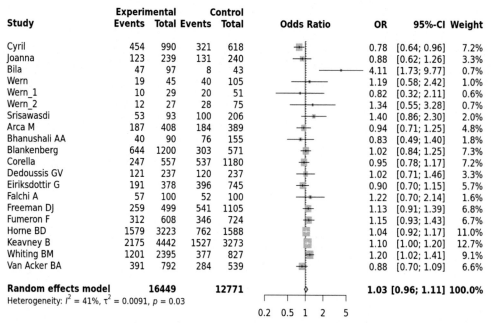

Study	Experimental		Control		Odds Ratio	OR	95%-CI	Weight
	Events	Total	Events	Total				
Cyril	454	990	321	618		0.78	[0.64; 0.96]	7.2%
Joanna	123	239	131	240		0.88	[0.62; 1.26]	3.3%
Bila	47	97	8	43		4.11	[1.73; 9.77]	0.7%
Wern	19	45	40	105		1.19	[0.58; 2.42]	1.0%
Wern_1	10	29	20	51		0.82	[0.32; 2.11]	0.6%
Wern_2	12	27	28	75		1.34	[0.55; 3.28]	0.7%
Srisawasdi	53	93	100	206		1.40	[0.86; 2.30]	2.0%
Arca M	187	408	184	389		0.94	[0.71; 1.25]	4.8%
Bhanushali AA	40	90	76	155		0.83	[0.49; 1.40]	1.8%
Blankenberg	644	1200	303	571		1.02	[0.84; 1.25]	7.3%
Corella	247	557	537	1180		0.95	[0.78; 1.17]	7.2%
Dedoussis GV	121	237	120	237		1.02	[0.71; 1.46]	3.3%
Eiriksdottir G	191	378	396	745		0.90	[0.70; 1.15]	5.7%
Falchi A	57	100	52	100		1.22	[0.70; 2.14]	1.6%
Freeman DJ	259	499	541	1105		1.13	[0.91; 1.39]	6.8%
Fumeron F	312	608	346	724		1.15	[0.93; 1.43]	6.7%
Horne BD	1579	3223	762	1588		1.04	[0.92; 1.17]	11.0%
Keavney B	2175	4442	1527	3273		1.10	[1.01; 1.20]	12.7%
Whiting BM	1201	2395	377	827		1.20	[1.02; 1.41]	9.1%
Van Acker BA	391	792	284	539		0.88	[0.70; 1.09]	6.6%
Random effects model		16449		12771		**1.03 [0.96; 1.11]**		100.0%

Heterogeneity: $I^2 = 41\%$, $\tau^2 = 0.0091$, $p = 0.03$

0.2 0.5 1 2 5

Figure 11.5 Forest plot for the association of CETP gene polymorphism with CAD risk under overdominant model. *CAD*, Coronary artery disease; *CETP*, cholesteryl ester transfer protein.

Cholesterone esters transfer from high-HDLs to LDLs, TG-rich lipoproteins (TRLs) chylomicrons, and VLDLs, while triacylglycerols are transferred from TRLs to HDLs and LDLs. Previously, few meta-analysis studies were reported for the association of CETP polymorphism with CAD risk. A meta-analysis of CETP gene polymorphism with the risk of CAD was reported by Zhijun et al. [129] using Mendelian randomized approach. The results showed that CETP was strongly associated with risk of CAD on allele, recessive, and dominant contrasts while no association was observed in overdominant variant. Lisanne et al. [61] reported the meta-analysis of CETP gene polymorphism circulating on lipid levels with the risk of CAD. Qi Wang et al. [130] reported the meta-analysis of CETP gene polymorphism with MI risk. The results revealed that CETP gene polymorphism may be susceptible to MI, especially in caucasians. The results revealed that the HDL is not a risk factor for CAD while LDL may be associated with CAD risk. The current study results showed strong association of gene polymorphism of CETP with the risk of CAD in recessive, allele, and overdominant contrasts while no association was observed in dominant model. Sensitivity assay was analyzed to check the heterogeneity between studies by omitting each study. Overall, none of the studies significantly influenced the overall outcome of the study. Eggers test and funnel plot was used to analyze the publication bias. All the results were constant and no significant bias was observed.

Table 11.2 Characteristics of the studies for the association of CETP gene polymorphism with the CAD risk.

Study	Ethnicity	B1B1 cases/ controls	B1B2_Cases cases/ controls	B2B2_Cases cases/ controls	Total cases/ controls	HW-P value
Cyrus et al. (2016)	Asian	376/183	454/321	160/114	990/618	0.4369
Iwanicka et al. (2018)	Caucasian	80/63	123/131	36/46	239/240	0.3305
Ilanbey et al. (2020)	Asian	28/17	47/8	22/18	97/43	0
Chu et al. (2016)	Asian	8/6	19/40	18/59	45/105	0.8261
Chu et al. (2016)	Asian	5/5	10/20	14/26	29/51	0.8261
Chu et al. (2016)	Asian	7/14	12/28	8/33	20/75	0.2286
Srisawasdi et al. (2021)	Asian	36/65	53/100	4/41	93/206	0.8261
Arca et al. (2001)	Caucasian	153/134	187/184	68/71	408/389	0.8261
Bhanushali et al. (2010)	Asian	33/37	40/76	17/42	90/155	0.8261
Blankenberg et al. (2004)	Caucasian	407/175	644/303	149/93	1200/571	0.228
Corella et al. (2010)	Caucasian	224/482	247/537	86/161	557/1180	0.8261
Dedoussis et al. (2007)	Asian	83/78	121/120	33/39	237/237	0.8261
Eiriksdottir et al. (2001)	Caucasian	128/194	191/396	59/155	378/745	0.2286
Falchi et al. (2005)	Caucasian	30/52	57/52	30/18	100/100	0.8261
Freeman et al. (2003)	Caucasian	164/339	259/541	76/225	499/1105	0.8261
Fumeron et al. (1995)	Caucasian	209/258	312/346	87/120	608/724	0.8261
Horne et al. (2007)	Asian	1064/508	1579/762	580/318	3223/1588	0.5868
Keavney et al. (2004)	Caucasian	1477/1100	2175/1527	790/646	4442/3273	0.054
Whiting et al. (2005)	Caucasian	792/280	1201/170	402/170	2395/827	0.228
Van Acker et al. (2008)	Caucasian	275/171	391/284	126/84	792/539	0.228

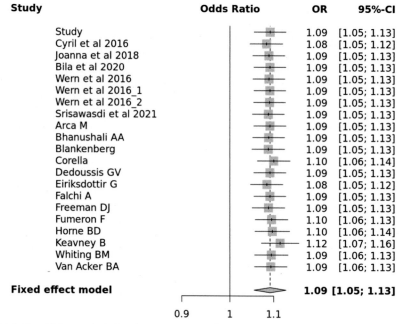

Figure 11.6 Sensitivity analysis for the association of CETP gene polymorphism with CAD risk. *CAD*, Coronary artery disease; *CETP*, cholesteryl ester transfer protein.

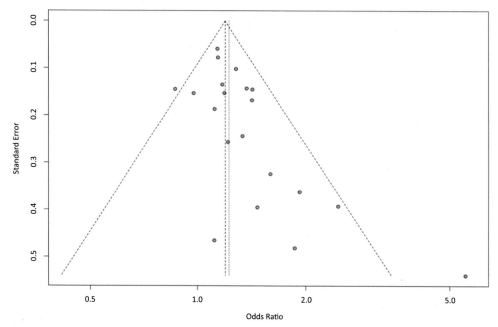

Figure 11.7 Publication bias analyzed by the funnel plot for the association of CETP gene polymorphism with CAD risk. *CAD*, Coronary artery disease; *CETP*, cholesteryl ester transfer protein.

Therefore to reconcile CETP gene polymorphism and the association with CAD, we performed this meta-analysis. From the meta-analysis results, CETP gene polymorphism rs2981582 was found to be associated with CAD risk. The results revealed that Asian people showed more significant risk factor than caucasian people. We emphasize that studies with a bigger sample size are required in the future to confirm the present findings.

11.15 Results and discussion of SMARCA4 gene polymorphism

In the present study, we selected a total of 8 articles for SMARCA4 rs1122608 gene polymorphism consisting of 6792 controls and 8322 CAD cases. Our collected data included 23 studies relating to CAD, out of which 8 studies assessed SMARCA4 rs1122608 gene polymorphism (Fig. 11.8). Table 11.3 represents the characteristic features of selected studies with case control for the SMARCA4 rs1122608 gene polymorphism association on breast cancer susceptibility. Of the eight studies, six studies were examined in Asian people [90,131−135], and two studies were examined in caucasian people [89,136].

In the present study of meta-analysis, eight articles were examined to find out the association of the rs1122608 gene polymorphism with CAD risk in. The results showed strong association in all the contrasts such as recessive, allele, and dominant and overdominant ($P<.05$) (Figs. 11.9−11.12). The ethnicity comparison and heterogeneity was checked by the subgroup analysis (Table 11.4). The results revealed that

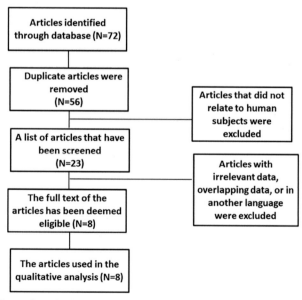

Figure 11.8 Flowchart of study design of SMARCA4 gene polymorphism with the risk of CAD. *CAD,* Coronary artery disease.

Table 11.3 Summary estimates for ORs and 95% CI in different ethnicities under various genetic contrasts.

Model	Ethnicity	Number of studies	Test of association			Test of heterogeneity			Publication bias
			OR	95% CI	P–val	P–val	I^2	I^2	P–val (Egger's test)
Allele contrast (A vs. a)	Overall	20	1.1214	[1.0648; 1.1810]	1.46	0.0404	0.3869	39%	0.0018
	Asian	9	1.2563	[1.1045; 1.4290]	0.001	0.0623	0.4611		0.0195
	Caucasian	11	1.0705	[1.0283; 1.1144]	0.001	0.2364	0.2174		0.1301
Recessive model (AA vs Aa + aa)	Overall	20	1.1221	[1.0337; 1.2181]	0.0059	0.016	0.4494	45%	0.017
	Asian	9	1.2783	[1.0328; 1.5821]	0.024	0.0296	0.5307		0.2127
	Caucasian	11	1.0433	[0.9831; 1.1072]	0.162	0.1828	0.2748		0.0594
Dominant model (AA + Aa vs aa)	Overall	20	1.1952	[1.1224; 1.2727]	2.69	0.101	0.3005	30%	0.0104
	Asian	9	1.4293	[1.1374; 1.7961]	0.002	0.0621	0.4613		0.0128
	Caucasian	11	1.1791	[1.0950; 1.2697]	1.290	0.295	0.1563		0.511
Overdominant (Aa vs AA + aa)	Overall	20	1.0292	[0.9560; 1.1080]	0.444	0.0312	0.4064	41%	0.8779
	Asian	9	1.0651	[0.8635; 1.3138]	0.555	0.0126	0.5888		0.3595
	Caucasian	11	1.0591	[1.0012; 1.1203]	0.045	0.3212	0.1291		0.1981

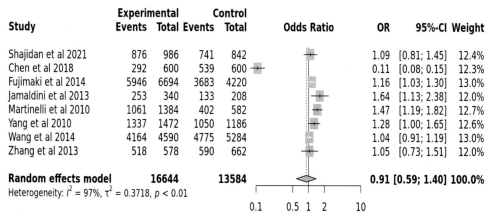

Study	Experimental Events	Total	Control Events	Total	Odds Ratio	OR	95%-CI	Weight
Shajidan et al 2021	876	986	741	842		1.09	[0.81; 1.45]	12.4%
Chen et al 2018	292	600	539	600		0.11	[0.08; 0.15]	12.3%
Fujimaki et al 2014	5946	6694	3683	4220		1.16	[1.03; 1.30]	13.0%
Jamaldini et al 2013	253	340	133	208		1.64	[1.13; 2.38]	12.0%
Martinelli et al 2010	1061	1384	402	582		1.47	[1.19; 1.82]	12.7%
Yang et al 2010	1337	1472	1050	1186		1.28	[1.00; 1.65]	12.6%
Wang et al 2014	4164	4590	4775	5284		1.04	[0.91; 1.19]	13.0%
Zhang et al 2013	518	578	590	662		1.05	[0.73; 1.51]	12.0%
Random effects model		**16644**		**13584**		**0.91**	**[0.59; 1.40]**	**100.0%**

Heterogeneity: $I^2 = 97\%$, $\tau^2 = 0.3718$, $p < 0.01$

0.1   0.5 1 2   10

Figure 11.9 Forest plot for the association of SMARCA4 gene polymorphism with CAD risk under allelic model. *CAD*, Coronary artery disease.

Study	Experimental Events	Total	Control Events	Total	Odds Ratio	OR	95%-CI	Weight
Shajidan et al 2021	386	493	325	421		1.07	[0.78; 1.46]	12.5%
Chen et al 2018	71	300	248	300		0.07	[0.04; 0.10]	12.1%
Fujimaki et al 2014	2636	3347	1601	2110		1.18	[1.04; 1.34]	13.2%
Jamaldini et al 2013	90	170	45	104		1.48	[0.90; 2.41]	11.6%
Martinelli et al 2010	405	692	138	291		1.56	[1.19; 2.06]	12.7%
Yang et al 2010	606	736	467	593		1.26	[0.96; 1.65]	12.7%
Wang et al 2014	1880	2295	2155	2642		1.02	[0.89; 1.18]	13.1%
Zhang et al 2013	232	289	263	331		1.05	[0.71; 1.56]	12.1%
Random effects model		**8322**		**6792**		**0.85**	**[0.54; 1.35]**	**100.0%**

Heterogeneity: $I^2 = 97\%$, $\tau^2 = 0.4147$, $p < 0.01$

0.1   0.5 1 2   10

Figure 11.10 Forest plot for the association of SMARCA4 gene polymorphism with CAD risk under recessive model. *CAD*, Coronary artery disease.

Study	Experimental Events	Total	Control Events	Total	Odds Ratio	OR	95%-CI	Weight
Shajidan et al 2021	490	493	416	421		1.96	[0.47; 8.26]	10.4%
Chen et al 2018	221	300	291	300		0.09	[0.04; 0.18]	13.4%
Fujimaki et al 2014	3310	3347	2082	2110		1.20	[0.73; 1.97]	14.1%
Jamaldini et al 2013	163	170	88	104		4.23	[1.68; 10.68]	12.6%
Martinelli et al 2010	656	692	264	291		1.86	[1.11; 3.13]	14.0%
Yang et al 2010	731	736	583	593		2.51	[0.85; 7.38]	12.0%
Wang et al 2014	2284	2295	2620	2642		1.74	[0.84; 3.60]	13.4%
Zhang et al 2013	286	289	327	331		1.17	[0.26; 5.25]	10.1%
Random effects model		**8322**		**6792**		**1.27**	**[0.54; 2.98]**	**100.0%**

Heterogeneity: $I^2 = 89\%$, $\tau^2 = 1.2857$, $p < 0.01$

0.1   0.5 1 2   10

Figure 11.11 Forest plot for the association of SMARCA4 gene polymorphism with CAD risk under dominant model. *CAD*, Coronary artery disease.

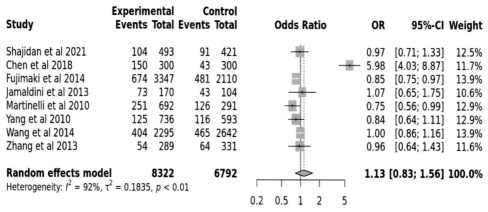

Figure 11.12 Forest plot for the association of SMARCA4 gene polymorphism with CAD risk under overdominant model. *CAD*, Coronary artery disease.

Table 11.4 Characteristics of the studies for the association of SMARCA4 gene polymorphism with the CAD risk.

Study	Ethnicity	GG Cases/ controls	GT_Cases	TT_Cases	Total cases/ controls	HW-*P.* value
Abudureyimu et al. (2021)	Asian	386/323	104/91	3/5	493/421	0.83
Chen et al. (2018)	Asian	71/248	150/43	79/9	300/300	0.0016
Fujimaki et al. (2015)	Asian	2636/1601	674/481	37/38	3347/2110	0.74
Jamaldini et al. (2014)	Caucasian	90/45	73/43	7/16	170/104	0.74
Martinelli et al. (2010)	Caucasian	405/138	251/126	36/27	692/291	0.93
Yang et al. (2010)	Asian	606	125	5	736/593	0.74
Wang et al. (2014)	Asian	1880	404	11	2295/2642	0.83
Zhang et al. (2013)	Asian	232	54	3	289/331	0.96

Asian people showed strong association in all the contrasts such as recessive, allele, and dominant and overdominant while caucasian people showed no association in all the genetic contrast models such as recessive, allele, and dominant and overdominant. In the supplementary material, we presented detailed results from HWE for random and fixed models (Table 11.3), and subgroup analyses (Table 11.4).

Publication bias was assessed to investigate the influence of all the discrete data. The publication bias was performed for the association of rs1122608 gene polymorphism with risk of CAD. According to publication bias, all the results were constant except two studies (Chen et al., 2018, Jamaldini et al., 2014) indicating that our results were statistically stable (Fig. 11.13).

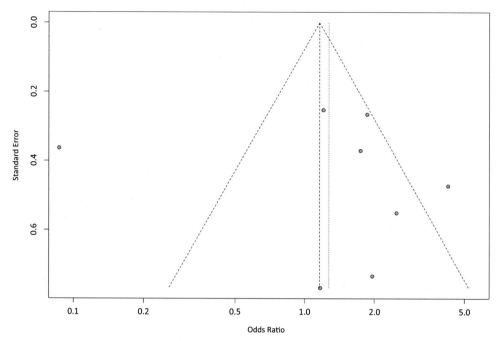

Figure 11.13 Publication bias analysed by the funnel plot for the association of SMARCA4 gene polymorphism with CAD risk. *CAD*, Coronary artery disease.

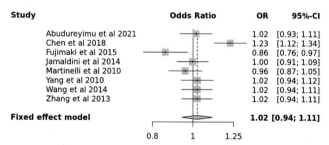

Figure 11.14 Sensitivity analysis for the association of SMARCA4 gene polymorphism with CAD risk. *CAD*, Coronary artery disease.

The striking heterogeneity may be due to a number of studies deviating from HWE (two studies containing low controls and cases). As a result, sensitivity analysis was conducted in order to determine the summary effects as well as the extent of heterogeneity between studies before and after excluding studies that were HWE-deviating. Based on the results of each individual study, it was found that no single study had a significant effect on the overall outcome of the study (Fig. 11.14) (Table 11.5).

Table 11.5 Summary estimates for ORs and 95% CI in different subgroups under various genetic contrasts.

Model	Ethnicity	Number of studies	Test of association			Test of heterogeneity			Publication bias
			OR	95% CI	P-val	P-val	I^2	I^2 (%)	P-val (Egger's test)
Allele contrast (A vs a)	Overall	8	0.9101	[0.5902;1.4034]	0.66	0	0.96	97	0.0018
	Asian	6	0.7634	[0.4450;1.3096]	0.32	0	0.97		0.0195
	Caucasian	2	1.5113	[1.2541;1.8214]	1.43	0.62	0		0.1301
Recessive model (AA vs Aa + aa)	Overall	8	0.8516	[0.5374;1.3495]	0.49	0	0.96	97	0.017
	Asian	6	0.7055	[0.4014;1.2402]	0.22	0	0.97		0.2127
	Caucasian	2	1.5426	[1.2133;1.9614]	0.00	0.83	0		0.0594
Dominant model (AA + Aa vs aa)	Overall	8	1.2676	[0.5393;2.9791]	0.58	0	0.89	89	0.0104
	Asian	6	0.9665	[0.3176;2.9413]	0.95	0	0.90		0.0128
	Caucasian	2	2.2681	[1.4423;3.5666]	0.00	0.12	0.56		0.511
Overdominant (Aa vs AA + aa)	Overall	8	1.1337	[0.8253;1.5571]	0.43	0	0.92	92	0.8779
	Asian	6	1.2311	[0.8327;1.8200]	0.29	0	0.94		0.3595
	Caucasian	2	0.8129	[0.6375;1.0364]	0.09	0.21	0.35		0.1981

11.16 Conclusion

Meta-analysis is a formal, epidemiological, quantitative design that methodically assesses the outcomes of previous studies to determine the conclusions about that body of research. Based on the literature search, 8322 patients and 6792 controls were chosen for the meta-analysis. Previously a few meta-analyses were conducted for different gene polymorphism with risk of CAD. A meta-analysis of rs1122608 gene polymorphism with the risk of CAD was reported and the lipid profile checked [137]. The results revealed that rs1122608 gene polymorphism showed strong association with CAD risk and TG levels. They revealed that G allele was not significant in the female population but a significant aspect in the male population. Xia et al. [138] reported the meta-analysis of gene polymorphism of ADIPOQ with the CAD risk in different ethnicities. The results revealed that ADIPOQ gene polymorphism showed strong association in East Asians, caucasians, and South Asians. The present study results were correlated with the previous meta-analyses. The current meta-analysis results showed strong association in all the genetic variants such as allelic, recessive, dominant, and overdominant. A subgroup study was also performed to check the heterogeneity and differences between association rs1122608 gene polymorphism in Asian and caucasian populations. The results showed that Asian people were at higher risk for CAD than caucasian people.

ATP-dependent helicase BRG1 is encoded by the SMARCA4 gene and belongs to SWI/SNF (switching defective/sucrose nonfermenting) complex. As per the literature, SMARCA4 is known to be one of the commonly mutated subunits, increasing an understanding of the mechanisms by which mutation of SMARCA4 drives cancer and of the susceptibilities produced carries key disease significance [139]. A case control study was conducted by Fujimaki et al., in the Japanese population to check the association between SMARCA4 gene polymorphism and risk of CAD. A study was conducted by Jamaldini et al. [140] in Iranian population to check the association of SMARCA4 gene polymorphism and CAD risk. The results revealed that intron SMARCA4 gene was associated with the risk of CAD. Previously a few studies also identified rs12232780, rs11879293, rs1529729, and rs2072382 variants and their effects on lipid parameters and dyslipidemia-related disease [37,95,141].

In the present investigation, we performed the meta-analysis to reveal the association of rs1122608 gene polymorphism with CAD risk. As a result of deviations from the HWE law of molecular association study, an error of accuracy may be attributed to inherited factors or methodological shortcomings. Hence, scores of HWE testing are important for the meta-analysis. In the present study, the results of rs1122608 gene polymorphism were fit for HWE. The publication bias assay was performed for the rs1122608 gene polymorphism using a funnel plot and all the results were statistically stable. Sensitivity assay was analyzed to check the heterogeneity between studies by omitting each study. Overall, none of the studies significantly influenced the overall outcome of the study. Eggers test and funnel plot was used to analyze the publication bias. All the results were constant and no significant bias was observed. From the present meta-analysis results, rs1122608 gene polymorphism was found to be associated with CAD risk. According to the subgroup study, Asian people were more at risk for CAD than caucasian people. To confirm the findings of the present study in the Caucasian population, more studies will be needed in the future with larger sample size.

Author contributions

Dr. GKS, Mr. SKY, and Dr. KL drafted the manuscript of this chapter and searched some of the literature on that particular topic, as some of the work was done in the field of systemic review and meta-analysis; we collected and compiled all the existing literature from various databases. Dr. PR, Dr. RS, Dr. VRU, and Dr. SFJ did the forest and funnel plot analysis. Dr. RB, Dr. PG, Dr. CK, and Dr. SJ did the statistical validation, revised the manuscript, and checked for grammar and spelling errors. Therefore all the authors are equally contributed and are considered as equal first authors.

References

[1] World Health Organization. Cardiovascular diseases (CVDs), <http://www.who.int/mediacentre/factsheets/fs317/en/index.html>; 2009.

[2] Won HH, Natarajan P, Dobbyn A, Jordan DM, Roussos P, Lage K, et al. Disproportionate contributions of select genomic compartments and cell types to genetic risk for coronary artery disease. PLoS Genet 2015;11(10):e1005622.

[3] Pauling L, Itano HA, Singer SJ, Wells IC. Sickle cell anemia, a molecular disease. Science. 1949;110 (2865):543−8.

[4] Wellcome Trust Case Control Consortium. Genome-wide association study of 14,000 cases of seven common diseases and 3,000 shared controls. Nature. 2007;447(7145):661.

[5] Kathiresan S, Willer CJ, Peloso GM, Demissie S, Musunuru K, Schadt EE, et al. Common variants at 30 loci contribute to polygenic dyslipidemia. Nat Genet 2009;41(1):56−65.

[6] Deloukas P, Kanoni S, Willenborg C, Farrall M, Assimes TL, Thompson JR, et al. Large-scale association analysis identifies new risk loci for coronary artery disease. Nat Genet 2013;45(1):25−33.

[7] Sayols-Baixeras S, Lluís-Ganella C, Lucas G, Elosua R. Pathogenesis of coronary artery disease: focus on genetic risk factors and identification of genetic variants. Appl Clin Genet 2014;7:15.

[8] Orho-Melander M. Genetics of coronary heart disease: towards causal mechanisms, novel drug targets and more personalized prevention. J Intern Med 2015;278(5):433−46.

[9] Khera AV, Emdin CA, Drake I, Natarajan P, Bick AG, Cook NR, et al. Genetic risk, adherence to a healthy lifestyle, and coronary disease. N Engl J Med 2016;375(24):2349−58.

[10] Roberts R. A breakthrough in genetics and its relevance to prevention of coronary artery disease in LMIC. Glob Heart 2017;12(3):247−57.

[11] Cohen JC, Boerwinkle E, Mosley Jr TH, Hobbs HH. Sequence variations in PCSK9, low LDL, and protection against coronary heart disease. N Engl J Med 2006;354(12):1264−72.

[12] Qian LJ, Gao Y, Zhang YM, Chu M, Yao J, Xu D. Therapeutic efficacy and safety of PCSK9-monoclonal antibodies on familial hypercholesterolemia and statin-intolerant patients: A *meta*-analysis of 15 randomized controlled trials. Sci Rep 2017;7(1):1.

[13] Genest Jr J, Bard JM, Fruchart JC, Ordovas JM, Schaefer EJ. Familial hypoalphalipoproteinemia in premature coronary artery disease. Arterioscler Thromb Vasc Biol 1993;13(12):1728—37.

[14] Cohen JC, Kiss RS, Pertsemlidis A, Marcel YL, McPherson R, Hobbs HH. Multiple rare alleles contribute to low plasma levels of HDL cholesterol. Science. 2004;305(5685):869—72.

[15] Willer CJ, Sanna S, Jackson AU, Scuteri A, Bonnycastle LL, Clarke R, et al. Newly identified loci that influence lipid concentrations and risk of coronary artery disease. Nat Genet 2008;40(2):161—9.

[16] Gupta R, Ejebe K, Butler J, Lettre G, Lyon H, Guiducci C, et al. Association of common DNA sequence variants at 33 genetic loci with blood lipids in individuals of African ancestry from Jamaica. Hum Genet 2010;128(5):557—61.

[17] Teslovich TM, Musunuru K, Smith AV, Edmondson AC, Stylianou IM, Koseki M, et al. Biological, clinical and population relevance of 95 loci for blood lipids. Nature. 2010;466(7307):707—13.

[18] Papp AC, Pinsonneault JK, Wang D, Newman LC, Gong Y, Johnson JA, et al. Cholesteryl Ester Transfer Protein (CETP) polymorphisms affect mRNA splicing, HDL levels, and sex-dependent cardiovascular risk. PLoS One 2012;7(3):e31930.

[19] Voight BF, Peloso GM, Orho-Melander M, Frikke-Schmidt R, Barbalic M, Jensen MK, et al. Cholesterol and risk of myocardial infarction: a Mendelian randomisation study. Lancet 2012;380 (9841):572—80.

[20] Oram JF. HDL apolipoproteins and ABCA1: partners in the removal of excess cellular cholesterol. Arterioscler Thromb Vasc Biol 2003;23(5):720—7.

[21] Barter PJ. The causes and consequences of low levels of high density lipoproteins in patients with diabetes. Diabetes Metab J 2011;35(2):101—6.

[22] Yang Q, Yin RX, Zhou YJ, Cao XL, Guo T, Chen WX. Association of polymorphisms in the MAFB gene and the risk of coronary artery disease and ischemic stroke: a case—control study. Lipids Health Dis 2015;14(1):1 -0.

[23] Dumitrescu L, Carty CL, Taylor K, Schumacher FR, Hindorff LA, Ambite JL, et al. Genetic determinants of lipid traits in diverse populations from the population architecture using genomics and epidemiology (PAGE) study. PLOS Genet 2011;7(6):e1002138.

[24] Ganna A, Magnusson PK, Pedersen NL, de Faire U, Reilly M, Ärnlöv J, et al. Multilocus genetic risk scores for coronary heart disease prediction. Arterioscler Thromb Vasc Biol 2013;33(9):2267—72.

[25] Fairoozy RH, White J, Palmen J, Kalea AZ, Humphries SE. Identification of the functional variant (s) that explain the low-density lipoprotein receptor (LDLR) GWAS SNP rs6511720 association with lower LDL-C and risk of CHD. PLoS One 2016;11(12):e0167676.

[26] Pasternak RC, Smith SC, Bairey-Merz CN, Grundy SM, Cleeman JI, Lenfant C. ACC/AHA/NHLBI clinical advisory on the use and safety of statins. J Am Coll Cardiol 2002;40(3):567—72.

[27] O'Keefe JH, Cordain L, Harris WH, Moe RM, Vogel R. Optimal low-density lipoprotein is 50 to 70 mg/dl: lower is better and physiologically normal. J Am Coll Cardiol 2004;43(11):2142—6.

[28] Mihaylova B, Emberson J, Blackwell L, Keech A, Simes J, Barnes EH, et al. The effects of lowering LDL cholesterol with statin therapy in people at low risk of vascular disease: *meta*-analysis of individual data from 27 randomised trials. Lancet (London, Engl) 2012;380(9841):581—90.

[29] Hokanson JE, Austin MA. Plasma triglyceride level is a risk factor for cardiovascular disease independent of high-density lipoprotein cholesterol level: a metaanalysis of population-based prospective studies. Eur J Cardiovasc Prev Rehabil 1996;3(2):213—19.

[30] Sarwar N, Danesh J, Eiriksdottir G, Sigurdsson G, Wareham N, Bingham S, et al. Triglycerides and the risk of coronary heart disease: 10 158 incident cases among 262 525 participants in 29 Western prospective studies. Circulation. 2007;115(4):450—8.

[31] Scherag A, Dina C, Hinney A, Vatin V, Scherag S, Vogel CI, et al. Two new Loci for body-weight regulation identified in a joint analysis of genome-wide association studies for early-onset extreme obesity in French and German study groups. PLoS Genet 2010;6(4):e1000916.

[32] Varbo A, Benn M, Tybjærg-Hansen A, Grande P, Nordestgaard BG. TRIB1 and GCKR poly-morphisms, lipid levels, and risk of ischemic heart disease in the general population. Arterioscler Thromb Vasc Biol 2011;31(2):451−7.

[33] Santoro N, Zhang CK, Zhao H, Pakstis AJ, Kim G, Kursawe R, et al. Variant in the glucokinase regulatory protein (GCKR) gene is associated with fatty liver in obese children and adolescents. Hepatology 2012;55(3):781−9.

[34] Zhang LX, Ying SU, Liang Y, Kui LI, Yong CH, Jian WA. Relationship between dyslipidemia and gene polymorphism in Tibetan population. Biomed Environ Sci 2012;25(3):305−10.

[35] Mirhafez SR, Avan A, Pasdar A, Khatamianfar S, Hosseinzadeh L, Ganjali S, et al. Zinc finger 259 gene polymorphism rs964184 is associated with serum triglyceride levels and metabolic syndrome. Int J Mol Cell Med 2016;5(1):8.

[36] Kooner JS, Chambers JC, Aguilar-Salinas CA, Hinds DA, Hyde CL, Warnes GR, et al. Genome-wide scan identifies variation in MLXIPL associated with plasma triglycerides. Nat Genet 2008;40 (2):149−51.

[37] Erdmann J, Großhennig A, Braund PS, König IR, Hengstenberg C, Hall AS, et al. New susceptibil-ity locus for coronary artery disease on chromosome 3q22. 3. Nat Genet 2009;41(3):280−2.

[38] Angelakopoulou A, Shah T, Sofat R, Shah S, Berry DJ, Cooper J, et al. Comparative analysis of genome-wide association studies signals for lipids, diabetes, and coronary heart disease: cardiovascular biomarker genetics collaboration. Eur Heart J 2012;33(3):393−407.

[39] Bressler J, Folsom AR, Couper DJ, Volcik KA, Boerwinkle E. Genetic variants identified in a European genome-wide association study that were found to predict incident coronary heart disease in the atherosclerosis risk in communities study. Am J Epidemiol 2010;171(1):14−23.

[40] Galkina E, Ley K. Vascular adhesion molecules in atherosclerosis. Arterioscler Thromb Vasc Biol 2007;27(11):2292−301.

[41] Khera AV, Kathiresan S. Genetics of coronary artery disease: discovery, biology and clinical transla-tion. Nat Rev Genet 2017;18(6):331−44.

[42] Palmer SJ. Pulmonary arterial hypertension: new software to accurately predict diagnosis. Br J Card Nurs 2017;12(2):98−100.

[43] Kupper N, Ge D, Treiber FA, Snieder H. Emergence of novel genetic effects on blood pressure and hemodynamics in adolescence: the Georgia Cardiovascular Twin Study. Hypertension. 2006;47 (5):948−54.

[44] Ehret GB, Morrison AC, O'connor AA, Grove ML, Baird L, Schwander K, et al. Replication of the Wellcome Trust genome-wide association study of essential hypertension: the Family Blood Pressure Program. Eur J Hum Genet 2008;16(12):1507−11.

[45] Rhee MY, Yang SJ, Oh SW, Park Y, Kim CI, Park HK, et al. Novel genetic variations associated with salt sensitivity in the Korean population. Hypertens Res 2011;34(5):606−11.

[46] Armando I, Van Villar AM, Jose AP. Genomics and pharmacogenomics of salt-sensitive hyperten-sion. Curr Hypertens Rev 2015;11(1):49−56.

[47] Shiffman D, Ellis SG, Rowland CM, Malloy MJ, Luke MM, Iakoubova OA, et al. Identification of four gene variants associated with myocardial infarction. Am J Hum Genet 2005;77(4):596−605.

[48] Samani NJ, Erdmann J, Hall AS, Hengstenberg C, Mangino M, Mayer B, et al. Genomewide asso-ciation analysis of coronary artery disease. N Engl J Med 2007;357(5):443−53.

[49] Reilly MP, Li M, He J, Ferguson JF, Stylianou IM, Mehta NN, et al. Identification of ADAMTS7 as a novel locus for coronary atherosclerosis and association of ABO with myocardial infarction in the presence of coronary atherosclerosis: two genome-wide association studies. Lancet 2011;377 (9763):383−92.

[50] Li X, Huang Y, Yin D, Wang D, Xu C, Wang F, et al. Meta-analysis identifies robust association between SNP rs17465637 in MIA3 on chromosome 1q41 and coronary artery disease. Atherosclerosis. 2013;231(1):136−40.

[51] Berger S, Raman G, Vishwanathan R, Jacques PF, Johnson EJ. Dietary cholesterol and cardiovascu-lar disease: a systematic review and *meta*-analysis. Am J Clin Nutr 2015;102(2):276−94.

[52] Farouk SS, Rader DJ, Reilly MP, Mehta NN. CXCL12: a new player in coronary disease identified through human genetics. Trends Cardiovasc Med 2010;20(6):204−9.

[53] Huang Y, Zhou J, Ye H, Xu L, Le Y, Yang X, et al. Relationship between chemokine (C—X—C motif) ligand 12 gene variant (rs1746048) and coronary heart disease: case—control study and meta-analysis. Gene. 2013;521(1):38—44.

[54] Burke AC, Dron JS, Hegele RA, Huff MW. PCSK9: regulation and target for drug development for dyslipidemia. Annu Rev Pharmacol Toxicol 2017;57:223—44.

[55] Almontashiri NA, Vilmundarson RO, Ghasemzadeh N, Dandona S, Roberts R, Quyyumi AA, et al. Plasma PCSK9 levels are elevated with acute myocardial infarction in two independent retrospective angiographic studies. PLoS One 2014;9(9):e106294.

[56] Kubo M, Kiyohara Y, Kato I, Tanizaki Y, Arima H, Tanaka K, et al. Trends in the incidence, mortality, and survival rate of cardiovascular disease in a Japanese community: the Hisayama study. Stroke. 2003;34(10):2349—54.

[57] Gaziano TA, Bitton A, Anand S, Abrahams-Gessel S, Murphy A. Growing epidemic of coronary heart disease in low-and middle-income countries. Curr Probl Cardiol 2010;35(2):72—115.

[58] National Cholesterol Education Program (US). Expert Panel on Detection, Treatment of High Blood Cholesterol in Adults. Third report of the National Cholesterol Education Program (NCEP) expert panel on detection, evaluation, and treatment of high blood cholesterol in adults (adult treatment panel III). The program; 2002.

[59] Shah T, Zabaneh D, Gaunt T, Swerdlow DI, Shah S, Talmud PJ, et al. Gene-centric analysis identifies variants associated with interleukin-6 levels and shared pathways with other inflammation markers. Circ Cardiovasc Genet. 2013;6(2):163—70.

[60] Smith SC, Allen J, Blair SN, Bonow RO, Brass LM, Fonarow GC, et al. AHA/ACC guidelines for secondary prevention for patients with coronary and other atherosclerotic vascular disease: 2006 update: endorsed by the National Heart, Lung, and Blood Institute. J Am Coll Cardiol 2006;47 (10):2130—9.

[61] Wu Z, Lou Y, Qiu X, Liu Y, Lu L, Chen Q, et al. Association of cholesteryl ester transfer protein (CETP) gene polymorphism, high density lipoprotein cholesterol and risk of coronary artery disease: a meta-analysis using a Mendelian randomization approach. BMC Med Genet 2014;15(1):1—7.

[62] Ginsberg HN, Elam MB, Lovato LC, Crouse III JR, Leiter LA, Linz P, et al. Effects of combination lipid therapy in type 2 diabetes mellitus. N Engl J Med 2010;362(18):1748.

[63] BIP Study Group. Secondary prevention by raising HDL cholesterol and reducing triglycerides in patients with coronary artery disease. Circulation. 2000;102:21—7.

[64] Gordon T, Castelli WP, Hjortland MC, Kannel WB, Dawber TR. High density lipoprotein as a protective factor against coronary heart disease: the Framingham Study. Am J Med 1977;62(5):707—14.

[65] Barter PJ, Caulfield M, Eriksson M, Grundy SM, Kastelein JJ, Komajda M, et al. Effects of torcetrapib in patients at high risk for coronary events. N Engl J Med 2007;357(21):2109—22.

[66] Schwartz GG, Olsson AG, Abt M, Ballantyne CM, Barter PJ, Brumm J, et al. Effects of dalcetrapib in patients with a recent acute coronary syndrome. N Engl J Med 2012;367(22):2089—99.

[67] Barter PJ, Brewer Jr HB, Chapman MJ, Hennekens CH, Rader DJ, Tall AR. Cholesteryl ester transfer protein: a novel target for raising HDL and inhibiting atherosclerosis. Arterioscler Thromb Vasc Biol 2003;23(2):160—7.

[68] Schierer A, Been LF, Ralhan S, Wander GS, Aston CE, Sanghera DK. Genetic variation in cholesterol ester transfer protein (CETP), serum CETP activity, and coronary artery disease (CAD) risk in Asian Indian diabetic cohort. Pharmacogenet Genomics 2012;22(2):95.

[69] Surakka I, Whitfield JB, Perola M, Visscher PM, Montgomery GW, Falchi M, et al. A genome-wide association study of monozygotic twin-pairs suggests a locus related to variability of serum high-density lipoprotein cholesterol. Twin Res Hum Genet 2012;15(6):691—9.

[70] Ordovas JM, Cupples LA, Corella D, Otvos JD, Osgood D, Martinez A, et al. Association of cholesteryl ester transfer protein—Taq IB polymorphism with variations in lipoprotein subclasses and coronary heart disease risk: the Framingham study. Arterioscler Thromb Vasc Biol 2000;20 (5):1323—9.

[71] Kondo I, Berg K, Drayna D, Lawn R. DNA polymorphism at the locus for human cholesteryl ester transfer protein (CETP) is associated with high density lipoprotein cholesterol and apolipoprotein levels. Clin Genet 1989;35(1):49—56.

[72] Dachet C, Poirier O, Cambien F, Chapman J, Rouis M. New functional promoter polymorphism, CETP/ − 629, in cholesteryl ester transfer protein (CETP) gene related to CETP mass and high density lipoprotein cholesterol levels: role of Sp1/Sp3 in transcriptional regulation. Arterioscler Thromb Vasc Biol 2000;20(2):507−15.

[73] Horne BD, Camp NJ, Anderson JL, Mower CP, Clarke JL, Kolek MJ, et al. Multiple less common genetic variants explain the association of the cholesteryl ester transfer protein gene with coronary artery disease. J Am Coll Cardiol 2007;49(20):2053−60.

[74] Boekholdt SM, Sacks FM, Jukema JW, Shepherd J, Freeman DJ, McMahon AD, et al. Cholesteryl ester transfer protein TaqIB variant, high-density lipoprotein cholesterol levels, cardiovascular risk, and efficacy of pravastatin treatment: individual patient meta-analysis of 13677 subjects. Circulation. 2005;111(3):278−87.

[75] Thompson A, Di Angelantonio E, Sarwar N, Erqou S, Saleheen D, Dullaart RP, et al. Association of cholesteryl ester transfer protein genotypes with CETP mass and activity, lipid levels, and coronary risk. JAMA. 2008;299(23):2777−88.

[76] Liu S, Schmitz C, Stampfer MJ, Sacks F, Hennekens CH, Lindpaintner K, et al. A prospective study of TaqIB polymorphism in the gene coding for cholesteryl ester transfer protein and risk of myocardial infarction in middle-aged men. Atherosclerosis. 2002;161(2):469−74.

[77] Whiting BM, Anderson JL, Muhlestein JB, Horne BD, Bair TL, Pearson RR, et al. Candidate gene susceptibility variants predict intermediate end points but not angiographic coronary artery disease. Am Heart J 2005;150(2):243−50.

[78] McCaskie PA, Beilby JP, Chapman CM, Hung J, McQuillan BM, Thompson PL, et al. Cholesteryl ester transfer protein gene haplotypes, plasma high-density lipoprotein levels and the risk of coronary heart disease. Hum Genet 2007;121(3):401−11.

[79] Borggreve SE, Hillege HL, Wolffenbuttel BH, de Jong PE, Zuurman MW, van der Steege G, et al. PREVEND Study Group An increased coronary risk is paradoxically associated with common cholesteryl ester transfer protein gene variations that relate to higher high-density lipoprotein cholesterol: a population-based study. J Clin Endocrinol Metab 2006;91(9):3382−8.

[80] Bhasin SK, Dwivedi S, Dehghani A, Sharma R. Conventional risk factors among newly diagnosed coronary heart disease patients in Delhi. World J Cardiol 2011;3:201−6.

[81] Schunkert H, Erdmann J, Samani NJ. Genetics of myocardial infarction: a progress report. Eur Heart J 2010;31:918−25.

[82] Rinkuniene E, Petrulioniene Z, Laucevicius A, Ringailaite E, Laucyte A. Prevalence of conventional risk factors in patients with coronary heart disease. Medicina. 2009;45:140−6.

[83] Schunkert H, Konig IR, Kathiresan S, Reilly MP, Assimes TL, Holm H, et al. Large-scale association analysis identifies 13 new susceptibility loci for coronary artery disease. Nat Genet 2011;43:333−8.

[84] Coronary Artery Disease C, Samani NJ, Deloukas P, Erdmann J, Hengstenberg C, Kuulasmaa K, et al. Large scale association analysis of novel genetic loci for coronary artery disease. Arterioscler Thromb Vasc Biol 2009;29:774−80.

[85] McPherson R, Pertsemlidis A, Kavaslar N, Stewart A, Roberts R, Cox DR, et al. A common allele on chromosome 9 associated with coronary heart disease. Science. 2007;316:1488−91.

[86] Coronary Artery Disease Genetics Consortium. A genome-wide association study in Europeans and South Asians identifies five new loci for coronary artery disease. Nat Genet 2011;43:339−44.

[87] Moes-Sosnowska J, Szafron L, Nowakowska D, DansonkaMieszkowska A, Budzilowska A, Konopka B, et al. Germline SMARCA4 mutations in patients with ovarian small cell carcinoma of hypercalcemic type. Orphanet J Rare Dis 2015;10:32.

[88] Wilson BG, Helming KC, Wang X, Kim Y, Vazquez F, Jagani Z, et al. Residual complexes containing SMARCA2 (BRM) underlie the oncogenic drive of SMARCA4 (BRG1) mutation. Mol Cell Biol 2014;34:1136−44.

[89] Fujimaki T, Oguri M, Horibe H, Kato K, Matsuoka R, Abe S, et al. Association of a transcription factor 21 gene polymorphism with hypertension. Biomed Rep 2015;3(1):118−22.

[90] Jamaldini SH, Babanejad M, Mozaffari R, Nikzat N, Jalalvand K, Badiei A, et al. Association of polymorphisms at LDLR locus with coronary artery disease independently from lipid profile. Acta Med Iran 2014;52:352−9.

[91] Liu Y, Zhou D, Zhang Z, Song Y, Zhang D, Zhao T, et al. Effects of genetic variants on lipid parameters and dyslipidemia in a Chinese population. J Lipid Res 2011;52:354−60.

[92] Zhong R, Liu L, Tian Y, Wang Y, Tian J, Zhu BB, et al. Genetic variant in SWI/SNF complexes influences hepatocellular carcinoma risk: a new clue for the contribution of chromatin remodeling in carcinogenesis. Sci Rep 2014;4:4147.

[93] Singh M, D'Silva L, Holak TA. DNA-binding properties of the recombinant high-mobility-group-like AT-hook containing region from human BRG1 protein. Biol Chem 2006;387:1469−78.

[94] Mulholland N, Xu Y, Sugiyama H, Zhao K. SWI/SNFmediated chromatin remodeling induces Z-DNA formation on a nucleosome. Cell Biosci 2012;2:3.

[95] Pan H, Niu DD, Feng H, Ng LF, Ren EC, Chen WN. Cellular transcription modulator SMARCE1 binds to HBV core promoter containing naturally occurring deletions and represses viral replication. Biochim Biophys Acta Mol Basis Dis 2007;1772(9):1075−84.

[96] Hoffman JI, Kaplan S. The incidence of congenital heart disease. J Am Coll Cardiol 2002;39 (12):1890−900.

[97] Bhardwaj R, Rai SK, Yadav AK, Lakhotia S, Agrawal D, Kumar A, et al. Epidemiology of congenital heart disease in India. Congenit Heart Dis 2015;10(5):437−46.

[98] Marelli AJ, Ionescu-Ittu R, Mackie AS, Guo L, Dendukuri N, Kaouache M. Lifetime prevalence of congenital heart disease in the general population from 2000 to 2010. Circulation. 2014;130 (9):749−56.

[99] Kilner PJ. Imaging congenital heart disease in adults. Br J Radiol 2011;84:S258−68 (Spec No 3).

[100] Bailliard F, Hughes ML, Taylor AM. Introduction to cardiac imaging in infants and children: techniques, potential, and role in the imaging work-up of various cardiac malformations and other paediatric heart conditions. Eur J Radiol 2008;68(2):191−8.

[101] Huang MP, Liang CH, Zhao ZJ, Liu H, Li JL, Zhang JE, et al. Evaluation of image quality and radiation dose at prospective ECG-triggered axial 256- slice multi-detector CT in infants with congenital heart disease. Paediatr Radiol 2011;41(7):858−66.

[102] Goitein O, Salem Y, Jacobson J, Goitein D, Mishali D, Hamdan A, et al. The role of cardiac computed tomography in infants with congenital heart disease. Isr Med Assoc J 2014;16(3):147−52.

[103] Tynan MJ, Becker AE, McCartney FJ, Jimenez M, Shinebourne EA, Anderson RH. Nomenclature and classification of congenital heart disease. Br Heart J 1979;41:544−53.

[104] Anderson RH, Becker AE, Freedom RM, Macartney FJ, Quero-Jimenez M, Shinebourne EA, et al. Sequential segmental analysis of congenital heart disease. Paediatr Cardiol 1984;5:281−7.

[105] Schweigmann G, Gassner I, Maurer K. Imaging the neonatal heart essentials for the radiologist. Eur J Radiol 2006;60(2):159−70.

[106] Section 2, Congenital heart disease. In: Jonathan G, Cornelia S-P, Andreas A, editors. Grainger & Allison's diagnostic radiology. 5th ed. Churchill Livingstone: Elsevier; 2008.

[107] Zamorano JL, Bax JJ, Frank E, Rademakers Juhani K. The ESC textbook of cardiovascular imaging. Springer-Verlag London Limited; 2010. p. 3−72.

[108] Black D, Vettukattil J. Advanced echocardiographic imaging of the congenitally malformed heart. Curr Cardiol Rev 2013;9(3):241−52.

[109] Alliburton SS, Abbara S, Chen MY, Gentry R, Mahesh M, Raff GL, et al. SCCT guidelines on radiation dose and dose-optimization strategies in cardiovascular CT. J Cardiovasc Comput Tomogr 2011;5(4):198−224.

[110] Fratz S, Chung T, Greil GF, Samyn MM, Taylor AM, Buechel ERV, et al. Guidelines and protocols for cardiovascular magnetic resonance in children and adults with congenital heart disease: SCMR expert consensus group on congenital heart disease. J Cardiovasc Magn Reson 2013; 15(1):51.

[111] Ntsinjana HN, Hughes ML, Taylor AM. The role of cardiovascular magnetic resonance in paediatric congenital heart disease. J Cardiovasc Magn Reson 2011;13(1):51.

[112] Cyrus C, Vatte C, Al-Nafie A, Chathoth S, Al-Ali R, Al-Shehri A, et al. The impact of common polymorphisms in CETP and ABCA1 genes with the risk of coronary artery disease in Saudi Arabians. Hum Genomics 2016;10(1):1−6.

[113] Ilanbey B, Kayıkçıoğlu M, Demirel Sezer E, Pehlivan S, Girgin Sagin F, Ozkinay F, et al. E. The role of cholesteryl ester transfer protein TaqIB polymorphism in young atherosclerotic heart disease. Int J Med Biochem 2020;3(1):8–13.

[114] Chu WC, Aziz AF, Nordin AJ, Cheah YK. Association of cholesteryl ester transfer protein and endothelial nitric oxide synthase gene polymorphisms with coronary artery disease in the multiethnic Malaysian population. Clin Appl Thrombosis/Hemostasis 2016;22(6):581–8.

[115] Srisawasdi P, Rodcharoen P, Vanavanan S, Chittamma A, Sukasem C. Association of CETP gene variants with atherogenic dyslipidemia among Thai patients treated with statin. Pharmacogenomics Pers Med 2021;14:1.

[116] Bhanushali AA, Das BR. Genetic variants at the APOE, lipoprotein lipase (LpL), cholesteryl ester transfer protein (CETP), and endothelial nitric oxide (eNOS) genes and coronary artery disease (CAD): CETP Taq1 B2B2 associates with lower risk of CAD in Asian Indians. J Community Genet 2010;1(2):55–62.

[117] Dedoussis GV, Panagiotakos DB, Louizou E, Mantoglou I, Chrysohoou C, Lamnisou K, et al. Cholesteryl ester-transfer protein (CETP) polymorphism and the association of acute coronary syndromes by obesity status in Greek subjects: the CARDIO2000-GENE study. Hum Hered 2007;63(3–4):155–61.

[118] Iwanicka J, Iwanicki T, Niemiec P, Balcerzyk A, Krauze J, Górczyńska-Kosiorz S, et al. Relationship between CETP gene polymorphisms with coronary artery disease in Polish population. Mol Biol Rep 2018;45(6):1929–35.

[119] Arca M, Montali A, Ombres D, Battiloro E, Campagna F, Ricci G, et al. Lack of association of the common TaqIB polymorphism in the cholesteryl ester transfer protein gene with angiographically assessed coronary atherosclerosis. Clin Genet 2001;60(5):374–80.

[120] Blankenberg S, Tiret L, Bickel C, Schlitt A, Jungmair W, Genth-Zotz S, et al. Genetic variation of the cholesterol ester transfer protein gene and the prevalence of coronary artery disease. The AtheroGene case control study. Z Kardiol 2004;93(Suppl 4):IV16–23.

[121] Corella D, Carrasco P, Amiano P, Arriola L, Chirlaque MD, Huerta JM, et al. Common cholesteryl ester transfer protein gene variation related to high-density lipoprotein cholesterol is not associated with decreased coronary heart disease risk after a 10-year follow-up in a Mediterranean cohort: modulation by alcohol consumption. Atherosclerosis 2010;211(2):531–8.

[122] Eiriksdottir G, Bolla MK, Thorsson B, Sigurdsson G, Humphries SE, Gudnason V. The -629C > A polymorphism in the CETP gene does not explain the association of TaqIB polymorphism with risk and age of myocardial infarction in Icelandic men. Atherosclerosis 2001;159(1):187–92.

[123] Falchi A, Giovannoni L, Piras IS, Calo CM, Moral P, Vona G, et al. Prevalence of genetic risk factors for coronary artery disease in Corsica island (France). Exp Mol Pathol 2005;79(3):210–13 45.

[124] Freeman DJ, Samani NJ, Wilson V, McMahon AD, Braund PS, Cheng S, et al. A polymorphism of the cholesteryl ester transfer protein gene predicts cardiovascular events in non-smokers in the West of Scotland Coronary Prevention Study. Eur Heart J 2003;24(20):1833–42 46.

[125] Fumeron F, Betoulle D, Luc G, Behague I, Ricard S, Poirier O, et al. Alcohol intake modulates the effect of a polymorphism of the cholesteryl ester transfer protein gene on plasma high density lipoprotein and the risk of myocardial infarction. J Clin Invest 1995;96(3):1664–71.

[126] Keavney B, Palmer A, Parish S, Clark S, Youngman L, Danesh J, et al. Lipid-related genes and myocardial infarction in 4685 cases and 3460 controls: discrepancies between genotype, blood lipid concentrations, and coronary disease risk. Int J Epidemiol 2004;33(5):1002–13.

[127] van Acker BA, Botma GJ, Zwinderman AH, Kuivenhoven JA, Dallinga-Thie GM, Sijbrands EJ, et al. Cholesterol does not protect against coronary artery disease when associated with combined cholesteryl ester transfer protein and hepatic lipase gene variants. Atherosclerosis 2008;200(1):161–7.

[128] Van Eck M, Ye D, Hildebrand RB, Kar Kruijt J, de Haan W, Hoekstra M, et al. Important role for bone marrow-derived cholesteryl ester transfer protein in lipoprotein cholesterol redistribution and atherosclerotic lesion development in LDL receptor knockout mice. Circ Res 2007;100(5):678–85 81.

[129] Okamoto H, Yonemori F, Wakitani K, Minowa T, Maeda K, Shinkai H. A cholesteryl ester transfer protein inhibitor attenuates atherosclerosis in rabbits. Nature 2000;406(6792):203–7.

[130] Blauw LL, Li-Gao R, Noordam R, de Mutsert R, Trompet S, Berbée JF, et al. (cholesteryl ester transfer protein) concentration: a genome-wide association study followed by Mendelian randomization on coronary artery disease. Circ Genomic Precis Med. 2018;11(5):e002034.

[131] Abudureyimu S, Abulaiti P, Xing Z, Li H, Liu SS, Li W, et al. The effect of four different single nucleotide polymorphisms on coronary heart disease in a Han Chinese Population in Xinjiang Region. J Cardio Cardiovasc Med 2021;5:025.

[132] Chen QF, Wang W, Huang Z, Huang DL, Li T, Wang F, et al. Correlation of rs1122608 SNP with acute myocardial infarction susceptibility and clinical characteristics in a Chinese Han population: a case-control study. Anatol J Cardiol 2018;19(4):249.

[133] Yang XC, Zhang Q, Li SJ, Wan XH, Zhong GZ, Hu WL, et al. Association study between three polymorphisms and myocardial infarction and ischemic stroke in Chinese Han population. Thrombosis Res 2010;126(4):292−4.

[134] Wang Y, Wang L, Liu X, Zhang Y, Yu L, Zhang F, et al. Genetic variants associated with myocardial infarction and the risk factors in Chinese population. PLoS One 2014;9(1):e86332.

[135] Zhang L, Yuan F, Liu P, Fei L, Huang Y, Xu L, et al. Association between PCSK9 and LDLR gene polymorphisms with coronary heart disease: case-control study and meta-analysis. Clin Biochem 2013;46(9):727−32.

[136] Martinelli N, Girelli D, Lunghi B, Pinotti M, Marchetti G, Malerba G, et al. Polymorphisms at LDLR locus may be associated with coronary artery disease through modulation of coagulation factor VIII activity and independently from lipid profile. Blood. J Am Soc Hematol 2010;116(25):5688−97.

[137] Liu S, Xiu B, Liu J, Xue A, Tang Q, Shen Y, et al. Association of rs1122608 with Coronary artery disease and lipid profile: a meta-analysis. Arch Med Res 2016;47(4):315−20.

[138] Zhang X, Cao YJ, Zhang HY, Cong H, Zhang J. Associations between ADIPOQ polymorphisms and coronary artery disease: a meta-analysis. BMC Cardiovasc Dis 2019;19(1):1−8.

[139] Jancewicz I, Siedlecki JA, Sarnowski TJ, Sarnowska E. BRM: the core ATPase subunit of SWI/SNF chromatin-remodelling complex—a tumour suppressor or tumour-promoting factor? Epigenetics Chromatin 2019;12(1):1−7 Moes-Sosnowska J, Szafron L.

[140] Nowakowska D, Dansonka-Mieszkowska A, Budzilowska A, Konopka B, Plisiecka-Halasa J, Podgorska A, et al. Germline SMARCA4 mutations in patients with ovarian small cell carcinoma of hypercalcemic type. Orphanet J rare Dis 2015;10(1):1−6.

[141] Guo X, Wang X, Wang Y, Zhang C, Quan X, Zhang Y, et al. Variants in the SMARCA4 gene was associated with coronary heart disease susceptibility in Chinese Han population. Oncotarget. 2017;8(5):7350.

Index

Note: Page numbers followed by "*f*" and "*t*" refer to figures and tables, respectively.

Printed in the United States
by Baker & Taylor Publisher Services